GREAT

The Breakthrough Investing Strategy That

COMPANIES,

Produces Great Returns over the Long-Term

GREAT

Cycle of Bull and Bear Markets Based on the

RETURNS

Twelve Traits of All Great Companies

JIM HUGUET

BROADWAY BOOKS   NEW YORK

This book was written to provide insight into an investing strategy. Neither the author nor the publisher is rendering legal, accounting, or financial services by publishing this book. Due to the unpredictable nature of the stock market and the risks inherent in any form of financial investment, this book offers no guarantees or assurances that the strategies discussed in this book will be successful. The author and the publisher will not be responsible for any loss, liability, or risk incurred as a result of the use or application of any information contained in this book. The book contains a number of historical graphs and tables; please note that past performance is not indicative of future results.

Jim Huguet owns stock in all of the Great Companies of America and the companies mentioned in Great Companies of the Future. He "puts his money where his mouth is."

GREAT COMPANIES, GREAT RETURNS. Copyright © 1999 by Jim Huguet. All rights reserved. Printed in the United States of America. No part of this book may be reproduced or transmitted in any form or by any means, electronic or mechanical, including photocopying, recording, or by any information storage and retrieval system, without written permission from the publisher. For information, address Broadway Books, a division of Random House, Inc., 1540 Broadway, New York, NY 10036.

Broadway Books titles may be purchased for business or promotional use or for special sales. For information, please write to: Special Markets Department, Random House, Inc., 1540 Broadway, New York, NY 10036.

BROADWAY BOOKS and its logo, a letter B bisected on the diagonal, are trademarks of Broadway Books, a division of Random House, Inc.

Visit our website at www.broadwaybooks.com

Library of Congress Cataloging-in-Publication Data
Huguet, Jim.
    Great companies, great returns : the breakthrough investing strategy, that
    produces great returns over the long term cycle of bull & bear markets : based on
    the twelve traits of all great companies / Jim Huguet. — 1st ed.
    p.   cm.
    ISBN 0-7679-0366-8
    1. Investments—United States—Case studies.   2. Stocks—United States—
Case studies.   3. Corporations—United States—Case studies.   I. Title.
HG4910.H84   1999
658.15'2—dc21
                                                                    99-19432
                                                                    CIP

FIRST EDITION

Designed by Susan Hood

00   01   02   03   10   9   8   7   6   5   4   3   2

*To my wonderful wife, Marie,
and our terrific daughters,
Kristin and Lauren*

CONTENTS

CONTENTS

GREAT COMPANIES, GREAT RETURNS

INTRODUCTION

This book explains how to single out the stocks of those few great American companies that every investor should own. It explains the twelve traits inherent in all Great Companies and details how you can construct a portfolio of Great Companies stocks that produces outstanding, tax-efficient returns in a variety of market conditions.

The investing strategy detailed in this book doesn't require you to know much about the ins and outs of the stock market, and it doesn't require you to spend lots of time monitoring its ups and downs. That's because this strategy is based upon identifying and buying into companies, not into stocks. But it's not about buying just any companies—it's about buying the stocks of a highly select group of Great American Companies that have delivered outstanding results for years, and will continue to outperform for the foreseeable future.

If you are like a number of my friends and associates, you have become disenchanted with the performance of your mutual funds. Since 88 percent of all domestic equity funds failed to beat the S&P 500 index in 1998, the odds are that you are ready to dump your managed funds. You may have grown so unhappy that you sold some or all of your managed funds and moved most of your money into index funds. On your own, you decided to venture out and buy the stocks of a few really good companies that you knew something about. These companies might have included Coca-Cola, Gillette, Merck, or General Electric. They are companies that you believe will continue to perform well over the long term regardless of the twists and turns of the markets. Over the last several years you noticed that these stocks outperformed the major indexes as well as the mutual funds you once owned.

Unfortunately most investment books and magazine articles tout the stocks to own *today*, or the ten hottest stocks for this year, not the stocks to own forever. These books and articles are focused on short-term returns, stocks that are selected by a computer, and investment strategies that cost you a bundle in taxes.

To counter these flawed approaches, this book presents a logical, easily understood investing strategy that should shape the core portfolio of virtually all investors, regardless of age or income. By "core," I mean at least 30 to 40 percent of all your investments should be in equities, the foundation on which your wealth should be built.

Had you invested equally in all fourteen stocks of the Great Companies of America on December 31, 1988, you would have beaten the S&P 500 index by 55.6 percent during the ten-year period ending December 31, 1998. Had you invested on December 31, 1993, and held your stocks for five years, your investment would have exceeded the S&P index by 49.65 percent. Long-term investors who invested on December 31, 1978, would have outperformed the index by approximately 41.95 percent. Nineteen ninety-eight returns would have equaled 28.75 percent compared to the S&P 500 index of 28.58 percent. More than that, you would have taken the steps required to implement a *core investing strategy*, a low-risk, tax-advantaged way to build wealth with large-cap stocks while allowing for international diversification. Core strategies differ from other investing strategies in that they are long term, tax efficient, easy to understand, and proven, and provide excellent returns relative to the level of risk. This differs from "black box" strategies that buy stocks rather than companies, cost you dearly in taxes, and often underperform the market at high levels of risk.

After reading this book you will:

• Have acquired a logical investment approach that has beaten the market by 55.6 percent during the last ten years.

- Understand why a core investing strategy is important, and why it makes sense regardless of your age or current wealth.
- Know the twelve traits that make a company a great investment.
- Know how to apply a checklist for identifying a great investment to a wide variety of companies in different businesses.
- Be able to sleep soundly, knowing that you are investing in the best-managed companies in the United States, and perhaps in the world.

Does this sound too good to be true? Let me tell you how it evolved.

THE DEVELOPMENT OF THE GREAT COMPANY INVESTING STRATEGY

Several years ago, after I sold my consulting company, I suddenly had more money than I had ever dreamed of but absolutely no idea how to invest the proceeds. I had spent most of my professional life building my consulting business and traveling all over the country. I had a 401(k) and owned a few mutual funds and some stocks, but when it came to the stock market, I was a novice. I decided that I quickly had to learn a lot more about investing and the market, or risk losing my one opportunity for financial independence.

My search for a sound investing strategy began with great optimism and enthusiasm. I was searching for an investing strategy that was easy to understand, had been proven over time, produced excellent tax-adjusted returns that beat indexing, and would result in a relatively low-risk portfolio. I really don't know if I was driven more by fear or greed (the two worst emotions an investor can possess), but I wanted to make sure I knew how to invest my money in the best way, leaving no stone unturned.

First, I thought it would be a good idea to study both the classic and new books about investing in the stock market. I picked up *The Intelligent Investor* by Benjamin Graham, the father of value investing, reasoning that since Warren Buffett is a disciple of Ben Graham, this would be a great place to start. I read books by Peter Lynch and a host of other writers on the dynamics and pitfalls of the market, and I read as much as I could about mutual funds. With the billions of dollars pouring into funds, I felt that I should be better informed.

GREAT COMPANIES OF AMERICA VS. S&P 500

December 1978 to December 1998

Legend:
- Great Companies of America
- Standard & Poor's 500 Index

Source: S&P Compustat

NOTE: PAST PERFORMANCE IS NOT INDICATIVE OF FUTURE RESULTS.

With this reading as background, I met with various money managers in an effort to understand their philosophies and approaches. I also read books about money managers and, through my reading and discussions, realized that each manager had a unique approach. Needless to say, some were more successful and convincing than others.

Next I attended investment conferences at various locations around the country. Then I purchased *Morningstar on Floppy* in hopes of finding the answer. I subscribed to *Barron's* and watched CNBC and Bloomberg for tips from the top. I attended the Money Show in Boston. I searched the Internet and subscribed to all the top investment newsletters. All my research convinced me that I had to invest heavily in stocks if I was to retire and have a decent lifestyle. In the long run, I discovered, the returns on stocks are so stable that stocks are actually a safer investment than government bonds or treasury bills. But despite all this studying, I still didn't know which stocks I should put my money in. As a result of my efforts I learned the following:

- *Approximately 62 percent of the domestic equity mutual funds fail to beat the market in any given year.* I found out the hard way that funds that beat the market one year normally "tanked" the next. Even more discouraging was another realization: funds that beat the market several years in a row often had so much money pour in that the nature of the fund changed and performance declined.
- *Timing the market was impossible.* I was invested with one of the most famous market timers, the "guru" who called the 1987 crash, when she exited the market in July of 1996. I, along with other investors, sat on the sidelines while the market soared to new heights. It seems that everyone on Wall Street can pontificate ad nauseam on why the market went up or down, but none can reliably predict *when* it will go up or down.
- *Short-term in-and-out investing gains are quickly eaten up by taxes.* It was exciting to see a stock's value jump by 20 percent in one month, but the taxes paid on the short-term gain dampened my enthusiasm for this investing approach.

- *Momentum investing was overhyped.* The momentum traders could turn a portfolio 300 percent to 400 percent in one year. This generated huge commissions for my broker but less than impressive tax-adjusted returns for me. I wondered, if companies were good enough for the manager to buy in the first place, why not keep the stocks longer? I also wondered why, if the stocks were so good, the stock price dropped so rapidly when something happened. I was told I just didn't understand momentum investing.
- *The articles identifying the "Next Microsoft," "The 10 Hottest Mutual Funds for 1999" or "The Stocks You Can't Lose On" seemed to over-promise and underdeliver more often than I could imagine.* While all of the authors presented compelling reasons for their selections, performance seldom met expectations.

Investment professionals weren't as much help as I expected either: Some approaches were so complex that they defied comprehension while others defied common sense and logic. There were a few people who were helpful, but you really had to dig to find them. People who could not explain their investment approach referred to themselves as "stock pickers," a term that made me more than a little nervous. Chartists/Technical analysts seemed to have charts for every occasion, but few had the right chart for the present situation. History may repeat itself in the stock market, but I have found that chartists are no better than market timers at predicting the future. There were very few really outstanding money managers. Most of those who were successful either added numerous funds to their portfolios, became more involved in managing than stock picking, or sold their businesses and took the money and ran.

I was at a loss. I asked friends for advice but found that they didn't even know as much as I did, a scary thought indeed. I momentarily contemplated investing everything in index funds. Perhaps it was crazy to think about beating the market. But somehow I just couldn't resign myself to mirroring the indexes. I reasoned that there had to be an approach that would not only beat indexing, but was also logical and easy to understand.

About this time, my twenty-plus years of consulting experience kicked in. I had learned long ago that if I was trying to solve a difficult problem and the answer wasn't forthcoming, I hadn't dug deeply enough for the facts. I had found that if I really opened my mind and focused on the issue, the answer would leap out at me. I always knew it was the right answer because it was so simple and obvious.

I renewed my research efforts, but this time my research took a different direction. For over thirty years I have had the honor and privilege of working for or consulting with what I considered to be well-managed companies like Procter and Gamble (my first employer out of college), Bristol-Myers Squibb, Coca-Cola, Colgate-Palmolive, Gillette, Johnson & Johnson, and others. During these assignments, I met and got to know many of the managers within these companies. They were a very talented and impressive group. All of a sudden, it hit me. Why not let these outstanding managers go to work for me? Not as consultants, but as managers of my money.

I would invest in the best-managed companies in the world. So I turned to books and articles about the best-managed companies in the U.S. and around the world. I read about a number of outstanding companies that were highly regarded by the management gurus and the major business magazines. Surely this was the answer. However, as I began to compare shareholder returns of these wonderfully managed companies, I found that many of them failed to meet or exceed the S&P 500 index. It was then that I realized that investing in companies that were simply well managed didn't provide the investment answer I was seeking.

Disappointed, but not discouraged, I reasoned that well-managed companies did not always produce great returns, and that companies that looked good from a financial perspective might not measure up when management was really scrutinized. However, if I could isolate a few companies that were well managed, highly regarded within their industry, and attractive from a Wall Street perspective, I might have the answer. I concluded that if I invested in these companies, their managers would help me beat the market over the long term. Additionally, I realized that I would be able to sleep at night knowing that my money was in the hands of the best managers and greatest companies in the U.S. I also knew that if this approach worked, my taxes and trading costs would be minimized because I would buy and hold these stocks for a long time.

Reviewing a variety of statements by Warren Buffett, I found that Buffett, arguably the greatest investor of our time, endorsed the strategy of investing in great companies. His approach wasn't fully detailed, but the basics were contained within the Berkshire Hathaway annual reports (a real treat to read) and the speeches and interviews Buffett had given over the years.

But What Makes a Great Company?

I quickly realized that the most difficult part of this strategy would be defining a Great Company. Answering this question raises two absolutely critical questions that investors and analysts must answer before they invest:

- Do great returns make a great company?
- Do great companies make great returns?

If you believe that great returns make a great company, then all you need to do is enter the financial screens that you believe are important in identifying a great stock, compare a cross section of stocks with these screens, and buy the stocks that pop out of your computer. This approach is often referred to as quantitative management or modeling. Any money manager with fifty or more stocks in her portfolio is using some type of quantitative approach. Those with over 100 stocks in their portfolios are using purely quantitative measures to select stocks. Since only 12 percent of all domestic equity mutual funds beat the S&P 500 index in 1998, perhaps there is a better way. That is why I believe that great companies make great returns.

It's easy to say, "Invest in great companies." It's a little tougher to define the elements that exist within *all* great companies. The confusion exists because the experts evaluating a company typically view it from only one perspective. For example, the management experts who wrote *In Search of Excellence* and *Built to Last* sought companies that were *well managed*. They talked about culture, management, and focus. Unfortunately, they didn't examine or rate the qualities of the businesses in which the companies were engaged, a critical factor from the perspective of the chairmen and CEOs of great companies.

Investment analysts examine a company's *returns* from the perspective of the professional investor. However, what's important to the investment expert is often meaningless to the management expert and may differ greatly from the CEO's perspective. For example, CEOs of the great companies felt that a company should operate as a global entity, deriving at least 40 percent of its revenues from overseas. The financial experts never mentioned this international presence as important. Finally, there is the *operational* perspective of the CEO. These men and women live in the real world of quarterly returns and boards of directors. Some of the factors that are important to them are not of concern to the management and investment experts, and vice versa.

Previous experts attempting to define a great company reminded me of the proverbial three men trying to describe an elephant in pitch darkness. The one feeling the trunk had a very different perspective from the one holding the elephant's leg, and the man holding the tail had yet another perspective. Like accurately describing the elephant, defining a great company requires taking into account a variety of perspectives. Only when you combine all the perspectives into a single definition and identify the specific qualities common to all great companies, can you spot a truly great investment opportunity . . . and no one had ever done that.

Ultimately, I was able to distill a list of twelve factors common to all great companies—factors that became invaluable in separating the great companies from the merely good ones.

I developed the original list of companies to study from the annual *Fortune* issue that lists "America's Most Admired Companies." *Fortune* asks "top executives, outside directors, and securities analysts to evaluate the companies in their industry on each of eight criteria." My list was supplemented by other well-managed companies identified in several highly regarded management books. As I finalized the selection of companies for my Great Companies stock portfolio and began to match returns to my strategy, I realized that I had developed an investing strategy that had handily beaten the S&P 500 index over five, ten, and twenty years. Additionally this strategy met my original criteria:

It delivered returns that, over time, were superior to indexing.

It provided tax-advantaged returns, since I would hold the stocks for the long term.

It was logical and easy for the average individual investor to understand.

It was efficient because commissions and management fees would be low.

It focused on safe, secure, large-cap stocks, the kinds of stocks and companies I feel comfortable owning.

Once I had formulated the strategy, I decided to show it to several investing professionals and get their input. The first person I discussed the concept with was Ralph Goldman of PaineWebber. Ralph works with many of the top money managers in the United States and is highly regarded within the investment community. To my surprise, Ralph was extremely supportive. "I've looked at literally hundreds of money managers," he said, "but your approach is truly unique and is a logical core investing strategy." More than that, he immediately began to purchase some of the stocks for his personal portfolio. It's one thing for someone like Ralph to say he likes an investing strategy, and quite another for him to put his money where his mouth is.

With increased confidence in the Great Companies strategy, I decided to write a book based on investing in Great Companies to help ordinary investors build wealth. Since I started writing this book, I have asked a number of my friends, very bright people in their forties and fifties, how they invest their money, and have found that most people I know don't really have a plan for building wealth. They typically explain that they are too busy managing their careers and spending time with their families to devote the time needed to managing their money. A few have purchased speculative stocks on tips. Most of these people have lost a lot more than they've made. Some have purchased stocks in what they view as outstanding companies, but when queried admit that they really don't have a formalized system for defining what makes these companies great investments.

The more I study this approach and its results, the more convinced I become that the Great Companies strategy should form the foundation of virtually every investor's portfolio. I have invested over seven hundred thousand dollars of my own money in these Great Companies, and have developed a Great Company of America managed account for investors.

WHO CAN BENEFIT FROM THE GREAT COMPANY INVESTING STRATEGY?

This book was written for investors who are:

Frustrated that the performance of their stock portfolio is below their expectations. They now realize that most mutual funds fail to beat the relevant index in a given year, and have learned the hard way how difficult it is to select a market-beating mutual fund.

Confused about the world of investing. They have read books, attended conferences, subscribed to newsletters and magazines, and are totally confused by the contradictory messages they have received.

Short of time. These investors are busy with their careers and simply don't have the time to develop a sound investing strategy.

Relying primarily upon indexing. These investors got tired of investing in funds that failed to beat the index. They turned to indexing out of frustration, but believe that there has got to be a better way to invest.

Just beginning their investing journey. Novice investors will be able to read and understand the investing strategy that is outlined in this book.

Successful investors. These investors have been successful but are searching for another strategy that is compatible with their investing approach and will add diversity to their portfolio.

Paying too much in taxes. Investors who are realizing significant short-term gains but paying high taxes will find the investing strategy outlined in this book of real value.

Preretirement investing. If you are searching for a relatively low-risk investment strategy that produces excellent returns over time, you will find this book of value.

Retirement investing. If you are retired and are concerned about outliving your money, you may find that this approach is far more attractive than fixed-income investments.

Financing college. If long-term capital growth with relatively low risk is important to you, then this approach should be of interest.

Just starting out. If you are just starting to build wealth, then you will see tremendous value in this approach.

Great Companies, Great Returns provides all types of investors with a core strategy that has been proven effective over time. Its logical approach has been endorsed by some of the most highly regarded investors. It will help the reader understand what to look for in a company by explaining the twelve factors common to all Great Companies. Personal interviews with the chairmen and CEOs of Great Companies will provide the reader with a better understanding of what makes for a great company from an operational perspective and reveal how specific companies have been able to achieve greatness. Finally, specifics on how the reader can get started investing in the Great Companies will be presented. This book will prove beyond a doubt that the Great Companies investing approach outperforms the market at low levels of risk and with minimal tax impact.

Let me emphasize that the Great Companies Strategy is a long-term approach (ten to twenty years) rather than a get-rich-quick in-and-out approach to the market. If you are seeking the magic answer, you have picked up the wrong book. However, if you are looking for an index-beating core strategy, then you have picked up the right one.

The book is organized as follows:

Chapter 1: *Why Great Companies Produce Great Returns.* What a core investing strategy is and why the Great Companies strategy is appropriate for virtually every investor.

Chapter 2: *What is a Great Company?* The twelve traits of all Great Companies as well as the fourteen companies that passed our screens.

Chapter 3: *The Twelve Traits of the Great Companies.* The twelve traits are explained in detail.

Chapter 4: *The Great Companies*. Profiles of each company, including candid interviews with the chairmen and CEOs of four Great Companies that reveal never-before-published insights.

Chapter 5: *Applying the Great Companies Strategy*. How investors can modify the screens used to identify the Great Companies and develop new stock portfolios based on the Great Companies criteria.

Chapter 6: *Turning Your Portfolio into a Great Companies Portfolio*. The step-by-step process investors can follow to convert their current portfolios into Great Companies portfolios.

Chapter 7: *Great Companies Investing Options*. The various investing options, including direct purchase, brokers, mutual funds, individually managed accounts, and hedge funds.

Chapter 8: *Managing and Monitoring Your Great Companies Portfolio*. Passive and active strategies for managing the portfolio, and how to track a portfolio once it is in place.

Chapter 9: *Reducing the Worry Factor*. Ways you can cope with the risks inherent in investing in the stock market.

Investing in Great Companies is a strategy that won't go out of style, for it has been proven over the years in a variety of market cycles. Furthermore, the strategy's focus on maximizing returns while minimizing risks and taxes meets the needs of virtually every investor. I suggest that you read the book as it is organized, for it is important to understand the concept of core investing strategies before you study the qualities of a great company.

Chapter 1

The Great Companies Approach to Investing

———◦◦◦———

Why Is Investing So Confusing?

Like most investors today, you have probably concluded that you should invest some of your money in the stock market. You may have purchased a couple of mutual funds or even bought a few blue chip stocks, but this is different. The money you are investing now may well determine when you can retire and what life will be like after retirement. Will you live the "good life," or will you be forced to cut back?

You begin your investing journey by reading what the financial gurus have to say about "the market" and asset allocation. Some say we are entering a great bear market, while others confide that the bull is still charging. Some say the market is overpriced, while others say it is underpriced. Some say buy, while others scream sell. This should be your first clue that the market is complex. If it weren't so complex, everyone would come up with the same right answer.

Your quest to understand how best to invest leads you to articles about indexing, value investing, and growth investing. Each expert touts his or her approach as the best way. Then you are shocked by the reality that last year 88 percent of the domestic equity managed funds failed to beat the S&P 500. You wonder how experts can have such conflicting points of view. Why don't they beat the market year in and year out? To the novice investor, these differences of opinion are confusing and extremely unsettling. You reason that these market experts are smart people who have made a lot of money in the market. If they don't know what to do to beat the market, how can you have any chance at all of successfully investing your money?

You then read articles like the one that appeared in the *New York Times*, explaining why analysts couldn't always be counted on for meaningful advice relative to mergers and acquisitions:

> In sorting this out, investors get little help from Wall Street analysts, who often play along. After all, companies can come down hard on naysayers. Thomas K. Brown, until recently a banking analyst for Donaldson Lufkin & Jenrette, long criticized the acquisition strategy of the First Union Corporation, which has made more than 70 acquisitions since 1985. As a result, he said he was excluded from one-on-one meetings at First Union's headquarters in Charlotte, N.C.
>
> Another analyst, who asked not to be identified, recalled being threatened with a lawsuit by one serial acquirer after publicly questioning its purchases. Why the heavy-handed treatment? "So much depends on the stock price, he surmised."
>
> Analysts can also be reluctant to look too closely at any one transaction for fear that their company might lose the lucrative investment banking fees on the acquirer's next deal.
>
> A result of this combination of complexity and analysts' see-no-evil, speak-no-evil approach is that the guidepost usually followed by investors—the analysts' estimated growth rate of earnings—can vary so wildly for these companies as to be nearly meaningless.

The confusion is compounded by the incessant phone calls you receive from people who can't pronounce your name, calling on behalf of a firm that has three initials followed by the word "securities," announcing that their soothsayer, someone you never heard of, has just found the next Microsoft. These "advisors" casually explain that you will surely double your money if you invest in the companies that they are recommending. But you'd better invest today, for a big announcement is going to be made that will send the stock through the roof.

Desperate and feeling totally inadequate, you decide to call a friend who you think understands the market. Surely, he must have the answer, for he is always talking about how much he has made in the market. Typically, your friend knows less than you think but—like most people—will never tell you about some of the real mistakes he has made. So your friend throws out some names, tells you how much he has made, and "sets you up" with his broker. Six months later you are underperforming the market. The mutual funds that did so well last year are down this year. The stocks your broker recommended have declined in value. You are disappointed and disillusioned. Will you ever be able to retire? You feel inadequate and scared. You aren't sure where to go next.

The complexities of the market seem to build. You find that there are different classes of stock with different rights. Some shares are preferred; some may be voting shares and others nonvoting shares. Investors who believe the stock will decline "short" the stock. Investors who believe the stock will rise will be "long." Some investors buy options; others buy puts and calls. Some investors trade on margin, others don't. Some use derivatives, others hedge the market.

You learn about the various exchanges in the U.S. where stocks are traded. The major exchanges are the New York Stock Exchange, the American Stock Exchange, and NASDAQ, but there are also the Philadelphia Exchange, the Pacific Exchange, and the Chicago Board of Trade. You can buy foreign stocks with ADRs or GDSs. There are foreign stocks that trade on exchanges throughout the world. You can run money offshore or onshore. If you want someone to make investments for you, you can use a broker or a money manager, invest in a hedge fund, or purchase a mutual fund—either closed-end or open-end, load or no-load. Some mutual funds charge a front load, while others have a rear load. Prices may be referred to as the asking price, the bid price, or the NAV. Some people look at PE ratio, others at dividend yield.

Investment approaches may include value investing, momentum investing, market timing, indexing, sector investing, and various hybrids. There are IPOs, MBOs, and LBOs to consider. Bonds make this whole mess even more complex, for there are zero coupon bonds, municipal bonds, junk bonds, high-quality bonds, convertible bonds, and bond insurance. Then there is the market impact of interest rates, exchange rates, world events, and the economy. A variety of indexes are used to measure the market, including the DJIA, S&P 500, New York Exchange Index, Russell Indexes, Value Line, Wilshire Indexes, the NASDAQ, and a host of others. There are bear markets when the market goes down, and bull markets when the market goes up. There are market peaks and market bottoms. There are people who chart the market and others who use astrology to predict market direction. There are earnings projections and earnings disappointments. Some people track insider sales and other insider purchases. There are stock buy-backs and new issues. Some analysts look at free cash flow; others try to calculate intrinsic value. There are books, magazines, and newsletters published by investing gurus. There is the *Wall Street Journal, Investor's Business Daily, Barron's,* and the *Financial Times.* Additionally, there are videotapes containing the investing secrets of the "chosen," seminars where the experts speak, and financial news networks.

You realize that the stock market provides a wonderful opportunity for naïve or confused investors to "lose their shirts." Unfortunately, many investors don't have a clue how to invest in the market. They are intimidated by all the investing advice they read or hear. They bounce from one mutual fund or stock to another. They don't have an investing strategy, don't understand the companies whose stocks they own, and are motivated by fear and greed. A formula for disaster.

It Doesn't Have to Be This Way

The good news is that you don't have to be one of these casualties of the market, and you don't need to understand all aspects of the market to make money in it. Most people, even professional investors, don't understand all the ins and outs of the market, and never will. But you do need to understand some investing basics. First, you need to understand that you are buying companies, not stocks, and that some companies are far better than others. The smart investor should focus on individual companies rather than all the ins and outs of the market. Second, you must realize that long-term investing offers a number of benefits, including tax advantages and reduced trading costs. Third, you must be aware that there is always news, either good or bad, that is impacting the market. Fourth, you should adopt investing strategies that make sense to you. The bulk of your wealth should be invested in what we define as a core investing strategy.

Finally, you can become a successful investor and make a lot of money in the market without becoming a market expert. Rather than focusing on understanding the stock market, this book helps you focus on understanding what makes for a Great Company. If you study the principles contained in this book and practice them over the long run, you will be able to identify companies that should outperform the market long term. The strategy of investing in Great Companies has been proven over time.

In summary, you shouldn't feel inadequate if you don't understand all aspects of the market. What you need to focus on is implementing a core investing strategy based on investing in Great Companies, and this book will help.

THE BIG BENEFITS OF A CORE STRATEGY

The Great Company strategy detailed in this book is based upon five very important principles:

1. *The greatest returns come from purchasing stocks.* The following chart from Ibbotson Associates clearly makes this point.
2. *Large-cap companies enjoy a number of critical strategic advantages over their smaller-cap counterparts.* These advantages will be discussed in detail later in the book.
3. *It is possible to identify the inherent qualities of Great Companies. These Great Companies have achieved and will continue to achieve business results that over time produce outstanding returns for their shareholders.* Rather than invest in companies that are down and out, or companies that look great but falter, the investor should invest in Great Companies. These are companies that have been

Stocks, Bonds, and Cash After Taxes

1925 - 1997

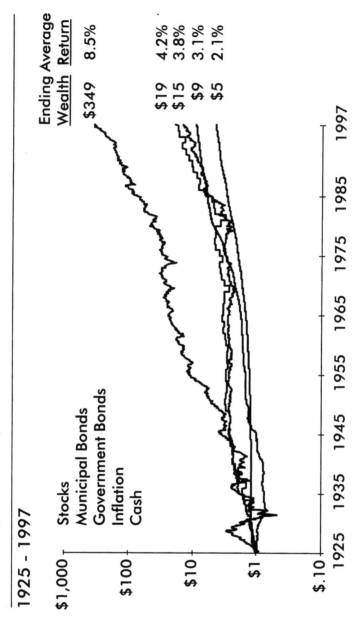

	Ending Average Wealth	Return
Stocks	$349	8.5%
Municipal Bonds	$19	4.2%
Government Bonds	$15	3.8%
Inflation	$9	3.1%
Cash	$5	2.1%

great in the past, are great today, and will continue to be great in the future. They are more than simply blue chip stocks, they are Great Companies, and there are very few of them—we found only fourteen, but the achievements of these fourteen companies are incredible.

4. *Purchasing the stocks of these Great Companies and owning them over time will provide the patient investor with index-beating returns while minimizing risks, taxes, and investment expenses.* It is virtually impossible to time the market. The time-proven way to win in the market is to purchase shares in Great Companies and hold the stock over time.

5. *By adjusting the allocation of funds among Great Companies for changes in intrinsic value and company and sector momentum, an investor can significantly improve returns.* While Great Companies remain great over time, their intrinsic values change relative to the price of these stocks. The intrinsic value of a company is an estimate of a company's future net worth. Momentum has to do with a company's growth relative to the market. Even with Great Companies, there are times when the company is growing faster than the market and occasions when the market is growing faster than the company.

THE GREAT COMPANIES STRATEGY VS. TRADITIONAL INVESTING STRATEGIES

The Great Companies strategy differs from traditional investing strategies in a number of key ways. As an investor it is important that you understand these differences.

Value Investing

The value approach was originally presented by Benjamin Graham in his book, *The Intelligent Investor,* an investment classic that serves as the basis for all modern-day value investors and outlines the concept in detail.* The approach centers on searching for stocks that offer "a significant margin of safety relative to price." Graham believed that

---

* For full bibliographic information on this and other materials referenced in this book, please see the Sources on page 313.

without a basis for determining whether a security is undervalued or overvalued, the investor is at risk of being swept away by the "tides of pessimism and euphoria which sweep the security market." This strategy dictates that the stocks that should be most attractive to investors are these that are relatively unpopular with the market. This process takes great discipline and a strong conviction that the securities the investor purchases are indeed a true bargain, and not simply companies that are going downhill and will eventually fade from sight.

In presenting his criteria for stock selection, Graham identified the following seven factors as key:

1. Adequate size of the enterprise.
2. A sufficiently strong financial condition.
3. Earnings stability.
4. Continuous dividends for at least the past twenty years.
5. Ten-year growth of at least one-third in per-share earnings.
6. Moderate price/earnings ratio, no more than fifteen times average earnings in the past three years.
7. Moderate ratio of price to assets.

Graham also presented his formula for determining what he described as the "intrinsic value" of an enterprise. This formula sought to calculate the future fundamental value of a company based on its ability to produce profits, or its true worth to its owners, as opposed to the company's share price or perceived value. The concept of intrinsic value is something that Warren Buffett uses today. Buffett stated in Berkshire Hathaway's 1993 annual report that the company's long-standing goal is to increase Berkshire's "per-share intrinsic value at an average annual rate of 15 percent."

Other value managers have added their own twists in determining the value of an enterprise. For example, Mario Gabelli utilizes a concept that he refers to as "private market value." This is the price an informed industrialist would pay to own the enterprise. Still other investors have added their own unique spins, but the concept of value investing developed by Benjamin Graham seems to run through all of these permutations and remains the base upon which value investing is practiced today. The investor who wants to learn more about value investing should consider reading *The Intelligent Investor* by Benjamin Graham, *The Quest for Value* by G. Bennett Stewart III, or *Value Investing Made Easy* by Janet Lowe.

Momentum /Growth Investing

The momentum or growth strategy relies upon a combination of earnings and/or revenue growth calculations. Analysts using this approach seek out companies whose earnings or revenues are increasing at rapid rates, and for whom continued growth is forecast. This strategy is based on the idea that a rapidly growing company will continue to grow for some time, and that investors who purchase shares in the enterprise in its early stages will be handsomely rewarded as the stock price rises. Typically, the PE ratios of these companies are relatively high and may well be in the 30 to 40 PE range versus the value investor's typical range of 12 to 15. The momentum investor purchases shares in the growth company regardless of its PE, book value, or size. Theoretically, once the investor believes that growth rates will slow, or the stock price reaches a preestablished target, the investor sells. Normally, when a growth stock's earnings slow, the price plummets, since many growth stocks carry abnormally high PE's. Therefore, it is critical to sell the stock before the company reaches this precipice.

Variations on Growth and Value Investing

In an effort to enhance the performance of a portfolio, some investors vary the value and momentum investing approaches. Some investing professionals believe that timing the market allows them to increase returns. Timing assumes that the investor is capable of knowing when the market or a particular stock will rise or fall at some point in the future. A market timer believes that by using forecasting techniques, technical analysis, market sentiment, or other methods, the timer can predict when to be in or out of the market. The strategy is to sell when the market is high and invest when the market is low.

I do not believe that it is possible to accurately time the market. But let's assume that you found a magic genie who gave you the power to time the market one day each year. Let's further assume that for forty years you invested one thousand dollars in an index fund on the one day of the year when the market was at its lowest. At the end of the forty years your portfolio would have grown at the rate of 11.7 percent per annum. Had another investor who knew nothing about timing decided to simply invest the thousand dollars on the first day of the year, this investor's portfolio would have increased 11.1 percent per annum. Now let's assume that the dumbest timer in the world is given a thousand dollars to invest. Naturally, the dumb timer invests every year at the market peak. No doubt the dummy's returns would be far lower than those of the timer with the genie. Wrong! The world's worst timer's portfolio would have grown by 10.5 percent. Surprisingly, the actual results of the great timer and the dumb timer are far closer than we would have imagined. I know how tempting it is to time the market, especially when all the soothsayers are calling for a "25 percent decline" or a "major market correction." But remember that they are no better at timing the market than you are.

Another variation of the value and momentum investing strategies is sector investing. Investors who practice this approach believe that within the market certain industry sectors have more upside potential for stock appreciation than others. For example, the sector investor might believe that computers and airlines have more upside growth potential than automobiles and retailing. In this case the manager would invest heavily in these high-potential sectors and avoid other sectors with less perceived potential. In theory, sector investing is similar to timing the market, for the idea is to invest when a sector is about to rise and sell just before it declines.

Comparing Value and Momentum Investing

The value and momentum approaches are very *different* in several ways:

VALUE	MOMENTUM
Focuses on financial analysis	Focuses on earnings growth rate
Normally used with large caps	Typically used with small/mid caps
Longer-term buy-and-hold approach	Stocks are turned frequently

Value and Momentum Investing

➤ Free cash flow   ➤ Earnings growth
➤ Intrinsic value   ➤ Price
➤ Earnings stability   ➤ Private market value
➤ Dividends record

Company with a low stock price relative to its potential value

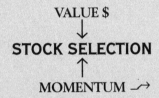

VALUE $
↓
STOCK SELECTION
↑
MOMENTUM ↝

Company whose earnings are growing rapidly relative to the markets, other sectors, or firms within the sector

➤ Company growth in excess of competitors
➤ Sector growth relative to the market
➤ Early-discovery companies
➤ Accelerating earnings momentum

The value and momentum approaches are *similar* in that:

- *They both ignore the quality of management within the company.* Neither approach places a value on superior management or deducts for weak management. We believe that in the long term, quality management determines a company's success.
- *Neither approach considers the type of industry in which the company is operating.* Although some industries provide more favorable operating environments than others do, the quality of the business environment is not considered in either approach.

- *Neither approach places a premium on market share or franchise value, critical factors in determining future growth potential.* It's hard to imagine how many marketing benefits Gillette's razors and blades enjoy because of the company's superior market share, but they are numerous. First, Gillette is able to realize higher net sales prices than its competition. Gillette's share of dollars is always greater than its share of units. Second, Gillette benefits from increased space and facings at retail because of its superior market share and velocity from the shelf. Since over 85 percent of all consumer products are purchased from the shelf or rack rather than a display, superior shelf position and space are key strategic advantages. Also, Gillette probably pays fewer promotion dollars than its rivals. Next to cost of goods, trade promotion is the greatest line-item expense for most CPG (Consumer Products Group) companies. Savings here can have a huge impact on the bottom line. This strong business franchise means that Gillette doesn't have to "buy" the business and results in increased profits. Additionally, the company enjoys greater leverage for the advertising dollars spent because of its huge volume base. All these benefits—plus others that Gillette receives because of its share advantage—illustrate the point that market share offers numerous advantages that can result in increased margins and an even greater competitive advantage.
- *Neither approach considers the company's record of increasing shareholder returns over time.* While history does not necessarily predict the future, a company that has delivered outstanding returns to shareholders on a three-, five-, ten-, and twenty-year basis should be more valuable than one that provides only sporadic returns.
- *Neither approach promotes the concept of purchasing and holding the stock for a long time.* Under the value approach the investor should sell the stock once the share price exceeds the intrinsic value of the stock. Following the momentum strategy, the stock should be sold just before earnings begin to slow. As we will demonstrate later, these activities increase taxes and expenses, something you should seek to minimize.

The Advantages and Disadvantages of Indexing

ADVANTAGES	DISADVANTAGES
➤ Lower fees	➤ Assumes the individual should invest in all industries
➤ Breadth/diversity of stocks	➤ Assumes there are 500 leading companies worthy of your investment dollars
➤ Beat 88 percent of mutual funds in 1998	➤ Forces you into a momentum investing style
	➤ Impossible to balance the portfolio
	➤ Yields average returns

Indexing

The third major approach is indexing. Although it is a close cousin of the growth strategy, it should be addressed separately because of its popularity. The indexing approach became popular when investors realized that most mutual funds fail to outperform the major indices in a given year. They became disenchanted with their mutual fund managers and turned to indexing. Indexers purchase stocks in companies that are found within one of the major indexes (typically the S&P 500 or the Dow Jones) against which the fund is benchmarked. Using a computer program, the manager continually balances the portfolio to approximate the structure of the various stocks that compose a particular index.

The primary advantages of indexing are:

- Management fees are low since little work is needed to analyze and manage the fund.
- Results are in line with the benchmarked index, and some people

Great Companies Approach vs. Others

GREAT COMPANIES APPROACH
➤ Buy Great Companies
➤ Hold the stock
➤ Adjust portfolio weighting

VALUE APPROACH
➤ Buy the stock
➤ Sell once price exceeds intrinsic value

MOMENTUM APPROACH
➤ Buy the stock
➤ Sell just before earnings decline

INDEXING
➤ Buy 500 stocks
➤ Portfolio weight driven by market cap

are happy with average returns, given the poor showing of managed funds.
• There is diversity in the fund, since the investor actually owns the stocks of as many as 500 companies.

The negatives of indexing are reflective of the concept. Since the underlying goal of indexing is to reflect the rise and fall of an index, this approach:

• Assumes that all industries should be represented (we believe some businesses are better than others).
• Assumes that there are as many as 500 companies worth owning (there aren't 500 great companies in the U.S.—or the world, for that matter).

Great Companies Approach vs. Value and Growth/Momentum Investing

Value and Growth strategies focus on financial measures, not Greatness, and they focus on the stock, not the company. These approaches differ from the Great Companies approach in two key ways:

➤ The value manager believes that a company is a value at a point in time. The Great Companies approach dictates that a Great Company is a bargain forever.

➤ The momentum manager believes that a growth company's greatest weakness is time: eventually earnings will decline and the stock will collapse. The Great Companies approach views time as the most valuable ally of a Great Company.

- Does not actually mirror the market since small caps are not included.
- Forces investors into a hybrid momentum approach since stocks that are growing control more of the index.

In April 1997, *Forbes* magazine noted that "In short, we suspect index funds have become a dangerous placebo, giving many of us the illusion that the stock market is a much safer place than it really is."

Indexing vs. the Great Companies Approach

INDEXING	GREAT COMPANIES APPROACH
➤ Own numerous companies (500)	➤ Own 14 companies
➤ Invest in all businesses/industries	➤ Some businesses are far better than others
➤ Market cap determines portfolio weighting	➤ Intrinsic value determines portfolio weight
➤ Seek average returns	➤ Seek superior returns

THE GREAT COMPANIES STRATEGY VS. TRADITIONAL INVESTING STRATEGIES

The Great Companies strategy that is presented in detail in this book differs from traditional investing strategies in a number of ways.

The Great Companies strategy differs from the traditional value strategy, which views a company as a financial value at a point in time. The Great Companies strategy holds that a truly Great Company is a bargain forever. A well-managed company in terrific business that consistently increases its intrinsic value should be held for the long term.

The Great Companies strategy also differs from the momentum or growth strategy, which suggests that the investor purchase the stocks of companies that are growing faster than the market and sell these stocks just before the growth rate slows. This strategy is based on the fact that eventually earnings growth rates of high-growth companies slow and the stock price drops. The key is selling the stock just before the growth begins to decline. Therefore time is the greatest enemy of the growth company, because it is only a matter of time before growth slows. The Great Companies strategy holds that time is a Great Company's most valuable ally. Unlike the momentum investor, who sells a company once earnings peak, you should plan to own a Great Company for an extended period of time. These companies get better and better over time.

The Great Companies strategy differs from indexing in the following ways:

- *Indexing mandates that investors should be invested in all companies in the index.* The Great Companies approach is based on the idea that there are a very limited number of Great Companies, only fourteen, and investing in 500 companies means that you are investing in many companies and businesses that aren't that good. (Fifty companies accounted for half of the increase in the S&P 500 index in 1998. The other 450 companies contributed the balance.)

As we have seen, the elements of the Great Companies investment strategy are quite different from traditional investing strategies. Specifically:

- *PE ratios should not be a key driver of purchase price.* Rather, the investor should compare the Great Company's intrinsic value and intrinsic value momentum with the market price of the stock. Intrinsic value, not PE ratios, should drive portfolio allocation. It bothers me that some small-cap, high-risk growth companies that are unprofitable with PE's of 55 are seen as good buys, while companies like Procter and Gamble with a PE of 35 are viewed as being overvalued.
- *A company's ability to deliver consistent superior shareholder returns over time should be factored into the purchase equation.* Investors who purchase mutual funds tend to examine fund returns over time. Why shouldn't investors who purchase stocks do the same? The Great Companies have been far more successful in beating the indexes than virtually any mutual fund.
- *Some businesses provide better operating environments than others do.* Unfortunately, traditional investing approaches do not place a premium on the quality of the business environment.
- *Superior management wins.* In a world where competitors can

The Great Companies Selection and Allocation Process

IDENTIFY POTENTIAL GREAT COMPANIES

- Management books
- Magazine articles
- Consulting experience

ANALYZE ALL COMPANIES VS. OUR SCREENS

- Highly regarded by management experts
- Headquartered in the U.S.
- Publicly traded
- Large cap > $15 billion
- Fifty years in business
- Terrific business
- Superior businesses franchises
- People are the company's most valuable asset
- World-class management
- Delivers outstanding returns to shareholders
- Company is global—40 percent
- Converts changes to opportunities

SELECT THE GREAT COMPANIES

- Select those companies to be included in the portfolio

ALLOCATE PORTFOLIO

- Intrinsic value
- Intrinsic value momentum
- Company & sector momentum

purchase the same raw materials, computers, and other equipment, it's what the companies do with these assets that decides the winner, and superior managers do more with their assets to drive shareholder returns than average managers.

Today many investors are buying stocks, not Great Companies. Intricate analyses are conducted in order to time the market or sell a stock at its peak. The real difference between good companies and Great Companies is measured in a variety of qualities, most of which aren't tracked by the analysts.

THE SIMPLE PROCESS OF SELECTING THE GREAT COMPANIES

The Great Companies selection and allocation process is depicted in the graphic on the opposite page. The process began with the definition of a Great Company. Next we determined the unique qualities that all Great Companies have in common. Companies that met these criteria were then identified. Finally, funds were allocated among the companies based upon intrinsic value calculations and company momentum. (Portfolio weights are adjusted for changes in intrinsic value and momentum.)

Compared to other investment strategies, the Great Companies strategy is relatively simple and easy to understand. And as you will see later in this section, the Great Companies approach provides meaningful results for the patient investor; it is a perfect core strategy that meets all of the core strategy criteria.

WHERE THE STRATEGY DELIVERS: OUTSTANDING RETURNS

As impressive as the companies themselves are, the most significant accomplishments that we care about as investors are their performance results. These fourteen companies which we refer to as the Great Companies of America have significantly outperformed the major indexes.

No matter how you look at it, the performance of these companies

GREAT COMPANIES OF AMERICA VS. BERKSHIRE HATHAWAY, S&P 500

December 31, 1988 to December 31, 1998

Equal Weighted, Dividends Reinvested

Total returns on the S&P Indexes that have been calculated using PC Plus may differ from the total returns on the S&P Indexes calculated by Standard & Poor's.

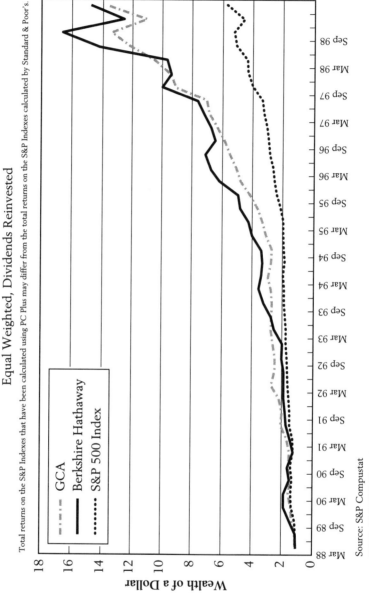

Source: S&P Compustat

NOTE: PAST PERFORMANCE IS NOT INDICATIVE OF FUTURE RESULTS.

is impressive. Furthermore, we believe that they will continue to deliver exceptional performance in the future, for this portfolio is composed of Great Companies that have and will continue to out-perform the market over time.

ADDITIONAL BENEFITS FOR THE PATIENT INVESTOR

In addition to outstanding returns, the Great Companies investing strategy provides individual investors with a number of key benefits:

- *Low volatility.* When we consider the volatility of these companies relative to the market average, we see that they have achieved this outstanding record of returns with very low standard deviations relative to the market in general and to successful mutual funds.
- *Solid, secure investment.* You can sleep well at night knowing that you are a shareholder in the finest companies in the world. These companies have huge market caps, which provides tremendous staying power. Furthermore, the fourteen companies have been in business an average of 112 years.
- *International diversity without the risks.* Since approximately 56 percent of the revenues of these companies come from outside of the U.S., you are receiving the advantages of an internationally diverse portfolio without the risks of purchasing international companies.
- *Responsible investments.* The companies in this portfolio are socially responsible companies. (For example, there are no marketers of alcohol or tobacco products in the portfolio.)
- *Great long-term investment.* Purchasing these companies is a long-term investment. You won't be actively trading your portfolio, which will save on commissions.
- *Diversified companies.* The companies in the portfolio are in a variety of businesses, which provides some degree of investing diversity.
- *Tax-efficient returns.* Since you won't be trading very often, this approach will be more tax efficient than buy-and-sell strategies.
- *Solid growth over time.* Many experts think of size as limiting growth but my research found just the opposite.

- *Simple and easy to understand.* You can feel comfortable using this approach because you can understand the investment process.

This strategy should form the core strategy on which most investors, regardless of their situation, build net worth.

Chapter 2

WHAT IS A GREAT COMPANY?

It was easy to come to the conclusion that buying the stocks of great companies and holding the shares for a long time made all the sense in the world. In fact, the only stock that I could ever imagine holding for five or ten years would be the stock of a great company. But what is a great company? How can you tell a great company from an imposter? How do you know that a company that has been great in the past will continue to be great in the future? I was at a loss. I had developed a "neat" investing strategy, but if I couldn't figure out and define what made for a great company, my neat strategy would be a dead strategy.

From my years of consulting experience with companies like Coca-Cola, Gillette, and Johnson & Johnson and my work experience with Procter and Gamble, I had learned that truly outstanding companies seemed to excel in three areas:

- *First, there were excellent people at all levels in the company.* These people kept the company on the leading edge of change and provided outstanding service to customers.
- *Second, these companies delivered outstanding returns to shareholders.* They consistently met their internal objectives and budgets, which in turn led to outstanding shareholder returns.

- *Finally, the chairmen and CEOs of these companies provided an important ingredient.* They knew which businesses to be in and which businesses to get out of. They had a clear vision of where the company was going and always steered it on the right course. And transitions from one leader to the next seemed almost effortless. When a CEO retired, he was replaced by someone who was a perfect fit for the company's needs at that point.

THREE PERSPECTIVES FROM DIFFERENT CORNERS

In order to properly define a great company from an investing standpoint, it was important to analyze a company from three different perspectives:

1. First, from the perspective of the *management experts*, the people who study companies from a "laboratory" viewpoint to determine why some companies are well managed and some aren't.
2. Second, from the perspective of the *financial experts and professional investors*, who focus on what drives shareholder wealth creation.
3. Third, from the *operational perspective* of the chairman or CEO of a corporation. The CEO is the person who must deal with the real-world challenges of achieving quarterly estimates and placating boards of directors.

While the three groups' perspectives on what makes for a great company would differ, by combining these three perspectives into one set of criteria I would be able to develop a series of "screens" for identifying a great company. I could then assess companies using these screens, and the great companies would pop out.

I found that the management experts viewed companies as individually functioning organisms that must excel in the overall business environment. They compared one company to another based upon how well the company is managed. They sought to determine if the company does things in the same way as other very well-managed, successful companies. Terms like *best practices, unique culture, focused, action oriented, highly regarded,* and *promotion from within* are frequently used by management experts to describe outstanding companies.

In Tom Peters and Robert Waterman's groundbreaking 1982 book *In Search of Excellence*, the authors extensively researched the world's top companies and defined an excellent company as follows:

> . . . the excellent companies were, above all, brilliant on the basics. Tools didn't substitute for thinking. Intellect didn't overpower wisdom. Analysis didn't impede action. Rather, these companies worked hard to keep things simple in a complex world. They persisted. They insisted on top quality. They fawned on their customers. They listened to their employees and treated them like adults. They allowed their innovative product and service "champions" long tethers. They allowed some chaos in return for quick action and regular experimentation.

A similar and equally outstanding book was written some twelve years later by James Collins and Jerry Porras. Published in 1994, *Built to Last* referred to what I call a Great Company as a "Visionary Company." Although the name differed, the definition was on target. The authors describe a Visionary Company as follows:

> A visionary company is like a great work of art. Think of Michelangelo's Scenes from Genesis on the ceiling of the Sistine Chapel or his statue of David. Think of a great and enduring novel, like *Huckleberry Finn* or *Crime and Punishment*. Think of Beethoven's Ninth Symphony or Shakespeare's *Henry V.* Think of a beautifully designed building, like the Masterpieces of Frank Lloyd Wright or Ludwig Mies van der Rohe. You can't point to any one single item that makes the whole thing work; it's the entire work—all the pieces working together to create an overall effect—that leads to enduring greatness. And it's not just the big pieces, but also the itty-bitty details—the turn of phrase, the change in pace at just the right moment, the perfect off-center placement of a window, a subtle expression sculpted into the eyes. As the great architect Mies van der Rohe put it, "God is in the details."

These two books provide an excellent understanding of what makes for a great company from the perspective of management experts and consultants, but it is also important to examine the qualities of a great company from the perspective of a money manager or financial analyst.

Taking a look at the literature with a financial/investor focus, I discovered numerous books on outstanding stocks to buy. Some books were limited to one hundred companies while others listed over four hundred. Since I believe that there are very few great companies, what these authors identified as a great stock and what I was calling a Great Company were not in sync. Moreover, as I reviewed previous works by some of these authors, I noticed that the list seemed to change from year to year. These stocks were stocks for the day or the year, not the next ten or twenty years. Furthermore, there was no effort to identify common traits beyond earnings growth that made these companies outstanding investments, outside of fairly routine financial analyses.

There was one book I found that sought to identify a Great Company from the perspective of a financial manager. The author noted that "If the job [selecting stocks] has been correctly done when a common stock is purchased, the time to sell it is—almost never." I liked his definition. Unfortunately, *Common Stocks and Uncommon Profits*, written by Philip A. Fisher and published in 1958, was somewhat dated and didn't list any specific companies to purchase. However, the author did provide a list of factors to examine when searching for a great company, including the following:

- A stream of profitable new products from an adequately funded research organization.
- An effective sales organization.
- Good profit margins that are consistently improving.
- A people-oriented company with management depth.
- A company with solid financial controls.
- A business that has growth potential but doesn't require major capital expenditures.
- A shareholder-friendly management group with great integrity.

It was obvious that Fisher believed that great companies delivered great returns, for he focused on the company rather than the stock.

This was the first investment book I had read that identified those qualities that made a company an outstanding investment. Most other books focus on the short-term numbers, rather than the factors that ensure that a company will be great over time. Significantly, the book suggests that investors become actively involved in researching companies before they purchase stock.

To supplement and contemporize Fisher's approach to identifying the best investments, I studied what the greatest investor of our time looks for in the companies that he purchases. Unfortunately, Warren Buffett hasn't written an investing book; however, he has been very generous in sharing his theories, wisdom, and experiences in speeches, lectures, interviews. He has also expressed his thoughts at the Berkshire Hathaway shareholder meetings and on the pages of the Berkshire Hathaway annual report. His definition from the 1996 annual meeting is wonderful in its simplicity:

> The definition of a great company is one that will be great for 25–30 years.

Obviously, Buffett and I were together in our belief that great companies should endure over time.

He expanded his definition of a great company in the following passage from the 1995 annual meeting:

> Wonderful castles surrounded by deep dangerous moats where the leader inside is an honest and decent person. Preferably, the castle gets its strength from the genius inside; the moat is permanent and acts as a powerful deterrent to those considering an attack; and inside the leader makes gold but doesn't keep it all for himself. Roughly translated we like great companies with dominant positions, whose franchise is hard to duplicate and has tremendous staying power of some permanence to it.

At last I had found someone who could provide the investing insight I was seeking into Great Companies. The fact that he is the most successful investor of our time makes me all the more confident in his definition of a great company from an investing perspective.

Finally, to get the CEO perspective, I conducted in-depth interviews with the chiefs of great companies like American International Group, Gillette, General Electric, and Pfizer to better understand what factors make up a great company. These corporate leaders claimed that there were a number of imposters: companies that had some of the qualities of a great company, but didn't measure up in all areas. They encouraged me to set the standard high and not to compromise when evaluating companies.

The chairmen and CEOs have a different perspective from the investment types and consultants, for they live in the operational world of quarterly returns, employees, and customers. They appreciate the importance of a terrific business. They relish having strong market shares and new products. They are driven by change and innovation, and the complexities of making a global business operate as if it were in one building rather than fifty countries. They interface with world leaders and politicians. The world is their market and they are players in the game of global business leadership.

The CEOs define great companies concretely, in terms of the qualities they possess rather than in flowery words. They believe that great companies are huge (in excess of $15 billion market cap) and global (not international or multinational, but fully integrated global corporations), with over 40 percent of revenues derived from international markets. They also believe strongly that great companies are in terrific businesses with capable leaders that consistently build shareholder wealth. These companies and their individual businesses are structured to manage competitive risks while aggressively exploiting attractive opportunities throughout the world. They believe that change creates opportunities for their companies—great companies embrace change rather than fighting or fearing it.

After researching the managerial, financial, and CEO perspectives on what makes a company a great investment, I developed this definition of a Great Company: a company that has consistently and dramatically built shareholder value over time, and will continue to build shareholder value at above index rates for years to come. These Great Companies don't have good quarters or years; they consistently have good decades. More importantly, these companies will continue to enjoy success into the foreseeable future. While they have occasionally stumbled, these are companies that have stood the test of time. They have weathered recessions, depressions, wars, and continue to shine. These companies are in great businesses, not by accident, but as a result of internal leadership. They look at change as an opportunity rather than a threat. These aren't blue chip companies or members of the "nifty fifty," they are the crown jewels of the best economic system on the globe. They are not just great American companies, these are companies that can compete with and win against any company anywhere in the world, and they do, day after day after day.

Ultimately, I concluded that a Great Company is a company whose stock I would be willing to purchase now and own forever.

I realize that forever is a long time, but if a company couldn't pass the "forever" test, then it wasn't a truly great company. With this definition as my guide, I began to search for the specific qualities that differentiated great companies from other companies.

Identifying the qualities shared by all truly great companies was complicated by the fact that the management experts, the investors, and the CEOs had somewhat differing opinions on the qualities of a great company. However, I soon realized that this diversity of opinion would ensure that the companies we identified would be great from a variety of perspectives, and this diversity would strengthen rather than weaken our criteria.

To really examine a company from these perspectives requires time, contacts, understanding, and experience. Most analysts don't have the time to conduct this type of in-depth analysis, and few have the necessary breadth of experience. Furthermore, most analysts are more comfortable looking at the numbers rather than the qualities of a company. As noted earlier, these analysts are also under pressure to deliver favorable reports about companies. While they might state that a company's earnings will be down this quarter, few analysts would suggest that a company is in a bad business and advise investors to avoid it on a long-term basis.

Let me say that many analysts do provide a valuable service, and that it's not my intention to knock their profession or lessen appreciation for their contributions. However, many analysts tend to focus on results rather than causes, and these causes are critical in identifying great companies.

What the Management Experts Think

I began the task of identifying the qualities that define great companies by studying *In Search of Excellence*. Peters and Waterman identified eight key traits that they found in all excellent companies. These included:

1. *A bias for action.* A preference for doing something—anything—rather than sending a question through cycles and cycles of analyses and committees.
2. *Staying close to the customer.* Learning customers' preferences and catering to them.
3. *Autonomy and entrepreneurship.* Breaking the corporation into small companies and encouraging them to think independently and competitively.
4. *Productivity through people.* Creating in *all* employees the awareness that their best efforts are essential and that they will share in the rewards of the company's success.
5. *Hands-on, value-driven management.* Insisting that executives keep in touch with the firm's essential business.
6. *Sticking to the knitting.* Remaining with the business the company knows best.
7. *Simple form, lean staff.* Few administrative layers, few people at the upper levels.
8. *Simultaneous loose/tight properties.* Fostering a climate where there is dedication to the central values of the company, combined with tolerance for all employees who accept those values.

From these criteria, Peters and Waterman then identified fourteen companies that they placed in a group called "exemplars," which embodied the eight factors listed above throughout their organizations: Bechtel, Boeing, Caterpillar Tractor, Dana, Delta, Digital Equipment, Emerson Electric, Fluor, Hewlett-Packard, IBM, Johnson & Johnson, McDonald's, Procter and Gamble, and 3M.

Collins and Porras's extensive research into the history and evolution of the eighteen companies analyzed in the groundbreaking book *Built to Last* revealed five key concepts that separated their visionary companies from the comparison benchmark companies:

1. *Big Hairy Audacious Goals (BHAGs)*. They have a commitment to the challenging, audacious—and often risky—goals and projects toward which a visionary company channels its efforts.
2. *Cult-like Cultures*. Great places to work, but only for those who buy into the core ideology.
3. *Try a Lot of Stuff and Keep What Works*. High levels of action and experimentation.
4. *Homegrown Management*. Promotion from within bringing to senior levels only those who've spent significant time steeped in the core ideology of the company.
5. *Good Enough Never Is*. A continual process of relentless self-improvement with the aim of doing better and better.

The eighteen firms identified as visionary companies included American Express, Boeing, Citicorp, Ford, General Electric, Hewlett-Packard, IBM, Johnson & Johnson, Marriott, Merck, Motorola, Nordstrom, Phillip Morris, Procter and Gamble, Sony, Wal-Mart, Walt Disney, and 3M. The authors did not consider stock market performance of these eighteen companies. In fact, they noted that "contrary to business school doctrine, 'maximizing shareholder wealth' or 'profit maximization' has not been the dominant driving force or primary objective of the visionary companies." However, the authors did include graphs that showed the shareholder returns of these companies, and the results were quite impressive.

WHAT BUFFETT THINKS

Next, I turned to Warren Buffett. He summarized his purchase requirements as follows:

When buying companies or common stocks, we look for first-class businesses accompanied by first-class managements.

Critical to Buffett's analysis is the quality of a company's business. He believes that the quality of the business is more important than the management.

> Ideally you want terrific management and a terrific business. And that's what we look for. But if you had to choose one, take the terrific business.

The following quotes help explain what Buffett defines as a great business:

> Look for the durability of the franchise. The most important thing to me is figuring out how big a moat there is around the business. What I love, of course, is a big castle and a big moat with piranhas and crocodiles.

> If you run across one good idea for a business in your lifetime, you're lucky; and fundamentally, this [Coca-Cola] is the best large business in the world. It has got the most powerful brand in the world. It sells for an extremely moderate price. It's universally liked, the per capita consumption goes up almost every year in almost every country. There is no other product like it.

> Distribution channels can make a fortune or nothing depending on how many channels there are. If there's one pipeline in between you can make a fortune. And that's what you are, for example, in the case of a daily newspaper. If there are a bunch of pipelines, you won't make anything.

> Generic products are not likely to affect Coke and chocolate brand names as much as cigarettes.

The following quotes define what he is searching for in management:

> Generally we like people who are candid. We can usually tell when somebody's dancing around something or when their re-

ports are a little dishonest or biased. It's just a lot easier to operate with people who are candid. And we like people who are smart.

Conversely, we do not wish to join with managers who lack admirable qualities, no matter how attractive the prospects of their business. We've never succeeded in making a good deal with a bad person.

A far more serious problem occurs when the management of a great company gets sidetracked and neglects its wonderful base business while purchasing other businesses that are so-so or worse. When that happens, the suffering of investors is often prolonged. Unfortunately, that is precisely what transpired years ago at both Coke and Gillette. (Would you believe that a few decades back they were growing shrimp at Coke and exploring for oil at Gillette?) All too often, we've seen value stagnate in the presence of hubris or of boredom that caused the attention of managers to wander. That's not going to happen again at Coke and Gillette, however—not given their current and prospective managements.

In summarizing what is key to Buffett, the critical points are as follows:

- *Great companies are in great businesses.* You absolutely can't have one without the other.
- *Great companies have built barriers such as brand franchises, market leadership, new products, and new technology that protect them from competitive attacks.* What's more, they continue to strengthen and fortify these barriers, and in so doing have made themselves virtually impenetrable to competition. I remember when the Clorox Corporation entered the detergent business. At the time, a good friend was the V.P. of sales at Clorox, a very well-run company. I suggested that P&G would fight Clorox to the death if Clorox launched a serious threat. He said that Clorox had a great new product and would capture a significant share of the market.

Clorox built plants and launched an aggressive program aimed directly at Procter's core detergent business. Within two years, Clorox was out of the detergent business and had lost millions of dollars. Procter had thrown everything at Clorox, *including* the "kitchen sink." It was impossible for Clorox to get by the crocodiles and piranhas in P&G's moat.

- *Great companies require very little capital to operate.* These companies are led by managers who effectively use funds to enhance shareholder value.
- *Great companies are focused. In Search of Excellence* refers to this trait by praising companies that "stick to their knitting."

Based on the most recent Berkshire Hathaway annual report, Buffett owns stock in the following publicly traded companies:

- American Express Company
- The Coca-Cola Company
- The Walt Disney Company
- Federal Home Loan Mortgage Corporation
- The Gillette Company
- McDonald's Corporation
- *Washington Post*
- Wells Fargo and Company

Buffett also owns a few shares in Berkshire Hathaway. In fact, Buffett is worth billions of dollars and is chairman of the board of one of the most successful companies in the United States. Had you invested $10,000 with the Buffett partnership in 1957 and used your money when the fund disbanded to buy Berkshire Hathaway, your original investment would be worth approximately $180 million—a compounded growth rate of slightly over 29 percent per annum.

WHAT THE CEOs THINK

I then considered the input I had received from the CEOs and CFOs of great companies during my interviews. These executives believed that the following factors were extremely important:

What Is a Great Company?

- *A great company is in great businesses.* Being in a good business is absolutely critical. Each CEO I spoke with either sold, spun off, or closed bad businesses shortly after being promoted to CEO. While Jack Welch is the leader in selling off and acquiring business, he certainly has a lot of company. The CEOs strongly believe that one of their most important roles is to ensure that their companies are in terrific businesses. Even today, these CEOs continue to change the mix of businesses they operate.

- *A great company is a fully integrated global company.* The executives I spoke with believed that the truly great companies function as well-coordinated global entities. This doesn't just mean that the company exports products to other countries, it means that the company has a fully integrated worldwide organization. They noted that great companies should derive at least 40 percent of their revenues/profits from international operations, and that these operations should be fully integrated. Ideally, they feel that these companies should market the same product all over the world. They also noted that great companies don't mentally divide their business into "U.S." and "international," for they are truly global companies and geographic barriers are meaningless to them.

- *A great company should have a market cap of at least $15 billion.* They pointed out that size offered a number of advantages and therefore great companies should have large market caps. These market caps allow them to make acquisitions, develop new products, stop competitors in their tracks, and prosper during economic downturns.

- *People are the most important asset of a great company.* Each executive I interviewed spends a significant portion of his time ensuring that the people in his company are being trained and prepared for the future. These companies promote almost exclusively from within, another important characteristic.

- *Great companies are focused on growth through innovation.* They look at change as a driver of opportunities and seek to convert these opportunities into revenues and profits. Each of the CEOs I interviewed invests heavily in R&D and believes that a sound R&D effort is a key to future growth.

- *Finally, great companies have a track record of excellent returns to shareholders and consistent earnings.* They are very much aware that Wall Street rewards consistent earnings growth, and that this factor is vital for increasing shareholder wealth.

What Makes for a Great Company?

QUALITIES	IN SEARCH OF EXCELLENCE	BUILT TO LAST	BUFFETT WISDOM	CEO INTERVIEWS
Highly regarded by experts	•	•		•
Terrific business			•	•
Companies with a past	•	•	•	•
Franchise / Moat			•	•
Measure of company value			•	•
Financial performance	•		•	•
Action oriented / Try a lot of stuff	•	•	•	•
Close to the customer	•		•	•
Stick to the knitting / Focus	•		•	
Hands-on / Value-driven	•		•	•
Simple form / Lean staff	•		•	
Productivity thru people / Cult-like cultures	•	•	•	•
Homegrown management		•	•	•
Good enough never is		•		•
Big hairy audacious goals		•		•
Simultaneous loose / tight properties	•			
Global company with 40% of revenues from overseas				•
Market cap in excess of $15 billion				•
People are the company's most valuable asset				•
Market leaders				•

After assimilating all of these viewpoints from the three different groups, I began to analyze and compare my data in order to identify differences and similarities. The chart on the opposite page summarizes the factors that are important to the management and financial experts, Warren Buffett, and the CEOs. From my analysis, I concluded that:

1. *The CEOs and Warren Buffett believe that the most important factor to consider is the quality of the businesses in which the company is engaged.* Interestingly, quality of business was not even considered by the management experts, who did not seek to rank or analyze the businesses of the companies they studied. Instead, they tended to focus on the quality of management.

2. *Both* In Search of Excellence *and* Built to Last *began their search for outstanding companies by assembling a group of highly regarded companies.* Buffett, by comparison, seems relatively unconcerned about how the companies he invests in are viewed by others. However, CEOs are very much aware of how the world looks at their companies.

3. *Financial performance is important to the CEOs, Buffett, and Peters and Waterman, but they use different measures to evaluate financial performance.* The CEOs look at consistency of returns, Buffett studies changes in intrinsic value, and Peters and Waterman consider more traditional financial criteria. The authors of *Built to Last* do not consider financial performance in their analysis of visionary companies, however they do include a chart that shows the investor returns their visionary companies have delivered over time.

4. *Buffett and the management experts seem to be biased toward large American companies.* While *Built to Last* did include Sony among its list of visionary companies, most of the firms they identified were headquartered in the U.S. While the CEOs did not express a bias, they did mention that it was far more meaningful to compare operating statistics of U.S. companies than to use overseas companies as benchmarks for comparison.

5. *The "moat effect," or the establishment of a sound franchise, which Buffett feels is critical in protecting a business, was seen as extremely*

important by the CEOs. The CEOs I interviewed spend billions of dollars on R&D, patents, and advertising to build wider and deeper moats. Jack Welch believes that GE must be either number one or number two in every business in which it competes, and either fixes or sells businesses that aren't market leaders.

6. *Innovation and new products were important from all three perspectives.* All those consulted realized that in order for a company to prosper and grow in the future, constant innovation is key to success. They believe that companies should be in tune with the needs of their customers and advances in technology. This combination will create value for the shareholders of the company and ensure long-term success.

7. *Creating a good working environment seemed to be important to everyone.* The CEOs were adamant that their most important asset was their people. Most of these executives view executive development as their most important role within their company.

The CEOs I interviewed were reluctant to mention companies that they thought were great companies. However, they were well aware of the companies that had passed our screens and felt that each company was certainly qualified to be on the list.

How the Results Compare

As a next step, I compared the twenty-nine companies selected by Collins/Porras and Peters/Waterman with the publicly traded stocks owned by Buffett and listed in the Berkshire Hathaway annual report. This comparison revealed some interesting findings:

- Buffett's two "inevitables," Coca-Cola and Gillette, aren't mentioned by the management experts.
- No one company appeared on all three lists.
- Only nine of the companies were found on two or more of the lists. Collins/Porras and Peters/Waterman had six companies in common: Boeing, Hewlett-Packard, IBM, Johnson & Johnson, Procter and Gamble, and 3M. Buffett owns shares of American Express, McDonald's, and Walt Disney, which are also included in the *Built to Last* and *In Search of Excellence* companies.

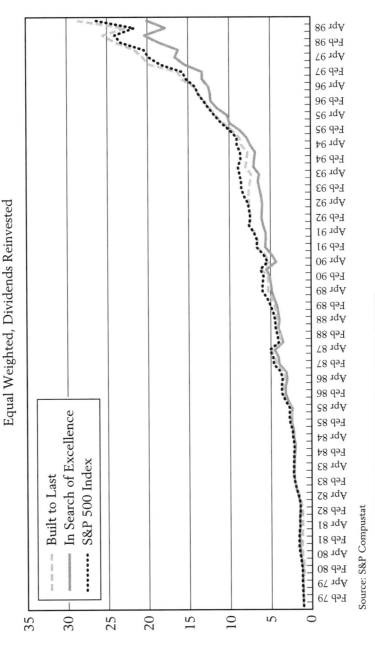

THE MANAGEMENT EXPERTS' PICKS VS. THE S&P 500

December 31, 1988 to December 31, 1998

Equal Weighted, Dividends Reinvested

Built to Last
In Search of Excellence
S&P 500 Index

Source: S&P Compustat

NOTE: PAST PERFORMANCE IS NOT INDICATIVE OF FUTURE RESULTS.

BUFFETT STOCKS VS. BUILT TO LAST, IN SEARCH OF EXCELLENCE, S&P 500

December 31, 1988 to December 31, 1998

Equal Weighted, Dividends Reinvested

Total returns on the S&P Indexes that have been calculated using PC Plus may differ from the total returns on the S&P Indexes calculated by Standard & Poor's.

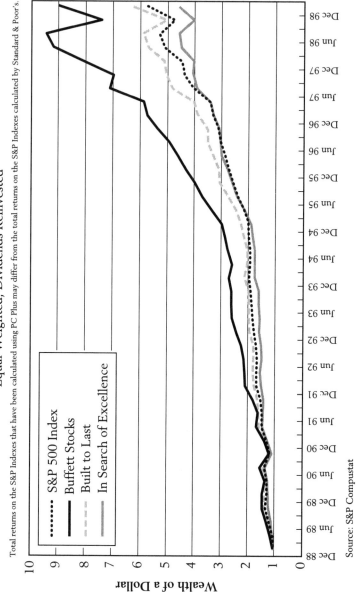

Source: S&P Compustat

NOTE: PAST PERFORMANCE IS NOT INDICATIVE OF FUTURE RESULTS.

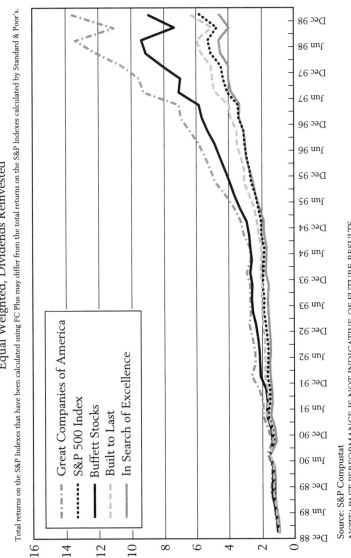

GREAT COMPANIES OF AMERICA VS. BUFFETT STOCKS, BUILT TO LAST, IN SEARCH OF EXCELLENCE, AND S&P 500 INDEX

December 31, 1988 to December 31, 1998

Equal Weighted, Dividends Reinvested

Total returns on the S&P Indexes that have been calculated using PC Plus may differ from the total returns on the S&P Indexes calculated by Standard & Poor's.

Legend:
- Great Companies of America
- S&P 500 Index
- Buffett Stocks
- Built to Last
- In Search of Excellence

Y-axis: Wealth of a Dollar (0, 2, 4, 6, 8, 10, 12, 14, 16)

X-axis: Dec 88, Jun 89, Dec 89, Jun 90, Dec 90, Jun 91, Dec 91, Jun 92, Dec 92, Jun 93, Dec 93, Jun 94, Dec 94, Jun 95, Dec 95, Jun 96, Dec 96, Jun 97, Dec 97, Jun 98, Dec 98

Source: S&P Compustat
NOTE: PAST PERFORMANCE IS NOT INDICATIVE OF FUTURE RESULTS.

- Using Buffett's definition of what makes for a great business, at least ten of the twenty-two companies selected by Peters/Waterman and Collins/Porras (45 percent) would have been eliminated from consideration, as follows:
    - Bechtel, Boeing, Delta, Caterpillar Tractor, Ford (capital and labor intensive)
    - Digital Equipment, Hewlett-Packard, IBM, Motorola (rapidly changing industry environment)
    - Phillip Morris (cigarette legislation)
    - Wal-Mart (retailing is a difficult business)

This analysis revealed that the companies Buffett invests in are indeed different from the companies identified by management experts as outstanding companies. This doesn't necessarily mean that Buffett is right and the management experts are wrong. Rather, it builds the case for looking at a Great Company from different perspectives.

Let's now examine the portfolio performance of the stocks selected by the management experts. The stocks of *In Search of Excellence* and *Built to Last* closely paralleled the S&P 500 over the past ten years. Let me state that it is somewhat unfair to evaluate the portfolios contained in the management books from the standpoint of shareholder returns since these books were never intended to be used as investment guides. However, if you believe as I do that one of the important roles of a great company is to build shareholder wealth, then the returns of these companies should be considered.

As you can see from the chart, the *In Search of Excellence* portfolio was slightly below the S&P 500 and *Built to Last* was slightly ahead over the past ten years. I used the S&P 500 because I believe it is more representative of today's market. Since many investors are quite happy with index funds, they would have found both the *In Search of Excellence* and the *Built to Last* portfolios to have been solid performers. Overall, both of the management experts' portfolios yielded solid returns. This stock market performance points out the importance of investing in well-managed companies.

I then compared Buffett's portfolio to the S&P 500 index and the management experts. As you might have guessed, Buffett's performance was outstanding. He beat the index and also handily beat the portfolios of the management experts. Buffett excelled by including the dimensions of a terrific business and the moat concept in his stock selection process, and using intrinsic value to provide for a safety margin.

Finally, I compared the performance of the Great Companies portfolio with those of Buffett and the management experts. The results were indeed impressive. The Great Companies outperformed all other portfolios.

Based on my research, I concluded that in order to identify great companies from both a management and financial perspective the following were important:

- *Starting with highly regarded companies is a good first step in understanding what makes for a great company.* In most cases, these highly regarded companies have earned their reputations.
- *Great companies must have demonstrated their ability to consistently build shareholder wealth over time.* There are sound reasons for being biased toward large companies headquartered in the U.S.
- *It's important for companies to have withstood the test of time. Built to Last* limited itself to analyzing companies that had been in business for fifty years, and this seemed to be a reasonable parameter.
- *The moat effect that Buffett and the CEOs embrace is very important.*
- *A company's ability to be innovative and develop new products is of critical importance.*

Since the factors that make for a great company from an investment standpoint are somewhat different than those that make for a great company from a management standpoint, and the CEOs present yet another set of qualities, and it was necessary to integrate these elements into one set of qualities that characterize all great companies in which you should invest. I was then able to identify the critical factors that investors like me needed to look for when selecting the companies that would make up their ideal portfolio:

QUALITIES OF GREAT COMPANIES
- Highly Regarded by Knowledgeable Experts
- Publicly Traded

- Headquartered in the United States
- In Business at Least 50 Years and Survived the Founder
- Market Cap in Excess of $15 Billion
- Global Company with at Least 40 Percent of Revenues/Profits from International Operations
- Outstanding Shareholder Returns
- Terrific Businesses
- Protected by Strong Barriers/The Moat Effect
- People Are the Company's Most Important Asset
- Outstanding Management Team That Keeps the Company in "Prime"
- Innovation-Driven Company That Turns Changes into Opportunities

These twelve qualities, derived from three separate sources, exist within all Great Companies. Only fourteen companies passed these twelve screens. These companies are, in alphabetical order:

- American International Group, Inc.
- Bristol-Myers Squibb Company
- Citigroup, Inc.
- The Coca-Cola Company
- Colgate-Palmolive Company
- General Electric Company
- The Gillette Company
- Johnson & Johnson
- Medtronic, Inc.
- Merck and Company, Inc.
- Merrill Lynch and Company, Inc.
- Pfizer, Inc.
- The Procter and Gamble Company
- Schering-Plough Corporation

As you read further, you will learn that these are indeed Great Companies, and should continue to remain great for years to come.

Chapter 3

THE TWELVE TRAITS OF GREAT COMPANIES

———◦◉◦———

YOU ARE BUYING COMPANIES IN BUSINESSES, NOT STOCKS

Investors must always be aware that they are buying companies, not stocks. These companies sell products or provide services, sell to and service customers, employ people to run the company, have a history of success or failure, and compete with other companies. While you may receive a paper stock certificate, it's the company behind the stock certificate that counts.

Investment advisors who recommend that investors purchase companies based on earnings growth, cash flow, and revenue growth without understanding the businesses of the companies that they recommend are looking at stocks, not companies. They believe that great returns/numbers make a great company. Many investment advisers follow this approach because it allows them to track and recommend a number of stocks without spending much time or effort on research. It takes time to really understand a company, especially a large global corporation that operates several different businesses. It's far easier and much less time-consuming to simply track the numbers or offer hot stock tips.

I strongly believe that investors should make an in-depth study of individual companies, not just review the companies' track records. I believe that great companies make great returns. The more an investor knows about a company and its businesses, the better the investment decision. In fact, investors should be able to easily write two paragraphs explaining why they invested in a particular company.

My twenty-plus years of consulting for a number of companies in a variety of different businesses helped me realize that the quality of the businesses in which a company was engaged and the quality of management within the company differed greatly from company to company, and from industry to industry. I found that these two variables, quality of business and quality of management, had a huge impact on a company's ability to generate free cash flow and thereby drive intrinsic value.

Over the years, I found that poorly run companies in bad businesses seldom survived. Normally, the combination of poor management and a difficult business is fatal. That's why it is so important to closely study IPOs (Initial Public Offerings). Many of these companies have not been around long enough to fail. I am quite familiar with an IPO that was in a very labor intensive business with questionable management at the helm. The company went public at $14.00 per share and within four months was trading at $28.00. After a disappointing earnings report (which I knew would come sooner rather than later), the stock plummeted by 50 percent overnight. It was a quick downhill slide to $6.00 and then merger. There are thousands of stories just like this one. Maybe the numbers and the industry differ, but the combination of poor management and a bad business are always fatal. The question isn't will they fail. The question is when will they fail.

I also found that there are a number of poorly managed companies in good businesses. These companies are poorly managed, but they are in such good businesses that the quality of the business compensates for the lack of management ability. These companies seldom make major strides within their industry, and their market share and profits remain relatively flat. Normally, they are acquired by one of the well-managed companies within the industry. Occasionally, a new management team is brought in to run the company and turns it around, but this is the exception rather than the rule.

Even when this turnaround occurs, the company finds that it does not have the size and clout to compete with the industry leaders, and is eventually sold. Tambrands falls neatly into this category. The company was in a solid consumer products business, feminine hygiene, but had generated disappointing results for shareholders. A new management team was brought in, led by a dynamic CEO who turned the business around. The CEO did a great job and as a result of his efforts, Tambrands was sold to Procter and Gamble, at a good return to Tambrand's shareholders. Other companies that fall into this category include Rubbermaid and First Brands. Both were acquired by large, well-managed companies after long periods of poor performance.

Interestingly enough, there are quite a few good companies in bad businesses. The management at these companies has figured out how to overcome the difficulties of the business, and successfully crafted a "silk purse" out of a "sow's ear." If their management teams hadn't been so effective, these companies would have either gone under or been acquired long ago. I will discuss IBP later in this chapter, but IBP is an example of a well-managed company in a very difficult business.

There are also a number of well-managed companies in good businesses. Many of these companies have grown and done reasonably well over the years, and many are highly regarded by "the Street." 3M is an excellent example of a well-managed company in a good business. But the rarest combination of all is the truly great company in a really great business. These are the true gems of the business world. They are the companies in which you want to invest for the long term.

The following excerpt, crafted by Warren Buffett and taken from Berkshire Hathaway's 1996 annual report says it best:

> Companies such as Coca-Cola and Gillette might well be labeled "the Inevitables." Forecasters differ a bit in their predictions of exactly how much soft drink or shaving-equipment business these companies will be doing in ten or twenty years. Nor is our talk of inevitability meant to play down the vital work that these companies must continue to carry out, in such areas as

manufacturing, distribution, packaging and product innovation. In the end, however, no sensible observer—not even these companies' most vigorous competitors, assuming they are assessing the matter honestly—questions that Coke and Gillette will dominate their fields worldwide for an investment lifetime. Indeed their dominance will probably strengthen. Both companies have significantly expanded their already huge shares of market during the past ten years, and all signs point to their repeating that performance in the next decade.

Obviously many companies in high-tech businesses or embryonic industries will grow much faster in percentage terms than will the Inevitables. But I would rather be certain of a good result than hopeful of a great one.

Of course, Charlie [Munger, Warren Buffett's business partner] and I can identify only a few Inevitables, even after a lifetime of looking for them. Leadership alone provides no certainties: Witness the shocks some years back at General Motors, IBM and Sears, all of which had enjoyed long periods of seeming invincibility. Though some industries or lines of business exhibit characteristics that endow leaders with virtually insurmountable advantages, and that tend to establish Survival of the Fattest as almost a natural law, most do not. Thus for every Inevitable, there are dozens of Imposters, companies now riding high but vulnerable to competitive attacks. Considering what it takes to be an Inevitable, Charlie and I recognize that we will never be able to come up with a Nifty Fifty or even a Twinkling Twenty. To the Inevitables in our portfolio, therefore, we add a few "Highly Probables."

Like Warren Buffett, at the end of our search for great companies we could not arrive at a "Twinkling Twenty"; in fact, we found that only fourteen companies passed our screens. Among these companies, some were clearly "inevitables," the rest, outstanding. It's important to understand the factors that separate these really great companies from the other companies in which you might invest.

———

It's one thing to understand the importance of investing in well-managed companies in great businesses; however, it's quite another to identify the qualities which, in combination, distinguish the Great Companies from other companies. I believe that these qualities not only separate the Great Companies from other companies for today, but will separate them from merely well-managed companies for years to come. This unbiased approach to identifying Great Companies will provide the investor with a select list of companies that should continue to be great. It should prove to be of value as you sort through companies in various sectors, market caps, or countries. We will discuss in detail how investors can use these screens in other ways later in the book.

The Great Companies screens take into account a number of factors in the analysis of a company. I am always amused to see an article claiming that some expert has found a simple secret for spotting great companies. The expert will claim that companies with great research and development departments are the companies to buy. Others will claim that buying companies that are market leaders is the best way to invest. Yet others shout that it's the quality of management. Still others feel that the quality of the board of directors is a key driver of success.

What they fail to realize is that identifying Great Companies should not be a one-dimensional process: it is the combination of qualities that makes for a Great Company. For example, if I were to ask you which part of your body was most important, you might respond, the brain, for our brain separates us from all of the other animals. Yet without your lungs to breath air, your heart to pump blood, and the blood vessels to carry the blood to your brain, your brain would be of little value. It's the same for a Great Company. In fact, the primary trait that distinguishes Great Companies from their lesser counterparts is that they are strong in virtually all of the critical areas that matter most.

Great does not mean perfect. While these companies have tremendous strengths that make them great and separate them from the pack of good companies, they do have weaknesses. These weaknesses tend to be minor and will not prove fatal, but the knowledgeable investor should be aware of these flaws.

The qualities of the Great Companies are presented in the order that they were applied to companies in the database. I evaluated our initial database of ninety-two companies using this sequence of twelve screens in order to identify what would end up being the fourteen Great Companies of America. As you will see, a number of very good companies were dropped from consideration as we progressed through the screening process. The fact that we did not include these companies among our Great Companies does not mean that they have provided investors with poor returns over time, or that they are unworthy of investment. It simply means that these companies did not meet our criteria for greatness.

Screen 1
HIGHLY REGARDED BY KNOWLEDGEABLE EXPERTS

We began our search for Great Companies by compiling a list of companies that were highly regarded by management experts and knowledgeable executives. By studying articles, surveys, and management books that sought to identify well-managed and highly successful companies, and using my consulting experience, I compiled a list of potential candidates. I studied numerous books that seek to define greatness or excellence among companies from a management perspective. A review of the literature includes:

- *In Search of Excellence* by Peters and Waterman. As mentioned earlier, this book identified eight factors that the writers felt determined excellence in corporations. The authors identified fourteen companies that possessed these qualities and deemed these firms to be excellent companies. Two of the companies identified as "exemplars" in this book are also included among our list of the fourteen Great Companies.
- *Built to Last* by Collins and Porras is similar to *In Search of Excellence* in that it sought to identify outstanding companies, detailed the five factors that made these companies great, and listed eighteen companies that met the criteria of a "visionary company." Our list of Great Companies includes five companies selected as visionary companies by the authors of *Built to Last*.
- *The Discipline of Market Leaders* by Treacy and Wiersema takes a slightly different approach. It studies eighty top companies in a va-

riety of industries and seeks to define the disciplines that make these companies market leaders. Since we believe that market leadership is a key element of being a great company, we reviewed the companies that were highlighted in this book. Because of the scope of the study, more companies were mentioned in this book than in the previous two. While the evaluation parameters were quite different, this book identified eleven companies that were also mentioned in the two other books.

- *Grow to Be Great* by Gertz and Baptista focuses on company growth. As they note on the cover, "No company ever shrank to greatness," and we believe that axiom to be true. Using their list of large-cap "Growth Champions" for reference, we found a significant correlation between profitable growth companies identified in this book and many of the companies named in the previous three books.

- Finally we reviewed *Competing for the Future* by Hamel and Prahalad, which addresses "breakthrough strategies for seizing control of your industry and creating the markets of tomorrow." While this book does not offer the reader a list of companies that the authors consider to be excellent in developing breakthrough strategies, it does mention a number of companies identified as superior in the previous texts.

We found that each book considered different factors in identifying superior companies. In a number of instances, the same companies were ranked as outstanding by authors who were relying on totally different criteria. For example, all five authors recognized Procter and Gamble, Hewlett-Packard, and Johnson & Johnson as being outstanding companies, but the criteria used for evaluation differed greatly.

We also turned to *Fortune* magazine in order to identify highly regarded companies. *Fortune* publishes a list of "America's Most Admired Companies" every year. This annual report focuses on the Fortune 1,000 companies, dividing them into various industry groups. According to *Fortune*, "More than 13,000 senior executives, outside directors, and financial security analysts were asked to rate the ten largest companies (or in some cases fewer) in their own industry by the eight key attributes of reputation." These eight key attributes included innovativeness; quality of management; value as a long-term investment; community and environmental responsibility; ability to attract, develop, and keep talented people; quality of products and services; financial soundness; and use of corporate assets.

The *Fortune* researchers then proceeded to rank 431 companies, divided into 49 distinct industry groups. The Great Companies were ranked either number 1 or number 2 (and in some cases held both positions) in seven of the eight industry groups in which they were represented. They earned an average score of 7.775, compared to the overall average of 6.61. Four of the Great Companies were ranked among the top 10 of all companies in the survey. Obviously, our Great Companies are a very select group.

I began the search for Great Companies with an initial list of ninety-two companies that were highly regarded by knowledgeable industry experts. I then began to screen each of these companies against the criteria that I had developed as a result of my analyses and conversations with the CEOs of four Great Companies.

Screen 2

PUBLICLY TRADED

With a database of companies to work with, I continued the screening process. The second screen was designed to eliminate companies that were not publicly traded from the list. Since we were searching for companies in which individuals could invest, we obviously sought out companies whose stocks were publicly traded and available for purchase. We gave no preference to any company based upon which U.S. exchange the stock was listed with. We simply wanted to ensure that each company was listed on an exchange like the New York Stock Exchange, the American Stock Exchange, or NASDAQ.

Unfortunately, this screen forced us to eliminate some privately held, well-managed companies like the following:

• *Ocean Spray,* a cooperative that turned a tart-tasting berry into a billion-dollar-plus profitable business, and fostered the growth of a brand that is a real powerhouse.

- *Mars, Inc.*, a wonderful company with a unique culture that has resulted in quality products and high market shares. Mars has a host of outstanding brands, and a solid international business.
- *Cargill*, with over 1,000 locations in sixty-five countries. *Forbes* lists Cargill's revenues at $51.5 billion.
- *Hallmark Cards*, a highly successful company that is a powerful market leader. I can only dream about the tremendous returns they must enjoy.
- *S. C. Johnson & Son*, one of the classiest, most professional companies I have been exposed to. They have a great corporate culture and some durable brand franchises, which they are expanding via acquisition.
- *United Parcel Service*, a dominant provider of freight and delivery services.

All of these companies stand out among their peers; however, since they are not publicly traded at this time, they were dropped from further consideration.

Screen 3
HEADQUARTERED IN THE UNITED STATES

Our next screen separated companies headquartered in the U.S. from those headquartered in other countries. While this screen would seem to be somewhat insignificant in determining a company's greatness, it was necessary since I wanted to focus on Great Companies headquartered in the U.S. for the following reasons:

- Accounting standards imposed on U.S. companies are rigid and ensure clear and accurate reporting.
- It is far easier to obtain comparable data on U.S.-based businesses than foreign corporations.
- It is easier for potential investors to purchase shares of U.S. stocks.

However, as I focused on this screen of U.S.-based companies, I came to realize that it was far more important than I had originally believed. Sure, it makes financial comparisons of companies easier and more accurate, but companies based in the U.S. also have a distinct advantage over other companies for the following reasons:

1. *Because America has a free-market economy, U.S. companies must be able to compete and win without the benefit of government protection from competitors.* Many other countries protect their national companies from outsiders. As a result, these companies have a more difficult time competing on a level global playing field. Our open-market environment has led to the survival of the fittest. It has forced U.S. companies to aggressively restructure and reengineer their operations. It has allowed them to use the strong business base they have developed in the U.S., a large and sophisticated market, to expand into other less developed and less sophisticated markets. The fact that the U.S. economy has been strong has further funded these expansion efforts.

2. *These U.S. companies have aggressively endorsed technology, and have used technology to distinguish themselves from their competitors.* As you read the GE interview with Jack Welch, you will discover how GE has used technology to redesign business models. GE's new technology-driven business models produce far more profit growth from historically low-growth businesses than anyone thought possible. Virtually all of our other Great Companies are also using technology to increase revenues and profits while reducing costs and improving service.

3. *Furthermore, as a result of the increased use of technology, U.S.-based companies have dramatically improved their R&D efforts, a key to future growth.* The end result is that better products come to market at lower costs and in less time. A January 1998 article in *Forbes* notes that in the past, "A pharmaceutical giant employing hundreds of researchers would count itself lucky to concoct 50 molecules a year that had some prospect as potential drugs. Now pharmaceuticals executives talk openly of concocting thousands—even millions—of test molecules. As before, only a few will turn into medically useful products, but there will be more of them, and they will come faster and cheaper."

4. *Today, many U.S. companies are mounting major quality initiatives.* The Six Sigma efforts of GE and others are improving quality

and increasing revenues and profits while reducing costs. These quality initiatives will provide U.S. companies with key operating advantages as they compete on a global basis.

All of these factors are contributing to the worldwide success of large, global, well-managed, technology-supported, U.S. companies in terrific businesses. I believe that we are entering an era when these companies will enjoy unprecedented growth in both revenues and profits. They are powerful and getting stronger. Many of them will dominate markets on a global basis.

My feelings on this issue were reaffirmed by the October 26, 1998 issue of *Fortune*, which ranked the "World's Most Admired Companies." Of the twenty-five world's most admired "All-Stars" (the twenty-five best companies in the world), twenty are headquartered in the United States, and nine of the twenty are included in our Great Companies.

This screen in no way implies that all Great Companies are head-quartered in the United States. Quite the contrary, there are a number of fine companies based in other parts of the world. As a result of this screen, I was forced to exclude some truly wonderful companies from the list.

Screen 4

IN BUSINESS FOR AT LEAST FIFTY YEARS AND SURVIVED THE FOUNDER

With our initial database somewhat reduced, we then screened the remaining companies for business longevity. I believe that a Great Company is a company that has stood the test of time. A Great Company has survived recessions, prospered from the onslaught of competition, flourished as it developed, and successfully marketed new products, and built market share or its business franchise against all odds. Most importantly, these companies created winning values and developed outstanding talent capable of taking over and leading them to future successes. It takes time for a company to develop these attributes, and only the truly Great Companies ever reach this pinnacle of success. I chose fifty years as the time frame, for I feel this time span will tell the investor a lot about the company and its management team.

During this phase of the screening process I also sought to eliminate companies whose founders were still involved in the business. Unfortunately, it is very difficult for some companies to survive and prosper once the founder is no longer actively involved. Experience has shown that outstanding founders don't always build outstanding companies that can survive and prosper after their departure. In many cases their skills and abilities are so strong that it is difficult for anyone to step up and fill the void.

As a result of this screen, we eliminated some outstanding companies from further consideration. Included among these companies were:

- *Microsoft*, the great American success story. Bill Gates is such a force at Microsoft that it is difficult to predict how the company will fare once Gates is no longer actively involved.
- *Berkshire Hathaway Inc.*, the company run by the second-wealthiest man in the United States and one of the greatest investors of our time, Warren Buffett. Buffett has established an investment track record that may never be broken. One thousand dollars invested in Berkshire Hathaway at the stock's peak in 1965 would now be worth approximately $1,686,195. Not bad for a relatively unknown investor from Omaha. While we couldn't list Berkshire Hathaway as a Great Company, I am proud to say that I am a shareholder.

By excluding these firms, we are not implying that Buffett and Gates aren't building Great Companies that will grow and develop long after these two men are no longer active in the business. We are simply suggesting that no one will know if they are building Great Companies until several years after their departure. Companies that were excluded by this screen include firms that will be the high-tech success stories of the twenty-first century. As we will discuss in chapter 5, by modifying this screen investors are able to develop what we refer to as the Great Companies of the Future, a group of companies that will lead the United States into a new and exciting, technology-driven future.

MARKET CAPITALIZATION IN EXCESS OF $15 BILLION

We next screened companies for market cap. The market capitalization of a company is calculated by multiplying the number of shares of stock outstanding by the closing price of the stock. For example, a company with five million shares outstanding that closed at $20 per share the previous day would have a market capitalization of $100 million. Normally the term "market capitalization" is shortened to "market cap" or "cap."

Companies that have market caps greater than $5 billion are referred to as large-cap companies, since they have a large market capitalization. Companies with market caps below $500 million are referred to as small-cap companies. Those firms with a market cap between $5 billion and $500 million are referred to as mid-cap stocks.

The chart on the following page reveals that over the long run, stocks produced the greatest returns for shareholders.

The Small-Cap Stock Anomaly

Further analysis of the data reveals that during the period 1974 to 1983 small-cap stocks showed remarkable growth, averaging in excess of 36 percent per year. Dr. Jeremy J. Siegel's outstanding investment book, *Stocks for the Long Run*, offers some very interesting findings regarding the small-cap phenomenon. Dr. Siegel found that ". . . If the nine year period from 1975–1983 is eliminated, the total accumulation in small-cap stocks over the entire period from 1926 through 1992 falls nearly 25 percent below that in large caps."

Data that PaineWebber analyzed from Ibbotson Associates reveals that $1 invested in small-cap stocks at the end of 1925 and held through the end of 1996 would have grown to $4,496, assuming reinvestment of dividends. That same $1 invested in the S&P 500 would have grown to $1,371. However, if the period 1975 to 1983 were excluded, the $1 in small caps would be worth $296, while the large-cap investment would be worth $368, 24.3 percent more. This nine-year period tremendously inflates small-cap returns and distorts the true long-term investment picture. If we were to eliminate this

Stocks and Real Assets

1977 - 1997

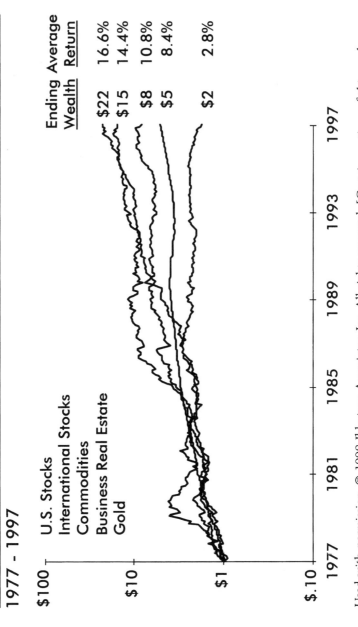

	Ending Wealth	Average Return
U.S. Stocks	$22	16.6%
International Stocks	$15	14.4%
Commodities	$8	10.8%
Business Real Estate	$5	8.4%
Gold	$2	2.8%

period from our analysis, then large-cap stocks would significantly outperform their small-cap counterparts.

Researchers at PaineWebber found that when examining statistical analyses of small-cap returns, it is important to note that many small-cap indexes are "paper portfolios" that cannot be replicated in the "real world" for several reasons:

1. *First, a significant portion of most small-cap indexes consists of stocks with very small market caps or thinly traded shares.* Institutional investors and money managers would be reluctant to own large positions in these companies.
2. *Second, publicly available small-stock indexes typically overstate the performance investors can receive because trade execution costs are not deducted from benchmark performance.* Since small caps typically trade at lower volume levels, their illiquidity produces wider bid/ask spreads. The typical result is substantially higher execution costs (brokerage costs, the difference between bid and offer price and market clearing price, and the adverse impact that trading has on a stock's price) for investing in small stocks and wider performance disparities with public indexes.
3. *Third, according to the* Journal of Portfolio Management, *the supposed historical price performance of some small- and mid-cap indexes is on a "survivor basis."* A portfolio that was created with the benefit of hindsight necessarily excludes the unsuccessful failures and includes only the successful survivors. By adjusting the companies in a small-cap index for this survivor effect, performance of the index could double what it might realistically be.

Detailed analyses of small-cap returns suggest that consistency of returns is lacking and that during normal times, the returns of small-cap stocks have not been as attractive as the historical data may seem to indicate. These findings suggest that the patient, long-term investor should be heavily invested in large-cap stocks. Large-cap stocks with market caps greater than $15 billion provide the investor with a number of additional key advantages:

1. *Large companies have far greater resources than small companies.* We believe that all truly Great Companies are large. The corollary

is that if small companies are so great, why aren't they big? We have observed and consulted with excellent small companies staffed by fine managers. Many of these companies are fine operators, but they aren't large Great Companies and there is a real difference. These smaller companies lack the financial resources of the Great Companies. Most don't have a surplus of outstanding managers capable of leading the company to greatness. And very few possess the clout and resources required to take on mega-opportunities in other parts of the world. They may be very good companies and record greater revenue percent increases than the Great Companies in the short run, but they can't compete with them in the long run.

2. *Obviously, large companies with significant market shares and business franchises are at a competitive advantage in the increasing-return arena.* For these market leaders have the potential for significant upside growth and have the opportunity to dominate the market. Microsoft is an excellent case in point. Rather than look at all large-cap stocks as lumbering dinosaurs, we should think of the outstanding large-cap companies as potential King Kongs, capable of dominating the marketplace. Dr. Siegel found that in the last five years, the average earnings growth of the nation's thirty largest companies has been 19.5 percent vs. just 11.6 percent for all the companies in the S&P index.

3. *If a company is to compete aggressively on an international basis, a key to future success, it must be capable of matching the resources and global distribution capabilities of other large international competitors.* Establishing a defensible international beachhead is expensive and often requires more resources and time than management of a small- to medium-size company can muster.

4. *Capitalizing on tomorrow's huge opportunities will require significant resources.* For example, how many companies will be able to seriously challenge Gillette for the worldwide razor-blade market? Not many! The amount of money required to compete on a global basis is huge and the costs will increase as the Great Companies grow bigger and stronger, making their fortresses virtually impenetrable to attacks by competitors.

5. *We believe that large-cap companies afford the investor a much greater level of investment security.* You will sleep well at night

knowing that you own the best-managed companies in the world. While large-cap companies can encounter problems and experience difficult times, their huge asset base affords them a number of advantages, including survival. I can't imagine one of our Great Companies losing half of its market share overnight. On the other hand this happens on a daily basis with the small-cap, momentum-driven companies. We believe that a Great Company with a large market cap is the height of shareholder security.

6. *A well-run large-cap company will receive a high financial rating, and this is important when borrowing.* Typically, the higher the credit rating, the lower the interest rate paid. Therefore, large, highly rated companies have access to large amounts of cash at relatively low interest rates.

7. *A large market capitalization can also be valuable when making major acquisitions.* It provides management with a resource against which it can borrow funds. In a pooling-of-interest transaction— one where the acquiring company swaps shares of its company for ownership in the company being acquired—a large cap can leverage its market value to finalize the acquisition or merger.

As a result of the previous analysis, we believe that large-cap stocks should form the core of most investors' holdings. *The Roaring 2000s,* a bestselling book on the economy of the future noted, "The more each leading company grows, the more it will enjoy greater economies of scale and brand-name advantages, making it impossible for marginal companies to compete." As we noted, large market cap provides a number of benefits. For the purposes of this screen, a large-cap stock was defined as having a market capitalization in excess of $15 billion. Companies with market caps below $15 billion were dropped from consideration.

This screen forced us to eliminate companies including the following:

• *The William Wrigley Company*—a firm with a wonderful brand franchise and a strong international presence.
• *Clorox*—a well-managed and rapidly growing consumer products company.

• *Mattel*—A company with a number of excellent brand franchises—and a firm I have consulted with.

S c r e e n   6

GLOBAL COMPANIES WITH AT LEAST FORTY PERCENT OF REVENUES/PROFITS FROM INTERNATIONAL OPERATIONS

The next screen sought to separate global companies from nonglobal companies. I believe that a fully integrated global presence will be critical for future earnings growth as markets make the transition from national to global. It's important to distinguish a truly global company from a firm that sells product overseas. In the book *Global Vision* the authors note that global companies differ from the three traditional international business models:

1. *The global exporter (the Japanese model).* These exporters usually develop local sales capacity in new markets by finding trading partners to serve as their agents. Global exporters are not configured to do business anyplace because most of their trusted and talented personnel are concentrated in the home business center. It is difficult to sustain the advantages of this type of business over time in a foreign market.
2. *The multinational (the U.S. model).* Multinationalism usually begins with the creation of national sales and service organizations, often followed soon after by national manufacturing organizations.
3. *The multilocal (the traditional European model).* Multilocals do not approach the world as one business system but rather as a set of individual markets, each to be approached separately.

Five factors distinguish global companies from these three models:

1. *"Global" is a business concept.* To be global means that you have a global strategy and a worldwide plan in terms of your products, marketing, manufacturing, logistics, and R&D.
2. *A global company has no boundaries.* Where a global company has its headquarters is transparent to the market or individual cus-

tomer. The global company is prepared to do business anywhere in the world.

3. *Not only does a global company serve its customers with excellence, but it has a delivery system that is highly sensitive to local customer needs and cultures.*

4. *A global company balances those aspects of the company that must be viewed and planned as a global system with those aspects that must be highly sensitive to local requirements.*

5. *The global company takes a long-term perspective.* It realizes that the globalization process takes time.

Having a viable global presence is critical for the following reasons:

- *A company must be capable of competing for sophisticated customers in a variety of markets if it is to leverage its products and brands on a worldwide basis.*
- *Some huge international markets are critical for amortizing product development and marketing costs.*
- *Some of these megamarkets are strategic because of the enormous potential volume they could deliver.*
- *If a company can build a major presence in the competitor's home market, it can siphon off profits the competitor might use to defend or attack in another market.*
- *A strong global presence enables a company to significantly leverage future acquisitions.* For example, Gillette's strong international presence will enable it to dramatically increase international revenues of Duracell (a recent Gillette acquisition). Likewise Procter and Gamble will be able to drive international revenues at Tambrands (a recent P&G acquisition), which are underdeveloped relative to P&G's.
- *Significant international experience and exposure provides a wonderful learning environment for the future.* During the crisis in Asia many of the Great Companies aggressively pursued and made key acquisitions. Their experiences in Latin America provided a road map that they followed in Asia. Several of the Great Companies had seen the crisis developing in Asia long before it hit the markets. They planned and executed strategies that turned the Asian crisis into an enormous opportunity.

In *The Roaring 2000s,* Harry S. Dent Jr. aptly summarized the importance of having a global presence when he wrote, "Many people will be surprised to see more large, established companies suddenly in trouble—not merely downsizing, but rapidly losing market share. On the other hand, the nimblest of our larger companies will see the urgency of moving into new markets and adopting the network organizational model that will sustain their leadership. The best will continue to realize the urgency of moving their mature, standardized products and services into the international markets, especially into the emerging third-world countries that are successfully industrializing."

Further, Dent noted that "The companies that you should watch, work for, or invest in are the gazelles. These are the 3 percent that have thrived during the last decade or companies like GE, Coca-Cola, and Gillette that are dominating emerging new markets overseas with proven products from the past."

Since it takes time to build an international business base, companies that don't generate at least 40 percent of today's profits and/or revenues from international operations are already at a serious disadvantage. On the other hand, companies with 40 percent or more of their revenues/profits from international markets are well positioned for the future.

Good companies that failed to pass this screen include:

- *Abbott Laboratories*—a fine company that came very close to passing this screen with 38 percent of its sales generated outside of our borders.
- *Walt Disney*—a well-known and highly respected industry leader.
- *Wal-Mart*—without a doubt, the best retailer in the United States.

While all three are fine companies and expanding internationally, their international business is underdeveloped when measured by our criterion.

Screen 7
OUTSTANDING SHAREHOLDER RETURNS

Those companies that cleared the first six screens were then screened for financial performance from a shareholder's perspective.

Since companies are expected to create wealth for their shareholders either through dividends or share price increases, or both, we considered all forms of shareholder returns when assessing returns. We examined two dimensions of shareholder returns:

- *Consistency of returns.* Did the company beat the S&P 500 year in and year out, or did it have one great year followed by a succession of poor-to-average years? We also compared company returns versus industry returns. We examined returns on a one-, three-, five-, ten-, and twenty-year basis. This forced us to exclude Motorola, IBM, and other very fine companies. A recent article in *Barron's* listed the fifteen companies with market caps over $10 billion that had the most consistent earnings growth over the past ten years. Four of the Great Companies were listed among the six top-rated firms. As Warren Buffett states, "you pay a high price for certainty." The fact that these companies deliver consistent earnings is further reflected in their PE ratios.
- *Level of returns.* We also considered total returns over twenty years (December 31, 1978, to December 31, 1998). During the twenty-year period measured, the S&P 500 grew at a rate of 17.78 percent per annum.

Overall, our Great Companies turned in index-beating results over three-, five-, ten-, and twenty-year periods.

As a result of this screen, we dropped the 3M Company from our list of Great Companies. While 3M passes a number of our screens and is noted for its innovation, the returns have fallen short of the level required for a Great Company. Xerox, once a Wall Street darling, continues its downslide and was also dropped.

Screen 8

TERRIFIC BUSINESSES

I believe that if you were to take one single element that is the most significant determinant of a Great Company, it would be this screen: Terrific Business. While some Great Companies are better managed than others, and some have provided shareholders with higher returns than others, **all Great Companies are in terrific busi-**

nesses. As we noted earlier, Warren Buffett is convinced of the importance of a terrific business, as he explained in a 1995 shareholders' meeting:

> Ideally you want terrific management and a terrific business. And that's what we look for. But if you had to choose one, take the terrific business.

It's important to understand that a terrific business is composed of two very important but quite distinct elements: the **industry** in which the company operates and the **business model** that the company employs. Historically, industries have changed very little over time (however, with the huge impact of technology, it is quite possible that industries that are unattractive from an investing perspective today may become far more attractive in the future). On the other hand, business models are dynamic and should constantly change and evolve. All Great Companies are continually adjusting their business models in order to take advantage of new opportunities that are emerging throughout the world. It's important for investors to understand how the industry in which a company operates and the business models the company employs should impact their investment decisions.

The Industry

From an investing perspective, some industries are far more attractive than others. While the management of a company in an unattractive industry might implement a new business model that generates more profitable growth and higher returns for shareholders than other companies within the industry, it is very difficult to alter the basic fundamentals of the industry.

As Buffett has noted, "Our conclusion is that, with few exceptions, when management with a reputation for brilliance tackles a business with a reputation for poor fundamental economics, it is the reputation of the business that remains intact."

Let me use an example to demonstrate the importance of being in a good industry. Imagine that you are a school bus driver and every morning after you drop off the children at school, you drive your bus back to a parking lot in the country. There is a straight stretch of road that you travel, and almost every morning as you reach this stretch, some guy in a red Ferrari 550 Maranello (a car with almost 500 horsepower that can reach speeds of 199 mph and sells for $200,000) comes up behind you and then blows by you as if you were standing still. He always toots the horn and waves as he shoots down the road. After a while, this begins to drive you crazy. Just once when he comes up behind you in his little red Ferrari, you dream of stomping down on the accelerator and pulling away from him. As you leave him in your dust, you wave out the window and toot. Unfortunately, this becomes an obsession, and eventually you reach the breaking point. You buy a Ferrari engine and have it installed in your bus. You take your bus out for a test ride and can't believe how fast it is with the new engine.

The next morning after you drop off the kids, a fiendish little smile comes over your face as you head into the straightaway. You glance in the mirror, and sure enough here comes your little friend. You've rehearsed this in your mind a thousand times. As he comes up to pass, you will downshift into second gear, pop the clutch, scream the tires, and blow him off the road. See you later, dude. As expected, he pulls out into the passing lane. It's the moment you have dreamed about. You grab the shift knob, downshift into second gear, pop the clutch, and your new Ferrari engine roars with the fury of 500 horses. The bus lurches forward, throwing you back into the seat. WOW! He's yours! You've won! He's dead meat! All of a sudden you look out the window and the guy in the Maranello comes screaming by you, gives a slight wave, and toots just like every other morning. How can this be? You have a Ferrari engine.

It's really pretty simple. You see, you have a bus, and try as you might, your bus will never, ever be (or beat) a Ferrari. Your bus is faster than all of the other school buses, but your bus is still a bus. Racing against the other buses, you look like a star, but against a Ferrari, you are history. It's the same with businesses. Some industries have very good fundamentals, and some industries do not. Companies in bad industries can become better than their competitors by bringing in a new management team, redesigning processes, cutting costs, building barriers, and improving returns. In fact, a company may become the most profitable company in its industry sector, but without implementing a new business model that alters the industry's dynamics, it's still a bus.

As Buffett noted, "In a difficult business, no sooner is one problem solved than another surfaces—never is there just one cockroach in the kitchen. Second, any initial advantage you secure will be quickly eroded by the low return that the business earns."And, in other remarks on the same subject, "When you're in an easy business, you're going to look like a genius. If you're in a tough business, you're going to look like a dolt. Having had that insight—after only twenty-three or twenty-four years—I got out of the textile business."

If you are familiar with IBP, you know that it is the largest processor of beef and pork in the world. I am convinced that IBP (Iowa Beef Processors)—with whom I have done consulting work for almost twenty years—is one of the better-managed companies in the country. IBP is responsible for revolutionizing the meat industry in the United States by replacing hanging carcass beef with boxed beef. In making this transition, IBP's outstanding management team totally reengineered the business from slaughter to distribution, including in-store merchandising. In the process they dramatically reduced costs and improved product quality. They dominated the beef industry, and followed the same model in pork.

I believe that IBP is without a doubt the best-run meat company in the world. Unfortunately, IBP is still in the beef and pork processing business, a commodity-oriented, price-sensitive, extremely competitive, labor-intensive business where supply is impacted by factors beyond IBP's control. IBP's Ferrari engine (its extremely capable management team) allows it to trounce the other buses (meat companies) in the industry, but IBP is still a bus.

In evaluating industries from an investing perspective, it's vitally important to understand the qualities that separate an unattractive industry from an attractive industry. Let's begin by examining the qualities of an unattractive industry.

Commodity Industries. Warren Buffett seemed to cover the subject when he noted that "In a commodity business, it's very hard to be smarter than your dumbest competitor." IBP is a very well-managed company, but it is in a commodity business, processing meat. The business is price competitive, labor intensive, cyclical (depends on demand for and supply of cattle), and dynamic. If you aren't the low-cost producer in a commodity-oriented business, you are in trouble. IBP continually tries to squeeze every penny out of the business.

There are literally hundreds of commodity-oriented businesses, including:

- Metals (steel and aluminum)
- Bulk chemicals
- Commodity food products, such as flour, coffee, orange juice, tuna, and produce. P&G, an excellent marketer and one of our Great Companies, exited the orange juice business after several years because it was so difficult to make money in a commodity-driven business with strong competition.
- Paper (often thought of as a commodity)
- Oil and gas
- Textiles

We would encourage investors to avoid price-driven, commodity-oriented industries.

Industries with High Labor Costs. Some industries have extremely high labor costs, which make it difficult to increase sales without proportionately increasing costs, the ideal strategy for increasing returns on capital. In the ideal business, you can increase sales by 10 percent with a 2 percent increase in manufacturing or labor costs. The pharmaceutical industry works along these lines. Pharmaceutical companies are able to increase sales as manufacturing expenses decline because their production processes are highly automated. In contrast, the consulting business is a high labor-cost business. If you sign new projects, you must hire people to work on them. You can reduce labor costs as a percentage of sales in consulting by bringing in less expensive consultants to do the "grunt work" for senior consultants, developing services that are more product oriented than custom consulting, and improving processes. However, at the end of the day the consulting business is a labor-intensive business.

Boeing is in a very labor-intensive business. Boeing signed a number of contracts to produce planes for customers all over the world, but the company experienced real problems delivering the planes on time because it was so difficult to hire skilled workers fast enough to build them. Unfortunately, this is the nature of the business, and the reason we dropped Boeing from our list of potentially great companies. The automobile industry is also labor intensive. While automotive companies are trying to automate their plants and reduce labor costs, they must battle labor unions every step of the way. I applaud the progress the automobile industry has made in reducing labor costs, but this will be a long and costly battle.

Capital-Intensive Industries. It is far better to be in a business that is not capital intensive than in one that requires heavy infusions of capital. For example, would you rather own a company that returned $5 million in profit on a capital base of $2 million, or a business with the same growth characteristics that delivered $2 million in profit on a capital base of $15 million? You would undoubtedly opt for the first company. Why? Because your return on capital invested is so much higher.

Warren Buffett noted that "The really desirable business is the one that doesn't take any money to operate because it's already proven that money will not enable anyone to get a position within the business. Those are the great businesses." He remarked, further, that "The airline business is a very tough business. It's capital intensive, it's labor intensive and it's a commodity product. You can't have a worse description than that. All you do is spend money." The airlines have tried to build brand loyalty, but price is still a dominant factor in selecting which flight to take. No airline passed our investing screens for Great Companies.

Industries That Are Harmful to Society. Industries that benefit society are better industries than those that are harmful to society. Phillip Morris was listed among the "visionary" companies by Collins and Porras. The company has an excellent return on capital, strong brand franchises, an international presence, and brand-loyal users. Unfortunately, this business is dangerous to the people who consume the product. As a result, the cigarette companies are continually involved in litigation with consumers who claim that the product they purchased caused them bodily harm. Fundamentally, the cigarette industry is very attractive because profit margins are good, production is highly mechanized, the product has a high level of consumption among users, branding builds loyalty, and a large segment of the population uses the product. However, the looming threat of lawsuits resulted in companies in the tobacco industry being dropped from further consideration.

Rapidly Changing Industries. Businesses that change rapidly carry with them some inherent risks. Consider some of the high-tech businesses, where you are a leader one day and a laggard the next. These companies can see their market caps dramatically reduced overnight. Investors who invest in these industries must be aware of the risks they face. While the returns in these industries may be extraordinary if the investor selects the right company, the losses may be equally devastating if the wrong company is chosen. Buffett remarked in the 1996 Berkshire Hathaway annual report:

> In studying the investments we have made in both subsidiary companies and common stocks, you will see that we favor businesses and industries unlikely to experience major change. The reason for that is simple: Making either type of purchase we are searching for operations that we believe are virtually certain to possess enormous competitive strength ten or twenty years from now. A fast-changing industry environment may offer the chance for huge wins, but it precludes the certainty we seek.

We have included several pharmaceutical companies among our Great Companies. While these firms are in an industry that is dynamic, we believe that virtually all industries will be subject to significant changes in the future as the technology wave sweeps over the world. Furthermore, pharmaceutical companies' new products are protected by patents for twenty years, thereby providing some degree of safety. While companies in the pharmaceutical industry are changing, we believe that this is a measured change and that the companies we have selected for inclusion in the portfolio do not present an unusually high risk for the investor. However, one must realize that any investment in common stocks presents certain risks.

Retailing. I have seen numerous cases where retailers that have developed a new concept or store format like Toys "R" Us, The Limited, and Home Depot are attacked by competitors. It appears very difficult to protect these new formats. Retailers with a hot format rush to open stores so they can reap the rewards before a competitor catches on. Ultimately, the company runs out of geography, or another retailer duplicates the format and same-store sales begin to level off or decline. Growth slows and shareholder returns begin to lag. I believe that the Internet will have an enormous impact on retailing as it exists today, thereby making an unattractive business even less attractive. I found Buffett's thoughts on this topic of interest:

> Retailing is a tough business. During my investment career, I have watched a large number of retailers enjoy terrific growth and superb returns on equity for a period, and then suddenly nosedive, often all the way into bankruptcy. The shooting-star phenomenon is far more common in retailing than it is in manufacturing or service businesses. In part, this is because a retailer must stay smart, day after day. Your competitor is always copying and then topping whatever you do. Shoppers are meanwhile beckoned in every conceivable way to try a stream of new merchants. In retailing to coast is to fail.

Nordstrom, an outstanding retailer and my choice for best men's store, was dropped from further consideration. While Nordstrom is an excellent company and is recognized in *Built To Last* as a visionary company, we were forced to drop it from our portfolio of Great Companies.

Fast food/restaurants. The fast-food/restaurant business is vulnerable to the same dangers as retailing. Another restaurant or fast-food company can open across the street and dramatically cut into sales and profits. The high labor costs, the initial investment required, and the difficulty in building barriers make for an unattractive business model. For this reason, we dropped McDonald's from the list of potential Great Companies.

Cyclicals (oil, paper, automotive companies, airlines). Companies in these industries were also dropped. You don't want to invest in an industry that produces great returns for three years and below-average returns for five years. You want to invest in industries that perform well regardless of the economic environment. This screen forced the exclusion of the big oil companies, the paper companies, the automotive companies, and the airlines, all of which are highly cyclical.

———

Companies in attractive industries are better investments than those in unattractive industries. For example, the consumer products industry in which Coca-Cola and Gillette—Buffett's "Inevitables"—operate is an attractive industry. Successful companies in this industry invest in research and development to constantly improve their existing products and develop new ones. Then they aggressively market these products to expand distribution, build brand franchises, and increase market share. Outstanding quality products, a good distribution base, and a strong brand franchise are excellent barriers to ward off competitors as we shall discuss in the next section. Later we will study Gillette's business model so investors can see how it provides Gillette with a sound operating environment.

The pharmaceutical industry, which is quite similar to the consumer products sector in a number of ways, possesses the characteristics of an industry that is attractive from an investing perspective. Pharmaceutical companies invest heavily in R&D to keep their pipeline of new products full. They secure patents for twenty years beginning with the discovery of a new compound. Because of development, clinical trials, and FDA approval, a new compound may have a protected life of only six to eight years before the patent expires; however, during this time period the pharmaceutical can generate huge profits. Unfortunately, when the patent expires, generic drug makers take over and the pharmaceutical company's sales drop dramatically. As a result, pharmaceutical companies work hard to increase the protected life span of a new product and to continually improve the product, thereby securing additional patents. Typically, it costs pharmaceutical companies very little to produce their products, so if they have a big success like Viagra, the dollars really roll in.

As new technology is integrated into the research process, R&D costs of pharmaceutical companies should decline, and the protected life span of new products increase, thereby making the fundamentals of the pharmaceutical industry even more attractive than they are today. The pharmaceutical companies are increasing their direct-to-consumer advertising budgets, which is leading more patients to make brand-name requests of physicians. This helps pharmaceutical companies build sound protective barriers around their products, which should result in increased sales and market share.

Many of the pharmaceutical companies are trying to have the best of both worlds. They not only sell pharmaceutical products, but also sell OTC (over-the-counter) products. The OTC business is like the consumer products business, where brands with broad market appeal are developed and marketed over time. These OTC products are not subject to the sharp sales declines of prescription drugs when patents expire, and they provide a nice complement to offset the inherent risks of the pharmaceutical business.

Many of the financial services businesses possess attractive industry characteristics. These businesses require very little investment in capital and equipment and can deliver attractive profits if properly managed. The financial services sector includes firms within the banking, insurance, and money management industries.

The Business Model

So far we have discussed the importance of investing in attractive industries, but a terrific business also relies on a sound business model that is driven by the needs of the company's consumers. *The Profit Zone*, a terrific book on business design by Adrian Slywotzky, refers to this as "customer-centric thinking," that is, designing the business model with the customer in mind and working backward. I believe that Gillette's business model, which was mentioned as being outstanding in a number of my interviews with CEOs, is worthy of further study.

I believe that the effects of Gillette's business model are so powerful that this one factor has contributed greatly to the company's outstanding shareholder returns. Business quality is something that Gillette's chairman, Al Zeien, guards very closely. For example, he has sold over twenty-two businesses that did not meet his criteria for an excellent business. Some didn't have the market potential to generate huge revenues, some bordered on being commodity businesses, and others had poor fundamentals. He got rid of them so he could focus on the really great businesses that Gillette has developed. Interestingly, Jack Welch remarked during our interview that GE is integrating elements of the Gillette model into its turbine and jet engine businesses.

Gillette's business is characterized by several important qualities, as follows:

Permanence. A very important characteristic of a good business model is its permanence. As you look at Gillette's business you know that men will grow beards and women will grow hair on their bodies for the foreseeable future. Therefore, they will need something to remove their unwanted hair. A few may choose electrolysis or some other method of hair removal, but most will use razors and blades. During my interview with Al Zeien, chairman and CEO of Gillette, he mentioned that one of the things that gave him comfort before he retired for the evening was knowing that each night men throughout the world were growing beards and women were growing unwanted hair, and that would continue forever. Gillette looks at all of its business from this perspective of permanence.

The bottom line is, a terrific business is one that will be around for years to come. While the business may change and evolve, as all businesses do, the core business proposition will remain. People will continue to wash clothes, take baths, shave, have headaches, get thirsty, protect themselves from risk, and get sunburns for years to come. Products that effectively cater to these needs will be around forever. You didn't want to be fully invested in the horse and buggy business when the car came along, and you don't want to buy businesses today that may become obsolete tomorrow.

High Consumption and Broad Market Appeal. Ideally, you want to invest in an industry that has high consumption levels and broad

---

Qualities of Terrific Businesses
Not All Businesses Are Created Equal

➤ Permanence
➤ High Consumption
➤ Broad Global Appeal
➤ Recession Proof
➤ System Sale
➤ High Return on Invested Capital

---

market appeal. This business velocity allows the company to enjoy the efficiencies of mass production and mass marketing. In Gillette's case, the fact that men shave every day makes the business that much more attractive. If the business has great appeal to a broad number of customers, so much the better. The fact that so many people drink a beverage several times a day, every day, means tremendous product velocity. If you are able to capture a significant share of a market with a product that has these characteristics, the economics of the business can quickly become very attractive.

Broad Global Appeal. As we move into a global economy, products or services that transcend cultures and countries will be treasured. One of the advantages of Gillette's business is that it is and has been a global business. Gillette sells the same product all over the world. This greatly simplifies the business and allows Gillette to develop a worldwide brand franchise built around a single product.

This global business base also allows Gillette to invest heavily in R&D. For example, Gillette spends approximately 15 percent of U.S. sales on research and development. Compare this to a high-tech company that spends around 10 percent on R&D. While Gillette budgets 15 percent of U.S. sales for R&D, the R&D budget is only 3 percent of worldwide sales. This heavy investment in R&D allows Gillette to continually improve on the products it is marketing, and ensures that the company stays ahead of its competitors. The fact that one standardized product is sold throughout the world constitutes a huge competitive advantage.

Recession Proof. Industries that are recession proof offer a margin of safety for investors. When there is a downturn in the economy, investors who are heavily invested in recession-sensitive businesses such as automobiles, housing, airlines, and hotels, will typically see their portfolios decline more than the market drops. Conversely, investors who are invested in businesses that are relatively recession proof (virtually no business is 100 percent recession proof) will typically experience much less of a decline. Therefore recession-proof businesses provide the investor with some margin of safety. While it is true that when the tide goes out (the market goes down) all ships ride lower (all stocks decline), the recession-proof companies tend to ride a little higher than the other ships.

Low Labor Costs. Good businesses have a relatively low cost of labor. This quality affords Gillette a number of advantages:

- *Increased revenues without increased labor costs.* Companies with low labor costs can typically increase sales revenues faster than they increase costs. This improves the overall profitability of the company and can also improve return on capital. For example, Gillette can increase production by a meaningful number of units without significantly increasing its labor pool.
- *Utilizing new technology to reduce manufacturing costs.* Many businesses that are not labor intensive will enjoy significant manufacturing efficiencies and increased profits as a result of installing new technology that speeds up the manufacturing process while reducing costs.

System Sale. Another characteristic of an attractive business is that it is a system sell. I believe that Gillette has one of the best business models in the world—perhaps even *the* best. If you purchase a Gillette razor, you also need to purchase Gillette's blades. The blades and razors together become the Gillette shaving system. As you use the razor, and most consumers use it every day to shave, the blades become dull and must be replaced with new Gillette blades since

---

Qualities of Terrific Businesses
Not All Businesses Are Created Equal

➤ Below the Radar
➤ Low Labor Costs
  "We don't want to be the most expensive
  wrench turners in town"—Jack Welch
➤ Broad Appeal
➤ Technology Driven

---

other blades don't fit the razor. Because of the way the product is designed, Gillette makes one sale with the razor, but continues to sell you Gillette blades as long as you use the razor. Since Gillette routinely improves its shaving system, and introduces entirely new shaving systems every few years, you become a long-term Gillette customer. Consider what Ford's business might look like if you had to purchase Ford gas, Ford tires, and Ford parts.

Technology Driven. Another critical component of Gillette's success is the use of technology. Technology forms the base upon which Gillette's R&D operations are built and extends to the machinery that produces the blades and razors it markets. This technology allows Gillette to differentiate its offerings from the competition and to bring new products to market faster and more efficiently than in the past.

Excellent Return on Capital. Outstanding businesses require little capital to start, and they are able to internally generate the capital they need to operate and provide shareholders with outstanding returns. Contrast this with the paper business, which requires a huge capital investment, is cyclical, and has relatively low margins. Because of the capital investment required, paper plants must operate around the clock at maximum capacity in order to turn a profit. A prolonged drop in volume destroys the profitability of this business—for both the paper company and the investor. In contrast, a high return on invested capital gives a company numerous options. It can repurchase shares, pass dividends along to the shareholders, invest in new businesses, expand globally, and acquire other firms. Or, it can use this money to create a huge cash reserve. The terrific businesses have a high return on invested capital.

"Below the Radar" Business. This is a quality that Jack Welch looks for in a business, and one I had not previously encountered. Welch feels that it is important to operate low-profile, or, as he refers it, "below the radar" businesses that aren't highly visible to competitors. He looks for a business where market shares aren't published every week and you can build the business without your competitors really knowing what you are doing.

You have only to look at the personal computer business to see an example of an above-the-radar business. No sooner are market shares published than one of the PC companies announces a major price reduction. This drives most of the other PC makers to lower their prices so that they don't lose market share. Welch looks for a business that just rolls along making money and growing. As far as he is concerned, the lower the profile, the better the business.

It's interesting to look at examples of companies in unattractive industries that have implemented innovative business models and, as a result, enjoyed huge increases in sales and profits. Let's examine two case studies:

- *First, let's examine Amazon.com, the online bookstore.* By using the World Wide Web as its distribution system rather than a chain of retail stores, Amazon hopes to turn a relatively unattractive business with low margins into a very attractive business with a very attractive profit structure. Amazon did this not by bringing in a new management team, or developing a new store format, but by completely redesigning the business model. *Business Week* reported in August 1998 that "Despite offering a million titles, vs. 175,000 for a Barnes & Noble superstore, Amazon carried only $17 million in inventory last quarter—2 percent of the inventory of Barnes & Noble. And while buyers pay Amazon instantly with their credit cards, it doesn't pay publishers for the books until about 46 days later—a tidy float that reverses the economics of physical stores. The result, $240,000 in sales per employee, vs. $100,000 at Barnes & Noble. Amazon.com CEO Jeffrey P. Bezos: 'We want to be like a small-town bookseller who knows your tastes.' Book distributor Ingram Book Group, Amazon's chief supplier, is even developing technology to print books one by one as orders come in—potentially changing the economics of publishing." Amazon.com is not a retailer that competes on the basis of store location and inventory; it competes based on knowing its customers and having superior software. Unfortunately, the retail book business is a very difficult business and Amazon has yet to report a profit.

- *A second example is Dell Computer Corporation, a company that also changed its business model.* In its start-up phase, Dell computers were sold through retail stores, and for the first five years of its existence Dell barely outperformed the S&P 500. Dell had to build computer inventories, then wait to be paid by retailers that controlled the price and promotion of their product line. Then Dell changed the model by going direct to the consumer. Now Dell's inventories are reduced, they don't have to cover the costs of a middleman, and they are building relationships with their consumers by providing them with made-to-order computers. *Fortune* reported in May 1998 that "Over the past three years sales have climbed from $3.4 billion to $12.3 billion and profits are up from $140 million to $944 million. Dell is growing more than twice as fast as any competitor and its worldwide PC market share has doubled. Among the Fortune 500, Dell ranks No. 7 in return on stockholders' equity—ahead of Coca-Cola, Intel and Microsoft. Over the past three years, its stock is up more than 26 times."

Dell's business model provides the following benefits:

- *Greater control of the market.* Direct contact with the customer provides Dell with greater control of its market environment. Dell marketers know who their customers are, where they are, and what products they own. This can be a huge competitive marketing advantage versus companies that are unable to market directly to their customers.

- *Inventory efficiency.* Since Dell doesn't build the computer until it has an order, the company doesn't have to build a product, ship it to a company that distributes the product, and then wait for payment. Assembly, shipment, and collection happen quickly at Dell. This improves cash flow and reduces inventory levels—both positive ways to improve returns on working capital. With this business model, Dell has not only streamlined its distribution system, but has also developed a competitive advantage.
- *Lower costs.* Companies that sell through intermediaries must typically share some of their potential profits with these companies. For example, companies that sell to supermarkets must pay merchandising allowances and slotting fees to the supermarket. These costs typically range from 7 percent to 15 percent of sales, a huge expense. People will argue that the retailer is providing value and should be paid for this value added; however, there is some question as to how much this service is worth. Retailers will claim that the direct distribution company must pay for shipping to individual consumers, and that this can be very costly. This may be a valid argument in some instances, but experience has shown that direct distribution can be very cost efficient. I believe that many distribution systems will be streamlined and that direct customer sales will increase as the Internet is developed commercially.

Even Great Companies are constantly seeking ways to improve their business models. For example, General Electric has dramatically changed some of its business models. As you will read in the interview with Jack Welch, a key element of GE's tremendous success has been the company's ability to take businesses like the steam turbine business and dramatically change the profit structure. GE did this by offering extensive service agreements to clients who own steam turbines. GE will not only service the turbines it produces, but will also service turbines manufactured by any GE competitor. GE has changed the business model for turbines, locomotives, jet engines, and MRI machines, and by doing so has changed the profit structure and nature of the business.

It isn't easy to totally change a business model, but companies that have successfully made this transition have reaped incredible rewards. *The Profit Zone* refers to companies that have successfully implemented innovative business models as "Reinventors." These reinventors have started with the customer and worked backward to design their business models. In doing so, they have enjoyed profitable growth that far exceeds that of other companies within their industries. However, radically altering the business model requires a total restructuring of the business, not simply bringing in a new team of managers, and few CEOs have the desire and ability to pull off this transition.

While changing a business model is difficult, all Great Companies are constantly thinking about how their business model may change in the future. It is worth taking the time to read the sections in *The Profit Zone* on General Electric and Coca-Cola. They will provide you with interesting insights into these two companies. *The Profit Zone* identifies some twenty-two different business models that can create significant profits for companies while driving shareholder returns and explains the GE and Coke models in detail.

Investors must consider both the industry and the business model when investing. Truly Great Companies operate within attractive industries and utilize dynamic models that are constantly evolving to deliver outstanding returns to shareholders.

Screen 9

PROTECTED BY STRONG BARRIERS/THE MOAT EFFECT

Another vitally important screen is the screen for protective barriers, or what Warren Buffett refers to as "the moat." Buffett's description of the importance of a moat or franchise is classic.

> Look for the durability of the franchise. The most important thing to me is figuring out how big a moat there is around the business. What I love, of course, is a big castle and a big moat with piranhas and crocodiles.

There are a number of barriers that management can build to protect a business, including the following:

Build a Strong Brand Franchise. Many companies seek to build a moat by creating superior brand franchises. In order to build a great brand franchise, a number of things are required, but two of the key elements are a good product and an extensive marketing/advertising program. Not surprisingly, two of the finalists for Great Company honors were among the top ten leading U.S. advertisers in 1995, and eight were among the top 100. These companies spend hundreds of millions of dollars on advertising in order to strengthen their moats.

The brand franchise or moat that is created provides these companies with a number of key benefits:

- *First, the great brand franchise creates value in the mind of the consumer, thereby allowing the company to charge and receive higher prices than its competitors.* Consider the following chart:

Procter and Gamble
Food, Drug, and Mass Merchandiser Shares
52 weeks ending 12/29/96

	POWDER LAUNDRY DETERGENT	PAPER TOWELS	MOUTHWASH
SHARE OF DOLLARS	37.2	36.7	17.5
SHARE OF VOLUME	30.4	26.7	16.6

Source: Information Resources, Inc.

Procter and Gamble was able to capture a higher share of the dollar market than the unit or volume share because of the value propositions of its brands. This provides P&G with greater pricing leverage and profits than its competitors.

Procter and Gamble is not alone in its ability to create profitable brand propositions. As can be seen in the following chart, both Gillette and Johnson & Johnson have been able to realize a greater dollar share than unit share through brand value creation.

Food, Drug, and Mass Merchandiser Shares
52 weeks ending 12/31/96

	TYLENOL (J & J)	GILLETTE RAZORS/BLADES
SHARE OF DOLLARS	29.1	67.0
SHARE OF VOLUME	19.3	48.4

Source: Information Resources, Inc.

Investors in companies like Johnson & Johnson, Gillette, and Procter and Gamble own companies that have built not only strong moats, but moats that provide the company with enormous pricing leverage.

• *Second, once a franchise has been solidly established in the mind of the customer, it is very difficult to destroy.* We have observed numerous examples where companies that built solid franchises neglected them for years. However, in-depth consumer testing revealed that many consumers still remembered and trusted the brands long after the company stopped aggressively supporting the brand.

• *Third, the franchise provides the sales force with instant credibility and increases their odds of closing a sale.* It's a real advantage to be selling for P&G the first time you attempt to sell to a major retailer. Likewise, I am sure a lot of doors are opened for the Avon lady because of her company's excellent reputation and franchise.

• *Fourth, retail-distributed brands typically pay less in promotional allowances and gain greater shelf space because of their brand power.* Since over 80 percent of the products sold in retail stores come from the shelf, having significant shelf presence is a key strategic advantage.

• *Finally, the efficiency of advertising increases as companies build huge franchises.* The marketer reaches a point of diminishing returns, and incremental sales become extremely profitable.

As the investor considers brands and business franchises, it's important to understand that not all brand and business franchises are created equal. In *Competing for the Future*, the authors discuss the concept of "banner brands," which "span multiple products and businesses, and help customers transfer great experiences with today's products into great interest and enthusiasm for tomorrow's products." The following excerpt from *Competing for the Future* details the real benefits of banner brands:

> To preempt competitors, customers around the world have to be genuinely eager to buy and try a company's new products. Think about what happened in 1982, when the Coca-Cola Company launched Diet Coke in the United States. Within two years Diet Coke became the number three U.S. soft drink. Leveraging the powerful Coke brand name, Diet Coke repeated the success in many markets around the world. While in no way disparaging the quality or uniqueness of Diet Coke, one could hardly credit the brand's supersonic take-off to product attributes alone. What existed in people's minds was a deep emotional bond with Coca-Cola, assiduously cultivated by some of the cleverest and least escapable advertising anywhere. In the absence of a preexisting brand franchise, Diet Coke would have faced the same slow, treacherous crawl onto retailers' shelves that faces Coke's wannabe competitors. If the goal is to preempt competitors, it helps to have built a preexisting "share of mind" with customers around the world.

Imagine the years it would have taken and the millions of dollars it would have cost to establish the XYZ brand of diet soft drink, even for Coke. Once the "banner brand" has been established, the leverage it provides for successfully launching new products is enormous.

The real power of "banner brands" is even greater in the global markets, where the launch of a single product can generate huge revenues and profits on an international basis. The authors conclude that "Those companies that have built banner brands that predispose customers to try their new products, that have secured access to critical channels around the globe, and have developed an internal capacity to quickly propagate new product innovations will, other things being equal, capture competitive high-ground."

It's interesting to note that many of the Great Companies on our list are moving to global branding. For example, P&G is realigning its agencies around brands rather than geographies. Ultimately, one agency will be responsible for a brand on a worldwide basis. This will allow companies like P&G, Gillette, and Coke to establish "Power Global banner brands." The combination of a strong franchise and a powerful international presence can result in an impenetrable empire.

Contracts/Agreements. Another way of strengthening the moat is through long-term agreements or contracts. For example, insurance companies have their customers sign long-term agreements. These agreements protect the insured from risk but also protect the insurer from competitive threats. Companies in the real-estate business that are leasing office space also rely on contracts. These contracts and agreements serve to strengthen the protective moat that surrounds the business.

Geographic Barriers. Geography can also be used to strengthen the protective moat. Consider the Hilton hotel at Chicago's O'Hare International Airport. If you want to spend the night at O'Hare and don't want to take a shuttle to your hotel, you have one choice—the O'Hare Hilton. While the Marriott, Hyatt, and Westin are all near the airport, along with at least twenty other hotels, there is only one hotel within walking distance, and you don't have to go outside to get to it (there is an underground tunnel from the terminal to the hotel). The O'Hare Hilton isn't necessarily the least expensive, the nicest, or the newest of the O'Hare hotels, but its location provides the Hilton with a moat that can be very powerful.

Other businesses, like grocery stores, convenience stores, fast-food restaurants, car dealerships, and airlines with their hub systems, try to use geographic location as a moat. If you have a one-of-a-kind location like the Hilton, this can be a powerful moat; however, if someone can open a business next door, your moat might serve to trap you in your castle as opposed to keeping the competition out.

Patents. If you have developed a new process or technology, a patent can keep your competitors from using it. This can provide a very powerful moat, especially if your company has developed a breakthrough innovation. Companies in the pharmaceutical industry are protected by securing patents on the new products they develop. These patents make it very difficult, if not impossible, for competitors to replicate their successes for a twenty-year period.

The U.S. Patent and Trademark Office (USPTO) received over 210,000 patent applications and issued over 120,000 patents in 1997. Both patent applications and patents issued are records that reflect the growth in technology and research. If you compare patents issued in the 1980s—around 71,000 patents annually—with the 120,000 patents issued in 1997, you will find that patents issued are up 69 percent. Unfortunately, patents have a life of their own. Once a patent expires, the protection it affords your company also expires. However, it can be a very powerful moat as long as it is valid.

Machinery. The machinery a company uses to produce its products can serve as a barrier to competition. That is precisely why Gillette produces most of the equipment that it uses to manufacturer many of its products. If Gillette purchased the machinery from a third-party provider, the provider could, in turn, sell the equipment to one of Gillette's competitors, thereby reducing Gillette's lead time on new products versus its key competitors. Gillette is quite willing to maintain the staff necessary to build this machinery because of the competitive advantage the company receives from it.

Low-Cost Producer. Being the low-cost producer can also strengthen the moat. Companies that have captured this advantage can price their products lower than the competition and still make a profit.

Low Price. Retailers like Wal-Mart use low price as a barrier. They can't necessarily be the low-cost producer, but they strive to be the low-cost distributor and merchandiser and pass these savings along to the consumer in the form of low prices.

Quality. If a company is able to consistently produce a superior product that cannot be acquired at a lower cost, then quality can become a barrier to competitive entry. IBP is a low-cost producer but it also strives to consistently deliver a quality product to its customers. GE's Six Sigma initiative is not only reducing costs and improving quality, it is also improving customer loyalty. GE's quality goal was described by Jack Welch, who said, "We want to make our quality so special, so valuable to our customers, so important to their success that our products become their real value of choice."

Customization. This can be another barrier. Think of the custom shirt manufacturers that will tailor a shirt to fit and manufacture the shirt from any cloth you choose. Dell prides itself on building computers to order. When you call Dell, a sales associate will ask you questions about your computing needs. Dell will then design a computer that meets your needs. I recently read about a company, CD World, that sells kiosks called Music Point. For roughly $18 per CD, customers can choose from among 50,000 songs to design their own personal CD. The kiosk is a data terminal connected by Sprint's high-speed fiber-optic network to a central music database. A blank CD is actually "burned" right in the kiosk. I believe we will see more and more of this mass customization, which will help companies build barriers around their businesses while increasing customer satisfaction.

There are any number of ways to build barriers around a business. In addition to the ones we have mentioned, some companies are using alliances; others may rely on assortment (especially retailers). It's important to realize that some barriers are much stronger and more durable than others. For example, a good brand name is very powerful and typically much more difficult for competitors to attack than a barrier based on geography. Likewise, a patent is much stronger than a barrier based on price.

The Great Companies build their barriers of the strongest materials, brands, and patents. The moats of these Great Companies are getting wider and deeper as they continue to add more crocodiles and piranhas. These moats will become increasingly difficult to breach with time. Frankly, I can't imagine trying to knock a brand like Coca-Cola from its worldwide position. I believe that those competitors that try to destroy the moats of the Great Companies will pay a heavy price.

S c r e e n   1 0

PEOPLE ARE THE COMPANY'S MOST VALUABLE ASSET

The Great Companies realize that it's not the brands or the machinery, it's the people who make the company great. They believe that their people are their most valuable asset. The CEOs of these companies believe that training and developing their people, instilling their values in their people, and providing for their people are the most important responsibilities they have.

These companies leave little to chance in the people area, right from the recruiting stage. They know the profiles of the people who will do well within their company, and they aggressively recruit at colleges and universities to bring only the best and brightest people into their companies. They closely follow the career development of these people as they progress through the company. There are constant progress evaluations and training programs to educate and develop them. They transfer people into various positions within the company and routinely give them experience in different product lines, businesses, or countries. Al Zeien, Jack Welch, and other CEOs of Great Companies spend several days each year personally reviewing the key people within their companies. Welch remarked during our interview that selecting the right people is the most important responsibility he has. Bill Steere of Pfizer remarked several times during our interview that people are Pfizer's most valuable asset.

As a result of their development efforts, the CEOs of the Great Companies are able to promote people from within the company. They very seldom, if ever, go outside the company to fill a senior position. They reward the people who perform with bonus plans, stock option programs, or both. They offer 401(k) plans and outstanding medical coverage. They measure workforce satisfaction with a combination of internal surveys and 360-degree evaluations (in a 360 program you evaluate your boss, and the people who report to you evaluate you). They loathe the unwanted turnover that occurs when a person they like and want to keep is lured away from the company. They measure turnover and constantly make adjustments to try and prevent it. I have always believed that employee turnover was the single biggest hidden cost of a corporation. Excessive turnover can destroy both profits and morale.

Consider the following example as you think about the costs of turnover. Suppose you hired someone to work for your company. You probably paid a fee to an agency or search firm to locate the candidate. Next, you had to train her to work for your company. Depending on the job, the training could cost, and often exceeds, as much as 20 percent of a person's first-year compensation. As she progresses, you provide her with additional training that is costly in terms of both time and travel. Assuming that she performs well and takes on additional responsibilities, her salary is increased and training expenses climb. This employee has become very valuable to your company, and represents a significant investment of both money and time spent on her development.

Now let's assume that this employee decides to resign and go to work for a competitor. Your company has lost someone who cannot be replaced overnight. Remember: You have five years invested in her, and even if you hire someone tomorrow, you are still five years away from achieving the same experience level. Suppose the new person who is hired doesn't work out, and after two years you let him go. Seven years later you are now back where you started. Let's suppose further that this new employee convinces one of his co-workers, a bright young "up and comer" in your company, to join him. You lose again. Let's further imagine that this person does well for your competitor and takes some of your business or develops a new product that cannibalizes the sales of your product. Other employees in your company see how well he is doing, and they call to see if there is room for them. How much has losing this person cost the company? How much have you lost in out-of-pocket, short-term dollars, and how much is long term? How many years of training have you lost that can never be replaced? By the way, since the people who leave are normally the really good people, you have also probably weakened your organization. What initially started out as a $40,000 loss suddenly turns into a $100,000 loss. If your company had 20,000 employees, the difference between 4 percent and 12 percent turnover could mean millions of dollars, not to mention the lost business opportunities that could never be recaptured.

Because of the positives of keeping great people over the long term, and the numerous negatives associated with turnover, these

Great Companies view their people as their most valuable asset and do everything possible to keep them. P&G has long been looked upon as a company with outstanding people. Having worked at P&G, I believe that one of Procter's greatest strengths is its aggressive recruiting program, which provides P&G with what many believe is the best talent in the consumer products industry, and has turned it into a prime recruiting ground for virtually every search firm doing business within the industry. The company is also very effective in keeping employees that it wants. P&G pulls out all the stops when a respected employee informs her supervisor that she is resigning. As a result, P&G is able to keep many talented people.

Screen 11

AN OUTSTANDING MANAGEMENT TEAM THAT KEEPS THE COMPANY IN "PRIME"

This screen focuses on the quality of management within a company. It is important to recognize that Great Companies are led by outstanding managers who create an environment where people can succeed. They work hard to help the company get to and stay in "Prime." I first became aware of the Prime concept by reading a book called *Corporate Lifecycles* by Ichak Adizes. Dr. Adizes believes that companies, like humans, have lifecycles. However, unlike humans, some companies are able to move into an area referred to as Prime— a place in their lifecycle where companies can exist without getting old. Reaching Prime is like finding the fountain of youth and remaining young forever. The corporate lifecycle is demonstrated in the graphic on page 108.

Dr. Adizes notes that companies, like individuals, grow and age. The lifecycle begins with Courtship (start-up) and progresses to Infancy (we know how much care and attention infants require), moves into Go-Go (when the business grows faster than the management can manage), and abruptly shifts into Adolescence (an incredibly difficult stage in which many companies fail or merge) before reaching Prime (the ideal spot on the curve—a place where companies grow but don't age). Companies may become sidetracked during any phase and be acquired, merged, or closed. Very few companies make it to Prime, and fewer still remain in Prime over time. For companies that are unable to remain in Prime, the path down the lifecycle is fraught with danger and may ultimately end in death.

We see numerous examples of growth companies that reach the Go-Go stage and then rocket into Adolescence. At this point everything goes wrong: earnings drop, sales flatten, and the stock price plummets. In many cases the company never recovers and is either acquired or goes under. This is why the momentum approach to investing is fraught with risk. Many of the momentum companies are in the Go-Go phase and it's simply a matter of time before they hit adolescence like a stone wall. It's virtually impossible for the investor to predict when a growth company will reach this point, but when it does happen the stock price may drop by 50 percent or more overnight, leaving the unsuspecting investor high and dry.

My goal in searching for Great Companies was to find companies that had reached and remained in Prime. A Prime organization is able to grow both sales and profits. "In Prime, the organization knows what to do and what not to do. They know when to pass up an opportunity and why to pass on it." The Prime organization embodies a number of key characteristics including:

- Institutionalized vision and creativity
- Results orientation
- Predictably excellent performance
- Growth in both sales and profits

According to Adizes, "Prime organizations know what they're doing, where they're going and how to get there. A Prime can tell you why they are going to make money. And they do. The Challenge of Prime is to stay in Prime." These Prime organizations are never happy with the status quo and are constantly searching for ways to improve. They have evolved almost cult-like cultures as they have grown and developed.

IBM is an example of a company that was in Prime, but rather than remain there, it faltered and slipped down the slope of the corporate lifecycle. IBM grew rapidly and was looked on as a shining example of American business. But the company didn't keep up with a rapidly changing business environment and fell from Prime. While it looks like IBM is aggressively trying to move back up the lifecycle curve to Prime, and seems well positioned to do so, until it proves it can reach and stay in Prime, we will not consider IBM a Great Company.

Significantly, this screen highlighted the strengths of some of our Great Companies, such as GE, which has long been viewed as a company with outstanding talent and a leader in new organizational structures. The boundaryless organization installed by GE is an innovative way to get people across various businesses to share their ideas and work together as a team. This teamwork has helped GE remain in Prime.

The Great Companies are in Prime, and most have been there for some time. They have each encountered problems and challenges along the way, but they have grown from these experiences. Rather than knock them out of Prime, these experiences made them even stronger and helped mold them into Great Companies, and their people into outstanding managers.

Screen 12

INNOVATION-DRIVEN COMPANIES
THAT TURN CHANGES INTO OPPORTUNITIES

The final screen focuses on innovation. I found through the interviews that the Great Companies are great innovators. Rather than fear change, these companies relish change, for it provides them with new opportunities, and that means increased revenues and profits. These Great Companies are organized to capitalize on new opportunities. Those that produce products have wonderful R&D organizations that create products of the future. These organizations are staffed by some of the best and brightest people in the company. Their job is to stay out in front and ahead of the changes. They search the globe for new technologies, products, or services that could play a key role in the future of the company. They disseminate this learning to the operating divisions, where these ideas are turned into new and better products. Likewise, the service companies in our group are always searching for opportunities to create and introduce new and

IN BUSINESS FOR AT LEAST 50 YEARS AND IN PRIME

CORPORATE LIFECYCLES

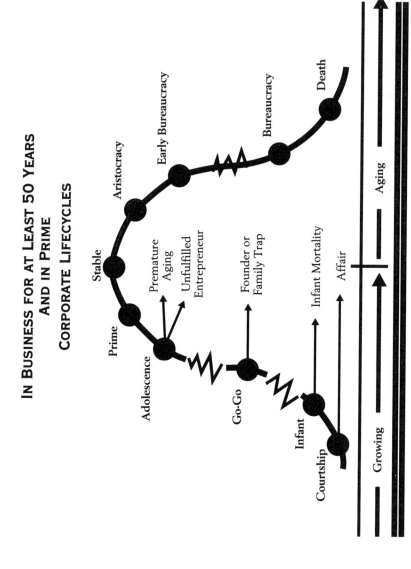

SOURCE: Corporate Lifecycles, Ichak Adizes, 1988.

better services that meet the needs of a changing customer base. Developing new products and services allows the Great Companies to continue to grow, which significantly enhances shareholder value.

Interestingly, the analysts at Credit Suisse/First Boston, under the leadership of Michael Mauboussin, have started measuring the value of these new products to shareholders. They have been working on what Mauboussin refers to as the "Competitive Advantage Period (CAP)." The Competitive Advantage Period is "the time during which a company is expected to generate returns on incremental investment that exceed its cost of capital." For example, if a company developed a cure for cancer, there would be a period of time when the sales of this new breakthrough product would dramatically drive the revenues and profits of the company that developed it. During this time, the company would have gained a competitive advantage over the market and its primary competitors. As a result of this competitive advantage, we would expect shareholders to send the stock price of the company to new heights because the company has extended its competitive advantage in the marketplace.

Mauboussin notes that the value of a company's CAP is determined by the company's return on capital, the rate of industry change (technology companies experience much more rapid rates of change than food companies), and the barriers to entry (the more difficult it is for a competitor to enter the business, the greater the value of the CAP). His research has shown that the average CAP for the U.S. stock market, as a whole, is estimated to be between ten and fifteen years. However, within the market, caps can range from under two years to over twenty years. His analysis has shown that companies with high CAPs like Coca-Cola and Microsoft—both in excess of twenty years—trade at high multiples because the market has placed a value on their long-term dominance.

I found his analysis of Microsoft fascinating:

We argue that approximately two-thirds of the increase in shareholder value was the result of a dramatic lengthening of the company's implied CAP. We calculate that Microsoft's CAP was eight to ten years the day it went public—using then-prevailing consensus estimates. Interestingly, the actual CAP at the time proved to be only about three years, as the company's actual results far exceeded expectations.

We calculate that Microsoft's current implied cap is 17–20 years. If the company still had an implied CAP of eight to ten years, the current market value would be roughly $33 billion. Therefore, we argue that two-thirds of the company's current valuation is the result of an expansion in its implied CAP. Without the concept of CAP, we believe that most of Microsoft's massive value creation cannot be explained.

Obviously, extending a company's Competitive Advantage Period can be very profitable for shareholders. It's something that the Great Companies do very well. These companies believe that acquisitions are not always the best way to exploit new opportunities. While they will occasionally purchase another company or division, most prefer to develop the opportunities they wish to pursue internally. Increasingly, these companies are exploring those opportunities through alliances with other companies. These alliances might involve some ownership of the company but could also be forged through marketing agreements.

This screen highlighted the strengths of several of our Great Companies, for example:

- *Pfizer spends over $2 billion each year on R&D, which ensures that the company's pipeline of new products is always full of exciting and profitable new products.* This R&D capability is key to Pfizer's success.
- *GE has used research and technology to reinvent its steam turbine, locomotive, jet engine, and MRI businesses.* GE has turned these areas, which had always been viewed as manufacturing businesses, into far more profitable sectors in which service is a key driver of profits.
- *Gillette has a research structure that is very similar to Hewlett-Packard's.* This has allowed Gillette to continuously improve its basic products and capture huge market shares in the shaving category.

Innovation and research are key drivers of success in each of our Great Companies.

SUMMARY

I began the process of selecting the Great Companies of America with ninety-two outstanding companies, many of which are among the best-known and most respected companies in the world. At the conclusion of the process only fourteen companies remained. The interviews and corporate profiles included in the next chapter will provide additional insight into these companies.

Chapter 4

THE FOURTEEN
GREAT COMPANIES

The previous chapter described the twelve qualities that exist in all Great Companies. This chapter presents an overview of each of the fourteen companies that passed the twelve screens. These companies are battle-tested champions. They have met the most difficult challenges imaginable and grown to greatness. As a group, their business profile is impressive:

- *These companies have been in business an average of 112 years.* The oldest company, Colgate-Palmolive, was founded in 1806. The youngest, Medtronic, celebrated its fiftieth anniversary in April of 1999. Only three of the companies were founded in the twentieth century. The rest were begun in the 1800s. All but Medtronic have survived world wars and the worst depression this country has ever experienced. They have all flourished despite numerous recessions and market declines. They have withstood the onslaught of international competitors. Despite everything that has been thrown at them, they have survived and flourished.
- *These companies averaged a 35.99 percent per-annum return for the past five years versus the S&P 500 average of 24.053 percent—a rate of return that exceeds the S&P 500 by 49.63*

percent. The Great Companies averaged 29.86 percent for ten years versus the S&P 500 at 19.192 percent.

- *These are global companies with broad business bases.* They operate in virtually every country in the world. International revenues represent slightly more than 56 percent of total corporate revenues. Coca-Cola is the leader, deriving some 80 percent of its revenues from international operations.
- *These companies have grown to become huge corporations.* Today their average market capitalization is almost $117 billion. The largest market capitalization of $333.3 billion belongs to General Electric. These are huge companies with tremendous staying power. Their size and credit-worthiness allow them to secure capital at very attractive rates.

The chart on page 115 recaps some of the key facts about the Great Companies of America.

Their achievements and awards are equally impressive:

- Five of the CEOs (Bill George of Medtronic, Lois Juliber of Colgate-Palmolive, John Pepper of Procter and Gamble, Sandy Weill of Citigroup, and Jack Welch of General Electric) were listed in *Business Week*'s "Top 25 Managers of the Year" in 1998.
- Four of the companies [General Electric (1), Coca-Cola (3), Johnson & Johnson (9), and Merck (10)] were among *Fortune*'s collection of "America's 10 Most Admired Companies."
- Nine of the Great Companies [General Electric (1), Coca-Cola (2), Pfizer (8), Merck (12), Johnson & Johnson (14), Procter and Gamble (15), Gillette (16), Citigroup (17), and Merrill Lynch (18)] were among twenty-five companies that were crowned as All-Stars by *Fortune* in its listing of "The World's Most Admired Companies."
- Eight of the fourteen Great Companies [General Electric (2), Colgate-Palmolive (9), Johnson & Johnson (12), Coca-Cola (15), Citigroup (16), Pfizer (19), Merck (20), and Procter and Gamble (24)] were included by *Business Week* in 1997 among the twenty-five companies that have the best boards of directors.

- Eight of the Great Companies [General Electric (1), Coca-Cola (2), Merck (4), Procter and Gamble (6), Pfizer (8), Bristol-Myers Squibb (10), Johnson & Johnson (11), and Gillette (15)] were included among the top fifteen wealth-creating companies in the November 9, 1998 issue of *Fortune*, which ranked "America's Greatest Wealth Creators." All the other Great Companies were in the top 70 of the 1,000 companies that were studied. They include Schering-Plough (23), American International Group (26), Citicorp (31), Travelers (40), Medtronic (50), Merrill Lynch (62), and Colgate-Palmolive (63). *Fortune* notes in the article that "over time, EVA (Economic Value Added) correlates far better with stock performance than does EPS (Earnings Per Share)."
- Four of the Great Companies [Procter and Gamble (2), Johnson & Johnson (13), Bristol-Myers Squibb (16), and Coca-Cola (23)] are among the twenty-five largest advertisers in the United States. Eight of the companies spent over $150 million in advertising during 1997. These companies have market-leading franchises, and they spend and fight to keep their shares and franchises.
- Six of the Great Companies [Merck (9), Procter and Gamble (19), Gillette (46), Medtronic (47), Johnson & Johnson (75), and Merrill Lynch (98)] were included in *Fortune*'s "The 100 Best Companies to Work for in America."

The interviews with the executives of Great Companies included here will prove that there really are companies out there that measure up to our twelve criteria. These people shared a number of things in common, including the following:

- *These executives view changes as opportunities.* They realize that enormous and rapidly occurring changes all over the world are placing tremendous burdens on their managers, but offering their companies new and exciting opportunities. They know that in order to realize these opportunities, their companies must be organized, disciplined, and focused and have the resources to exploit them. This focus on change enhances their ability to extend their competitive advantage period and thereby increase the value of their companies.
- *These executives think globally.* Their market is the world. While

Great Companies of America

COMPANY NAME	TICKER	SOURCE	U.S. HQ.	12/31/98 MKT. CAP. $ Billions	1998 FORTUNE Score	1997 % INTL Revenues	FOUNDED Year	MVA RANK Nov-98	5 Yr Avg	5 Yr vs S&P 500	10 Yr Avg	10 Yr vs S&P 500
American International Group	AIG	4,5	NY	101.4	7.3	53	1919	26	30.486	126.745	25.150	131.044
Bristol-Myers Squibb	BMY	4,5,6	NY	132.9	7.36	44	1887	10	40.262	167.387	23.730	123.647
Citicorp (now Citigroup)	C	1,3,4	NY	112.2	7.55	60	1812	31	29.920	124.390	20.500	106.810
Coca-Cola	KO	3,4,6	GA	164.9	8.68	67	1886	2	26.069	108.382	30.106	156.864
Colgate-Palmolive	CL	4,6	NY	27.2	7.27	70	1806	63	27.063	112.513	25.905	134.979
General Electric	GE	1,3,4	CT	333.3	8.18	42	1892	1	34.151	141.982	28.001	145.899
Gillette	G	4,6	MA	53	8.29	63	1895	15	27.720	115.244	29.524	153.833
Johnson & Johnson	JNJ	1,2,3,4,6	NJ	112.8	7.79	50	1885	11	32.413	134.754	25.247	131.550
Medtronic	MDT	4,5	MN	36.3	7.57	43	1949	50	49.443	205.557	41.873	218.178
Merck	MRK	1,3,4,5	NJ	174.2	7.99	43	1914	4	36.879	153.321	25.468	132.701
Merrill Lynch	MER	3,4	NY	23.9	8.13	47	1887	62	28.218	117.315	30.218	157. 449
Pfizer	PFE	3,4	NY	162.2	7.95	47	1849	8	51.194	212.836	35.938	187.252
Procter and Gamble	PG	1,2,3,4,5	OH	121.1	8.19	50	1837	6	28.518	118.564	26.385	137.479
Schering-Plough	SGP	4	NJ	81.2	6.6	50	1864	23	48.181	200.310	34.655	180.571
Average				116.9	7.75	56.4	1887	22.28	35.037	145.664	28.764	149.875
S&P 500									24.053	100	19.192	100

Sources: *Fortune* Magazine, S&P Compustat, Corporate Annual Reports, *Built to Last, In Search of Excellence, Discipline of Market Leaders, Grow to Be Great.*

Key: 1 = *Built to Last;* 2 = *In Search of Excellence;* 3 = *Discipline of Market Leaders;* 4 = *Fortune magazine* 3/2/98; 5 = *Grow To Be Great;* 6 = *Consulting Experience*

Average *Fortune* Most Admired score of 476 companies in 55 industries is 6.22.

NOTE: PAST PERFORMANCE IS NOT INDICATIVE OF FUTURE RESULTS.

their companies may be headquartered in the U.S., they are global businessmen building global organizations capable of doing business anywhere in the world. They don't look at Japan any differently than they view Texas. Japan is simply another market with its own unique challenges and opportunities.

- *They view management's role as ensuring that the company is in wonderful businesses.* They sell or close poor businesses. They don't chase every opportunity that comes along, but they aggressively pursue the ones that fit their strategies and cultures.
- *They are moat builders.* They are constantly searching for ways to reduce risks and protect their businesses from outside threats. Brand building and R&D are key activities for the manufacturing companies in our group.
- *These CEOs are leaders.* Their corporate jets are their offices in the air, and they use them to travel the world meeting with their customers and with foreign leaders, and motivating and guiding their employees. They don't hide behind their desks.
- *They believe in what they are doing.* At the conclusion of my interview with Al Zeien, chairman and CEO of the Gillette Company, he asked "How much of their personal net worth do you think the leaders of your Great Companies have invested in their company's stock?" He suggested that over 80 percent of each Great Company's CEO's net worth was invested in his company, while based on his experiences he doubted that most CEOs had more than 30 to 40 percent of their net worth invested in their companies. Zeien was right! All the CEOs that I spoke with have over 90 percent of their personal net worth invested in the company they lead. One executive mentioned that despite the urging of his financial planner, he has over 95 percent of his personal net worth invested in his company. **Do you want to invest with someone who has 90-percent-plus of his net worth riding on the decisions he makes, or someone who is more concerned about managing a portfolio composed of the stocks of other companies?**

I also found that each company I interviewed had *at least* one incredible strength. For example:

- *Gillette's* razor and blade business is the best business model I have seen. My belief was reaffirmed by Jack Welch of GE, who also commented on the strengths of Gillette's business model during our interview.
- *AIG*, the largest and arguably the best risk manager in the world, has structured its company so that the risks of one business offset the risks of another. A brilliant way to structure a business.
- *GE's* boundaryless learning organization allows this enormous, complex, global corporation to function and respond to challenges like a small-cap entrepreneurial firm.
- *Pfizer's* world class Research and Development is second to none.

The corporate profiles that follow provide investors with a basic understanding of each of the Great Companies. These overviews do not include up-to-the-minute financial performance data that would be outdated before the book was published. In fact, because these companies are so dynamic, and acquire and divest businesses so frequently, some of the corporate overviews may be obsolete before you read them. For this reason, corporate profiles are updated via our newsletter. An example of this type of change is Citicorp's merger with Travelers. Had this book been published at the beginning of 1998, the section on Citicorp would have been out-of-date by spring. The profiles of these corporations are constantly evolving as the Great Companies adapt to a new and dynamic global operating environment.

Fortunately, there are a number of sources that investors can access in order to stay abreast of the changes in the Great Companies. These sources include:

Corporate Publications. Documents published by the Great Companies include:

- *Annual reports.* These include financial performance updates; a description of the company's businesses and major achievements, and significant changes in the corporation; a listing of the people on the board of directors; and a list of key corporate officers.
- *Annual report, Form 10-K.* This document contains detailed financial data about the corporation.

- *Quarterly report, Form 10-Q.* These are published each quarter by the corporation and contain top-line financial performance data, plus an update on major changes impacting the corporation.
- *Special publications.* Corporations often distribute special publications during the course of the year. These may focus on a particular topic of interest to individual investors, and can be obtained by contacting the shareholder-services departments of the Great Companies.
- *Corporate websites.* All of the Great Companies maintain corporate websites, which often contain the most recent annual report, current publicity releases, a description of the companies' businesses, and a host of other data. Websites and addresses for the Great Companies are included in the corporate profiles.

Corporate Overviews and Analyses. These are published by independent research companies and are available to individual investors. Major providers of these overviews and analyses include:

- *Hoover's.* Provides detailed reports on over 3,400 companies, including all the Great Companies. These reports include an overview of the business, financial performance, a list of competitors, and other information. Hoover's may be contacted at its website (http://www.hoovers.com).
- *Value Line (800-833-0046).* Distributes company reports that include financial performance over time and rates companies in the areas of financial strength, price stability, growth, earnings predictability, safety, and other criteria. Value Line also provides a brief overview of each company business and identifies key executives. Furthermore, Value Line analysts provide an investment perspective detailing how they view the company.
- *Zacks.* Provides information on over 6,000 companies. Zacks may be contacted at http://www.zacks.com.

I hope you find the following corporate profiles of benefit, and the interviews as interesting and insight-filled as I did. Enjoy!

AMERICAN INTERNATIONAL GROUP, INC.

CORPORATE PROFILE

———=◉=———

Address: 70 Pine Street
New York, NY 10270
Ticker Symbol: AIG
Stock Exchange: New York Stock Exchange, London Stock Exchange,
  Paris Stock Exchange, Swiss Stock Exchanges
Phone Number: (212) 770-7000
Fax Number: (212) 943-1125
Website: http://www.aig.com

History and Business Background

AIG began in Shanghai in November 1919 when Cornelius Vander Starr, a twenty-seven-year-old American, arrived in this teeming river port. Starr was an entrepreneur and soon started an insurance company called American Asiatic Underwriters. AAU acted as a subagent for numerous American insurance companies. He saw the opportunity to expand beyond the fire and marine businesses to life insurance and formed another company, Asia Life Insurance Company. Within ten years it had established offices throughout Asia. Starr opened an office in New York in 1926 under the name American International Underwriters Corporation (AIU).

AIU grew rapidly in the 1940s and 1950s, expanding its operations throughout the world, including Latin America, Western Europe, the Middle East, North Africa, and Australia. By the end of the '50s, AIU was represented in approximately seventy-five countries around the world. Maurice R. (Hank) Greenberg joined the company in 1960 and quickly was asked to accept greater responsibility. Greenberg was appointed successor to Starr in 1968 and began laying the groundwork for what is today, by some measures, the largest international insurance company in the world. By the mid-1980s, AIG Companies had become the largest and the most profitable underwriter of commercial and industrial insurance in the United States. With over 40,000 employees worldwide, AIG has emerged as the preeminent U.S.-based global insurance and financial services organization. AIG Companies can insure almost anything, almost anywhere, and the company is now leveraging its varied operations to its advantage throughout the world.

The company's operations may be grouped as follows:

1. General Insurance Operations, including Domestic General—brokerage, Domestic Personal Lines, United Guaranty Corporation, Foreign General, and Reinsurance.
2. Worldwide Life Insurance Operations, including American International Assurance Company, Ltd. (operating throughout Southeast Asia), Nan Shan Life Insurance Company, Ltd. in Taiwan, Philippine American Life and General Insurance Company, American Life Insurance Company (operating in Japan and fifty countries worldwide), and AIG's Domestic Life Companies.
3. Financial Services Group consists of businesses that complement AIG's core insurance business, and those where AIG can add value and achieve a competitive advantage. These include International Lease Finance Corporation, AIG Financial Products Corporation, AIG Trading Group, Inc, and AIG Global Investment Group, Inc.
4. Recently, AIG completed the acquisition of Sun America, Inc., a leading provider of retirement and asset allocation products.

Evaluation of AIG using the Great Company screens:

- *Highly Regarded by Knowledgeable Experts:* AIG received a score of 7.30 in *Fortune*'s "Most Admired" 1998 ratings, well above the norm. The company was ranked 26th out of 1,000 in wealth creation by *Fortune.*
- *Publicly Traded:* NYSE.
- *Headquartered in the United States:* New York, NY.
- *In Business at Least 50 Years and Survived the Founder:* The company was started by C. V. Starr in 1919. Starr was succeeded by the current chairman, Maurice R. "Hank" Greenberg, in 1968.
- *Market Cap in Excess of $15 Billion:* AIG's market cap is currently $101 billion.
- *Global Company with at Least 40 Percent of Revenues/Profits from International Operations:* AIG, which was founded in Shanghai, is truly a global company. Today approximately 53 percent of operating income is derived from international operations.

- *Outstanding Shareholder Returns:* Average returns are shown below:

AIG Returns vs. S&P 500
ending December 31, 1998

	5 YEARS	10 YEARS
AIG	30.486%	25.150%
S&P 500	24.05%	19.19%

Source: S&P Compustat

- *Terrific Businesses:* The insurance business is a wonderful business with enormous cash flows. AIG is one of the few insurance companies in the world that shows a profit from its underwriting business.
- *Protected by Strong Barriers/The Moat Effect:* The company's operations are so diverse and so geographically scattered that AIG has made it very difficult for another company to compete head on. Its global network would be almost impossible to replicate today.
- *People Are the Company's Most Important Asset:* As you read the following interview with AIG chairman Hank Greenberg, you will see specific examples of how he and others at AIG live this principle.
- *Outstanding Management Team That Keeps the Company in "Prime":* AIG has recruited an excellent management team and implemented a unique incentive structure (explained in the interview) that keeps AIG management very focused on its core businesses.
- *Innovation-Driven Company That Turns Changes into Opportunities:* AIG continues to excel as a profitable innovator within the industry.

Key Competitors: AEGEON, Allianz, Allstate, American Family Insurance, AXA-UAP, Chubb, CIGNA, CNA Financial, General Re, The Hartford, John Hancock, Lloyd's of London, Mass Mutual,

MGIC Investment, Prudential, Reliance, St. Paul, Transamerica, Zarid Group.

Sources of Additional Information

CORPORATE PUBLICATIONS
- Annual report
- Form 10-K
- Form 10-Q
- *A Short History of AIG*—Available from AIG's corporate head-quarters, this brochure provides an in-depth look at the history of AIG.

RECENT ARTICLES
- "AIG: Aggressive. Inscrutable. Greenberg." *Fortune*, April 27, 1998.

INTERVIEW

MAURICE R. "HANK" GREENBERG

Chairman and CEO
American International Group, Inc.

World Leaders in Insurance and Financial Services

During my search for Great Companies I ran a number of screens in an effort to weed out companies that did not match my criteria for greatness. As I ran these screens, one company kept popping out at the top of all lists, American International Group, Inc. I had no idea what this company did and could not understand why it constantly rose to the top. As I began to research AIG, I found it odd that this company wasn't mentioned in *Built to Last*, an excellent book about well-managed companies. It wasn't included in *In Search of Excellence*, the original classic on excellent companies, either. Likewise *Competing for the Future*, a wonderful book on business strategies for the future, failed to mention AIG. *The Discipline of Market Leaders*, a book on how to "dominate your market," also excluded the company from its pages.

I began to wonder if this was some type of mystery company that didn't really exist. I couldn't imagine how these books had overlooked AIG, a company that virtually jumped off the pages screaming "AIG is a Great Company." As I dug deeper, I realized that while AIG might be a mystery to some people, the fact that its market cap was in excess of $100 billion meant that a few folks were very much aware of the company. The difficult part seemed to be precisely describing AIG. Some people describe AIG as the "World's Largest Insurance Company," which it clearly is. Others might describe AIG as the "World's Largest Airline," for AIG owns more commercial jets than any airline in the world. Still others might describe AIG as the company responsible for financing the building of the infrastructure in developing countries like China and Latin America, which it is also doing through billion-dollar-plus funds it has established. AIG has been broadly characterized as a global financial services company, but this is a hollow, meaningless characterization of this incredibly unique company, for *AIG is like no other company in the world.*

In order to begin to understand AIG you must look at all of its businesses and understand how they combine to form a truly Great Company. In my opinion, AIG is best described as the *world's largest and best manager of risks.* AIG executives manage every type of risk imaginable, from product tampering to life insurance, and from derivatives to ransom policies. In between, there is a business that owns airplanes, one that manages third-party funds for building infrastructure in developing countries, and so on. It is logical that a company that is in the business of managing risks has been internally structured to minimize them. Herein lies the beauty of AIG from an investing perspective. This is a company that manages risks, has been structured in an effort to minimize risks, and has quintupled its market cap in less than eight years. AIG is a risk-averse company that has trounced the S&P 500 index.

While I was conducting my research, I had the good fortune to informally meet with one of AIG's senior managers. He suggested that if I really wanted to understand AIG I should meet with the chairman and CEO of American International Group, Maurice R. "Hank" Greenberg.

It was with great anticipation that I traveled into the heart of New York's financial district, AIG's world headquarters, to meet with the chairman. Upon entering the waiting room adjacent to Greenberg's office, I was immediately impressed with the photographs and proclamations on the wall. There were photographs of Greenberg with every U.S. president for the past thirty years, beginning with Richard Nixon and including Gerald Ford, Jimmy Carter, Ronald Reagan, George Bush, and Bill Clinton. There was even a personalized note from Harry Truman. There were photographs of him with world leaders from India, China, and a host of other countries. This room was more like a "World Leader Hall of Fame" than an office.

Greenberg had obviously been running AIG for quite some time. In AIG's seventy-five-plus years in business, the company has only had two chairmen, C. V. Starr, the man who founded the company in Shanghai in 1919, and Hank Greenberg, who assumed the role of chairman in 1968, just over thirty years ago. What other publicly traded company with AIG's market cap can claim anything close to that kind of continuity? As you will learn later, that continuity is a key strategic advantage for AIG.

The fact that AIG was founded in Shanghai is also unique among the Great Companies, the rest of which were all founded in the U.S. AIG's Shanghai heritage provides its management with an interesting perspective on world business and a unique, almost family-like culture common to Asian companies. The advantages these qualities provide are addressed during the following interview.

The door opened and the man who has run AIG for over thirty years greeted me, a man who is seventy, looks fifty, and leads the company with the enthusiasm of a man in his thirties, Hank Greenberg.

The Interview

We began the interview by discussing how a company like AIG became a Great Company. Since Greenberg had run the company for thirty years, he had an excellent perspective on what it took to build a Great Company. Greenberg made it clear that "there is no magic bullet" for becoming a Great Company, and went on to explain that a number of things contribute to a company becoming great including:

- *The complete and total dedication of a number of people within the company who believe very intensely in it and have a passion to see it succeed.* People who don't believe intensely in the company, and who aren't willing to pay the price of success, will eventually leave and join companies where the pressure is less intense than it is at AIG. Greenberg said, "You either love the kind of pressure that exists within AIG—that inspires creativeness and achievement—or you go to a 'backwater' kind of company where you become a follower, rather than breaking new ground."

- *A leader with a vision who is able to carry out that vision over a period of time.* Great companies "start from the top down, rather than the bottom up." Since Greenberg believes that the leader must believe in the company and inspire everyone within the company to achieve a common mission, he likened his role as CEO to that of a missionary ensuring that everyone in AIG understands, embraces, and is focused on his beliefs. Since it takes years to build a Great Company, continuity at the top is critical.
- *A unique culture that has been built and nurtured over the years.* As we will discuss later, AIG is more like an extended family than a megaglobal corporation.
- *Specific objectives and goals that are always met.* The bottom line at AIG is performance. Perform and you can rise to the top of the company.
- *A global presence.* AIG is a truly global company with operations all over the world. After working for twenty years to open China for AIG, Greenberg has finally succeeded. He believes that in order for a company to achieve this global presence, the "leader has got to be there" to meet the leaders of these foreign countries. He said, "People often wonder why AIG is treated special in China." He said that it isn't because the company was organized and created in China. "We are treated special because I spent twenty years going there, year after year, opening that market."

A Global Company. Because of AIG's global strength, approximately 55 percent of its income is derived from foreign operations. When I asked, "How do you build a truly global company?" I was told that there is no book that explains how to do this because each situation is different. Greenberg identified four factors that are important in establishing an international presence:

1. *First, AIG does not export "made in America." Rather, AIG tries to adapt to the country and its way of doing business.* Greenberg believes that AIG's Chinese heritage provided the company with a unique perspective that became an advantage because AIG had a culture that tried to understand rather than change other cultures. This mindset of fitting in rather than controlling works well all over the world.

2. *AIG brings management skills, training, and technology that don't exist in many of the countries in which they do business.* This helps the local economy develop while establishing AIG as a company that is really trying to help. In this way, AIG is able to distance itself from potential competitors while establishing itself with a country's leaders as a preferred supplier.

3. *AIG installs local people as managers.* While AIG relies on a combination of locals and expatriates to manage its business in some countries, overall, 95 to 98 percent of AIG's employees in foreign countries are locals. AIG trains and develops these people, who can reach any level within the company. Today, one of AIG's vice chairmen is Chinese, another senior executive is from England, while another is from Brazil.

4. *Building a global presence takes time.* Opening markets that have been closed to outsiders and are dominated by monopolies that have existed for years "is not a one-time-trip event." It took Greenberg over twenty years to open China. He began this effort by visiting the country in 1975 and meeting with key leaders. His goal was to help these leaders understand the value of AIG as a business partner. He built on these relationships by working with the then-mayor of Shanghai (who is currently the vice premier of China and will soon become premier) to chair the first international business advisory council that China ever held, in 1990. This conference has become an annual event, and from this relationship Greenberg opened other doors in China. This has been a long process because not only was it necessary to convince the vice premier to open the market, but Greenberg also had to convince every member of the state council, as well as the president and the premier, that China should open its doors to AIG. These dealings involved individual meetings that took place over twenty years. Greenberg believes that this will be an extremely

important market to AIG over the next twenty-five years, and this long-term perspective is exactly how AIG looks at things. Which CEO of an AIG competitor will be given twenty years to open the doors to any country for his company? And would any other CEO have the tenacity and drive to make a "China" happen in a business environment driven by quarterly returns?

It's hard to imagine the vast opportunities that exist for AIG in a developing country of 1.2 billion people. *The Big Ten*, a book about emerging markets, notes that "It took Britain fifty-eight years to double its national income during the industrial revolution. It took the United States forty-seven years to do the same, beginning with the industrial takeoff in the mid-1800s. It took South Korea eleven years in the late 1960s. China is doing it faster than any of these countries did." If I were looking for a market to open, China would definitely be the place to start.

The AIG Culture. We then shifted our discussion to the topic of AIG's culture. Greenberg said that there were a number factors that defined the company's culture:

1. *The company was originally started as a private company in a foreign country.* This provided AIG with a global orientation. When other companies were thinking about international expansion, AIG was already functioning as an international company. Today AIG is a truly global company, and is comfortable operating in virtually every country in the world.
2. *When Greenberg took over, he reorganized the company and went public.* Rather than take out all of the money for themselves (which would have been worth millions to each manager), the management group at AIG established two private companies that held 30 percent of the company's stock. The funds, which represented the difference between book value and market value of the company at the time it went public, were placed into these companies. Greenberg felt that since others had gone before him and helped create value when the company was private, it was management's obligation to pass this value along to future generations of AIG managers. Today, a select group of senior managers

(chosen based on a number of factors, including performance and company contribution) has franchise rights to participate in the increase in value of these two entities, whose net worth is in excess of $12 billion. These companies will remain private so that future generations of AIG managers can also experience the opportunity to participate in their growth in value. The current senior management group of AIG must view this as a truly unique and wonderful benefit that encourages them to keep the management strong and directed. I know of no other company that offers a program remotely like AIG's.

3. *Another defining element of AIG's culture is its family orientation.* According to Greenberg, "In many ways, AIG is like a family." He stated that in every AIG office around the world, the senior management group treats its employees like family members. He pointed out that AIG has gone through "wars, revolutions—you name it—and has never left anyone behind. We always get our people out of extremely difficult situations, whatever they may be."

Greenberg believes in family values and feels that you should always help other members of your family, no matter what. He told the story of a senior AIG executive who had a massive heart attack in Japan the week before our interview. It happens that Greenberg has been the chairman of New York Hospital for seven years. Because of his involvement with the hospital, he was able to get the top cardiologist on the phone with the AIG executive's attending physician in Japan at two o'clock in the morning to make sure that everything possible was being done for the AIG manager. Greenberg offered the observation that this type of effort in caring for others was not unusual within AIG, and that anyone within the AIG family anywhere in the world could expect the same treatment. This family environment has enabled the company to build a truly global organization that works extremely well together as a global team. He said that a worldwide AIG meeting looks more like the United Nations than a "company meeting." These people "feel that they are a part of something that is so great, that they go back to their regions and become the best advertisements that AIG could have."

While Greenberg believes strongly in these values, the bottom line is performance. Members of his family perform, or they leave the family. I find it difficult to argue with his approach.

4. *A final defining element of the culture is that while AIG is very entrepreneurial, the company is also very focused.* AIG's goals and objectives are to "create consistent quality and predictable earnings. Therefore we pick and choose the kinds of businesses we want to be in." These businesses are selected in an effort to moderate volatility in a very volatile world. Greenberg structures the company the same way the company manages risks for others.

As a result of this focus, AIG has the most successful aircraft-leasing business in the world, International Lease Finance Corporation (ILFC). People couldn't understand why Greenberg bought what seemed to many to be a very unattractive business. However, at that time AIG had very strong bond and equity portfolios that were passive types of investments. So rather than buy another insurance company on one hand, or remain passive on the other, he sought to buy a business they knew something about, and a business in which they could add value (in this case via the company's AAA rating and worldwide relationships). Today, ILFC is extremely successful. This formula was also used in the development of AIG Financial Products Corp. and AIG Trading Group, Inc., companies that AIG developed internally.

AIG repeated this success again in the investment area. The company started up an asset management business to deal with the infrastructure needs of emerging countries. Greenberg had realized for years that there were huge infrastructure needs in Asia and Latin America that far outstripped what anyone believed would be necessary. These needs, which were enormous, included building roads, airports, and port facilities. He knew that without the infrastructure, these countries would not be able to develop economically. Therefore, AIG decided to develop an Asian infrastructure fund. Greenberg teamed up with Moeen Qureshi, who had served as interim prime minister of Pakistan and chief operating officer of the World Bank, and raised $1 billion to help finance the infrastructure needs of Asia. This fund provides investors with an expected rate of return of approximately 25 percent. A second Asia fund started in early 1998 has $2 billion in commitments. A Latin America infrastructure fund has also been developed, along with a "Silk Road" fund and an India infrastructure fund.

Amazingly, all of these businesses are linked together in a complex matrix that minimizes risks and leverages the company's global presence and contacts. For example, helping to build a country's infrastructure opens doors for AIG to sell insurance. If airports are built from these infrastructure funds, the airlines serving the airport will require jet airplanes that AIG can finance through its leasing business, and these airplanes must be insured. Since AIG is operating in many countries, the company's risks are minimized in case turmoil arises in any one country, and even this turmoil spells new opportunity for AIG.

Objectives and Strategies. AIG's objective is to grow consistently with predictable earnings while balancing its growth between foreign and domestic. Greenberg feels that balancing growth is almost impossible when currencies are being devalued, as they are today, so while balance is important, the real focus is on earnings consistency, and the results have been quite impressive.

AIG management makes money from managing risks and therefore looks at the volatility of markets as opportunities to be exploited rather than risks to be avoided. However, the company's management has identified and embraced key strategies designed to manage and minimize risk, including the following:

- *Function as disciplined underwriters.* AIG does not underwrite lines when rates are depressed. This ensures that the company will achieve its earnings goals.
- *Be focused and selective about the businesses that AIG enters.* Make sure that AIG understands the business and can add value.
- *Continue to be the low-cost operator within the industry.* This requires constant effort and attention. AIG is always seeking ways to reengineer and drive costs from the system. A key element of cost

reduction is the increased use of new technologies that reduce the cost of distribution, handling, and communication.

- *Focus on internal growth through new products and services, rather than external growth through acquisitions.* AIG's new products will result from changes in laws governing employment practices, turmoil overseas that creates political risks and kidnap/ransom risks, or product tampering that creates tampering-insurance opportunities. AIG is very alert and sensitive to changes in the world, and uses these changes to drive new sources of revenue. This strategy does not mean that acquisitions will be avoided, it simply means that they will be limited and, when considered, will be closely examined for fit within AIG as well as performance.

However, the biggest challenge facing AIG senior management is not the development of strategies: "When you have an organization of 40,000 people spread throughout the world, it's critical to make sure the implementation of these strategies is being carried out the way that you intended." Greenberg believes that ensuring that these strategies are implemented is a "seven-day-a-week, twenty-four-hour-a-day job." He believes that communication and training must be constant. The use of technology is also key in getting the message across. For this reason AIG has developed an alliance with MIT (the Massachusetts Institute of Technology) to make sure that AIG stays on the leading edge of technology.

Greenberg believes that the pace of change throughout the world has speeded up so dramatically that huge burdens have been placed on AIG managers. Companies must be able to respond faster, and "you must have an organization that keeps pace." He believes that companies can't hesitate to make decisions. Greenberg contends that "the demands on top management today are four to five times greater than they were ten or fifteen years ago." In this environment, managers must delegate a lot of responsibility, run faster, and execute better if they are to succeed.

Today, AIG has a market cap in excess of $100 billion and capital of $23 billion. Over the past five years, with dividends reinvested, AIG stock has risen 152 percent, compared to 79 percent for its peer group. Greenberg believes, and the numbers prove, that AIG is strong enough to survive and prosper while others are having a difficult time. But looking at past achievements and records isn't what he and AIG are all about. He believes that good managers are "restless, never satisfied." In his words, "Who cares about what you did last year?" It doesn't matter whether "the Yankees or the Dallas Cowboys won their league last year, who cares about that? I'm not interested in history, I am interested in the future."

BRISTOL-MYERS SQUIBB COMPANY
CORPORATE PROFILE

Address: 345 Park Avenue
 New York, NY 10154
Ticker Symbol: BMY
Stock Exchange: NYSE
Phone Number: (212) 546-4000
Fax Number: (212) 546-4020
Website: http://www.bms.com

History and Business Background
William Bristol and John Myers founded Clinton Pharmaceutical in 1887. The company's original business was the sale of bulk pharmaceuticals. Around 1900 the company was renamed Bristol-Myers and began to expand overseas. This was followed by several key acquisitions, including Clairol in 1959 and Mead Johnson (infant formula) in 1967. Bristol-Myers continued to develop and began expanding into pharmaceuticals, introducing new drugs for treating cancer and cardiovascular disease. A major development in the company's expansion was the acquisition of Squibb, a successful pharmaceutical company, in 1989. Since the merger, Bristol-Myers Squibb's returns to shareholders have dramatically improved.

Today, Bristol-Myers divides its businesses into five major sectors, as follows:

1. *Pharmaceuticals.* Represent approximately 62 percent of sales and include brands like Taxol, Pravachol, Avapro, Glucophage, Zerit, Plavix, Widex, and Serzone.
2. *Nutritionals.* Account for 10 percent of sales and include the products marketed by Mead Johnson, a global leader in nutritional products with brands like Enfamil, Enfalac, Pro Sobee, and others.
3. *Medical Devices.* Include products marketed by Zimmer (orthopaedic hips and knees) and Conva Tec (ostomy and wound care) and represent 9 percent of sales.
4. *Beauty Care.* Generates 12 percent of sales and includes Clairol and Matrix Essentials with such products as Herbal Essences, Nice 'n Easy, Aussie, Biolage, Miss Clairol, and others.
5. *Consumer Medicines.* Represent 7 percent of sales and include brands like Excedrin, Bufferin, Efferalgan, Dafalgan, and Keri Products.

Evaluation using Great Company Screens:

- *Highly Regarded by Knowledgeable Experts:* B-MS was ranked tenth in creating shareholder wealth by *Fortune.* The company was highly ranked in the "America's Most Admired Companies" survey with a score of 7.36.
- *Publicly Traded:* NYSE.
- *Headquartered in the United States:* New York, NY.
- *In Business at Least 50 Years and Survived the Founder:* Bristol-Myers was founded in 1887, while Squibb was founded in 1858.
- *Market Cap in Excess of $15 Billion:* Bristol-Myers Squibb's market cap is currently $132.9 billion.
- *Global Company with at Least 40 Percent of Revenues/Profits from International Operations:* Approximately 40 percent of revenues are derived from international operations. The company functions as a global company.
- *Outstanding Shareholder Returns:* The company's returns are shown below. Note how performance has improved vs. the S&P Index over the past five years.

Bristol-Myers Squibb Returns vs. S&P 500

ending December 31, 1998

	5 YEARS	10 YEARS
BRISTOL-MYERS SQUIBB	40.26%	23.73%
S&P 500	24.05%	19.19%

Source: S&P Compustat

- *Terrific Businesses:* Leading consumer brands coupled with an excellent pharmaceutical business makes for an excellent business model.
- *Protected by Strong Barriers/The Moat Effect:* The combination of strong brands and an excellent R&D capability is a powerful barrier.
- *People Are the Company's Most Important Asset:* The company has always placed a premium on its people.
- *Outstanding Management Team That Keeps the Company in "Prime":* Bristol-Myers Squibb has focused on the products and brands that are key to its future profits.
- *Innovation-Driven Company That Turns Changes into Opportunities:* The company's history of innovative new products has been a critical part of its current success.

Key Competitors: Abbott Labs, American Home Products, Amgen, Bayer AG, Eli Lilly, Gillette, Johnson & Johnson, Merck, Pfizer, Pharmacia and Upjohn, Procter and Gamble, Schering-Plough, Warner-Lambert, and others.

Sources of Additional Information

CORPORATE PUBLICATIONS
- Annual Report
- Form 10-K
- Form 10-Q

RECENT ARTICLES
- "The New Biotech Boom: A Star is Born." *Fortune,* January 13, 1997.

- "Staying Afloat While Asia Sinks." *Fortune*, January 12, 1998.
- "Stocks Large-Cap Fund Managers Love." *Fortune*, November 9, 1998.

CITIGROUP, INC.

CORPORATE PROFILE

Address: 153 E. 53rd Street
New York, NY 10043
Ticker Symbol: C
Stock Exchange: NYSE
Phone Number: (800) 285-3000
Website: http://www.citi.com

History and Business Background

No other Great Company has endured as much change in the last year as Citigroup. The year 1998 began with Citicorp and Travelers operating as two separate companies. By October, both companies had merged to form a new company, Citigroup, that had nearly $700 billion in assets. Rather than discuss the history of Citicorp and Travelers, I will focus on the new company, Citigroup.

Citigroup divides its businesses into three major sectors, as follows:

1. *Global Consumer Business.* The consumer business operates in some fifty-seven countries throughout the world and is divided into the following segments:
   - *Citibanking.* The only truly global consumer bank in the world.
   - *Salomon Smith Barney Private Client Group.* One of every six affluent investors in the United States is a Salomon Smith Barney client. This group sells financial products and offers advisory services.
   - *Private Banking.* Provides wealth management services for high-net-worth individuals throughout the world.

- *Cards.* Citibank is the leader in credit cards and has approximately 49 million card customers worldwide.
- *Consumer Finance.* Offers financing services to middle- and lower-income Americans.
- *Life Insurance.* Services include annuity products, life insurance, and long-term care insurance.
- *Personal Property Casualty Insurance.* Through Travelers, the company has more than 4.4 million automobile and home-owner's policies in force.

2. *SSB Citi Asset Management.* Citigroup has one of the largest asset-management businesses in the world. This business is divided into two segments:
   - *Salomon Smith Barney Asset Management.* Offers investment management services to pension funds, institutions, supranational organizations, wealthy individuals, and retail investors.
   - *Citibank Global Asset Management.* Manages assets for high-net-worth individuals, mutual-fund shareholders, and major institutional clients.

3. *Global Corporate Businesses.* Provides total solutions for companies, governments, and other institutions almost anywhere in the world. Divisions include:
   - *Salomon Smith Barney Investment Banking and Capital Markets.* Activities include managing IPOs, underwriting municipal debt, providing advice regarding mergers and acquisitions.
   - *Citibank in Emerging Markets.* The focus is on helping corporations in emerging markets achieve their goals.
   - *Citibank Global Relationship Banking.* Provides banking services to multinational companies all over the world.
   - *Commercial Property and Casualty Insurance.* Offers a variety of insurance services to commercial clients.

This new corporation is indeed a global powerhouse, capable of doing business virtually anywhere in the world.

Evaluation using Great Company Screens:

- *Highly Regarded by Knowledgeable Experts:* Prior to the merger, Citicorp was ranked as the second-best money center bank by *For-*

tune in "America's Most Admired Companies" survey. Travelers was ranked 7th among insurance companies with a score of 6.78, well above the average for all companies. Citicorp was accorded "Visionary" status in the book, *Built to Last*. Citicorp ranked 31st in wealth creation while Travelers was 40th among 1,000 companies studied.

- *Publicly Traded:* NYSE.
- *Headquartered in the United States:* New York, NY.
- *In Business at Least 50 Years and Survived the Founder:* Citicorp was founded in 1812.
- *Market Cap in Excess of $15 Billion:* Citigroup's market cap is currently $112.2 billion.
- *Global Company with at Least 40 Percent of Revenues/Profits from International Operations:* Combined, approximately 39 percent of revenues and 55 percent of Citigroup's profits came from international operations. Citigroup is indeed a global company, and the only global, full-service, consumer-banking company in the world.
- *Outstanding Shareholder Returns:* Citicorp's returns have exceeded the S&P returns, as shown in the following chart.

Citigroup's Returns vs. S&P 500
ending December 31, 1998

	5 YEARS	10 YEARS
CITIGROUP	29.92%	20.50%
S&P 500	24.05%	19.19%

Source: S&P Compustat

- *Terrific Businesses:* The banking and insurance businesses are both very attractive.
- *Protected by Strong Barriers/The Moat Effect:* The combination of Citicorp and Travelers has strengthened the barrier that protects both companies. While it will take some time to fully integrate the two businesses, the end result will be awesome.
- *People Are the Company's Most Important Asset:* Both companies have a high regard for their people and are considered to have some of the most talented people in the industry.

- *Outstanding Management Team That Keeps the Company in "Prime":* Citicorp's focus on its goal of becoming the largest full-service consumer bank in the world has ensured that the company has remained in "Prime."
- *Innovation-Driven Company That Turns Changes into Opportunities:* Citicorp and Travelers have long been regarded as innovators. For example, Travelers was the first company to offer accident insurance, the first company to write a double indemnity policy, and the first company to write an automobile insurance policy. Citicorp was the first U.S. bank to offer floating-rate notes, the first to offer "stretch" mortgages, and the first U.S. bank to reach $1 billion in assets. Both companies have rich traditions of innovation.

Key Competitors: Citigroup competes with a broad array of financial-services companies including AIG, American Express, Bank One, Credit Suisse/First Boston, Deutsche Bank/Banker's Trust, The Hartford, MBNA, Merrill Lynch, J. P. Morgan, Mass Mutual, Morgan Stanley, and Prudential.

Sources of Additional Information

CORPORATE PUBLICATIONS
- Annual reports of Travelers and Citicorp
- 10-Ks of both companies

RECENT ARTICLES
- "The King of Plastic." *Forbes,* December 15, 1997.
- "Citigroup." *Business Week,* April 20, 1998.
- "$1,000,000,000,000 Banks." *Business Week,* April 27, 1998.
- "One Helluva Candy Store." *Fortune,* May 11, 1998.
- "Two on Top." *Fortune,* May 25, 1998.
- "Citigroup: Scenes from a Merger," *Fortune,* January 11, 1998

THE COCA-COLA COMPANY

CORPORATE PROFILE

———

Address: One Coca-Cola Plaza
       Atlanta, GA 30313
Ticker Symbol: KO
Stock Exchange: NYSE
Phone Number: (404) 676-2121
Fax Number: (404) 676-6792
Website: http://www.cocacola.com

History and Business Background

Dr. John Styth Pemberton, a pharmacist, first introduced Coca-Cola in Atlanta in 1886. The product, sold in Jacobs Pharmacy for five cents a glass as a soda fountain drink, was described as "delicious and refreshing." In 1886 sales of Coca-Cola averaged nine drinks per day. Today, Coca-Cola operates in nearly 200 countries, has four of the top-selling soft-drink brands in the world, and in 1997 sold an average of one billion servings of Coca-Cola products daily. Had you purchased one share of Coca-Cola stock at $40 per share in 1919 when the company went public and reinvested your dividends, your share of stock would be worth in excess of $6.6 million today. Coca-Cola markets over 160 brands of beverage products throughout the world. The company is highly focused on the beverage business and sees enormous potential in the future. The company recently announced plans to acquire Cadbury Schweppes beverage brands in more than 120 countries around the world. The first page of its 1997 annual report notes: "This year, even as we sell 1 billion servings of our products daily, the world will still consume 47 billion servings of other beverages *every* day. We're just getting started."

Evaluation using Great Company Screens:

- *Highly Regarded by Knowledgeable Experts:* Coca-Cola is one of the most highly regarded companies in the world. For example, in 1998 Coca-Cola ranked third among *Fortune*'s "America's Most Admired Companies," second among its "World's Most Admired Companies," second among "America's Greatest Wealth Creators,"

GREAT COMPANIES, GREAT RETURNS

and its board of directors has been rated one of the best in the United States.

- *Publicly Traded:* NYSE.
- *Headquartered in the United States:* Atlanta, GA.
- *In Business at Least 50 Years and Survived the Founder:* The untimely 1997 death of Roberto Goizueta, the man who took Coca-Cola's market cap from $4.3 billion to $180 billion, is the reason this screen is so important. While Goizueta will be sorely missed, Coca-Cola will continue to prosper. Goizueta was replaced, almost seemlessly, by M. Douglas Ivester, an extremely capable leader who proved his capabilities while working with Goizueta on a variety of assignments. Truly Great Companies have the bench strength to overcome these kinds of tragedies.
- *Market Cap in Excess of $15 Billion:* Coca-Cola's market cap on 12/31/98 was $164.9 billion.
- *Global Company with at Least 40 Percent of Revenues/Profits from International Operations:* Coca-Cola is regarded by many as the most powerful brand in the world. The company derives approximately 67 percent of its revenues from international operations.
- *Outstanding Shareholder Returns:*

Coca-Cola Returns vs. S&P 500
ending December 31, 1998

	5 YEARS	10 YEARS
COCA-COLA COMPANY	26.07%	30.11%
S&P 500	24.05%	19.19%

Source: S&P Compustat

- *Terrific Businesses:* Coca-Cola is in a great business which was improved when the company spun off most of its bottling operations.
- *Protected by Strong Barriers/The Moat Effect:* The company has market-leading shares and the strongest brand in the world.
- *People Are the Company's Most Important Asset:* The company attracts and keeps outstanding talent. It works hard to develop its managers for additional responsibilities.

- *Outstanding Management Team That Keeps the Company in "Prime":* The company is highly focused on its core business, beverages. Although highly successful, it is always seeking to grow and realize new opportunities.
- *Innovation-Driven Company That Turns Changes into Opportunities:* Coca-Cola is an innovator in many aspects of its business.

Key Competitors: Cott, Pepsico, Quaker Oats, Triarc.

Sources of Additional Information

CORPORATE PUBLICATIONS
- Annual report
- Form 10-K
- Form 10-Q
- *The Chronicle of Coca-Cola since 1886*
- *A Taste For Quality*

RECENT ARTICLES
- "Doug Is It." *Fortune,* May 25, 1998.
- "I'd Like the World to Buy a Coke." *Business Week,* April 13, 1998.

BOOKS
- Greising, David. *I'd Like the World to Buy a Coke: The Life and Leadership of Roberto Goizueta.* New York: John Wiley, 1998.
- Pendergrast, Mark. *For God, Country & Coca-Cola.* New York: Collier Books, 1993.
- Allen, Frederick. *Secret Formula.* New York: Harper Business, 1994.

COLGATE-PALMOLIVE COMPANY

CORPORATE PROFILE

Address: 300 Park Avenue
New York, NY 10022
Ticker Symbol: CL

Stock Exchange: NYSE
Phone Number: (212) 310-2000
Fax Number: (212) 310-3284
Website: http://www.colgate.com

History and Business Background

Colgate-Palmolive was founded in New York in 1806. In the beginning, the company was in the starch, soap, and candle products businesses. As time passed, Colgate entered the toothpaste business (1877) and expanded its soap business to include perfumed soap. Colgate went public in 1908. During the 1930s, well ahead of its time, Colgate purchased French and German soap manufacturers and began to aggressively build its business in Europe. This focus on international business has resulted in a company that is truly global, with approximately 70 percent of its sales outside the U.S. For years, Colgate was more highly regarded internationally than it was in America. Today, Colgate has made major strides in the United States, one of its weakest markets, and for the first time has captured the leadership position in the U.S. toothpaste market.

Colgate-Palmolive's businesses are grouped into five major sectors:

1. Oral Care is the largest and represents 31 percent of revenues. Brands include Colgate Total, Ultra Brite, Colgate Toothbrushes, and Fluorigard Rinse.
2. Personal Care is the second-largest business with over 23 percent of the company's sales. Brands like Palmolive soap, Mennen, and Softsoap lead the way.
3. Household Surface Care represents 16 percent of Colgate's sales and includes brands like Ajax Cleanser and Palmolive Liquid.
4. Approximately 16 percent of the business is Fabric Care. This sector includes Fab and the company's fabric-softener brands.
5. Pet Nutrition, consisting of Hills, represents 11 percent of revenues.

Evaluation using Great Company Screens:

- *Highly Regarded by Knowledgeable Experts:* Colgate-Palmolive ranks third (behind Gillette and Procter and Gamble) in the Soaps and Cosmetics category among "America's Most Admired Companies." Colgate ranks sixty-third in wealth creation among the 1,000 companies that were rated by *Fortune*.

- *Publicly Traded:* NYSE.
- *Headquartered in the United States:* New York, NY.
- *In Business at Least 50 Years and Survived the Founder:* Colgate was founded in 1806.
- *Market Cap in Excess of $15 Billion:* Colgate-Palmolive's market cap is currently $25.4 billion.
- *Global Company with at Least 40 Percent of Revenues/Profits from International Operations:* Colgate derives approximately 70 percent of its revenues from its international operations. C-P leads all Great Companies in overseas sales development as a percentage of total revenues. Colgate is a truly global company focused on building global brands.
- *Outstanding Shareholder Returns:* Colgate's returns are as follows:

Colgate-Palmolive Returns vs. S&P 500
ending December 31, 1998

	5 YEARS	10 YEARS
COLGATE-PALMOLIVE	27.06%	25.91%
S&P 500	24.05%	19.19%

Source: S&P Compustat

- *Terrific Businesses:* Colgate's businesses are high-volume, high-household-penetration, consumer businesses, which lend themselves to branding. C-P is in good businesses.
- *Protected by Strong Barriers/The Moat Effect:* Colgate has achieved global leadership in toothpaste, liquid soap, all-purpose cleaners, and specialty pet food. These barriers protect Colgate's core business.
- *People Are the Company's Most Important Asset:* Colgate-Palmolive offers its employees a variety of benefits geared to keep them happy and productive.
- *Outstanding Management Team That Keeps the Company in*

"Prime": Now that Colgate's U.S. business is strong, the company is perfectly positioned for the future.

• *Innovation-Driven Company That Turns Changes into Opportunities:* Approximately 33 percent of the company's revenues are derived from products that did not exist five years ago. This focus on innovation and growth is paying handsome dividends for shareholders.

Key Competitors: Avon, Block Drug, Clorox, Dial, Gillette, Henkel, Johnson & Johnson, Procter and Gamble, Unilever, and others.

Sources of Additional Information
CORPORATE PUBLICATIONS
• Annual report
• Form 10-K
• Form 10-Q

GENERAL ELECTRIC COMPANY
CORPORATE PROFILE

Address: 3135 Easton Turnpike
Fairfield, CT 06431
Ticker Symbol: GE
Stock Exchange: NYSE
Phone Number: (203) 373-2211
Fax Number: (203) 373-3131
Website: http://www.ge.com

History and Business Background
General Electric was founded in New York in 1892 as the result of a merger between Thomson-Houston and Edison General Electric. Early GE products included motors, toasters, lightbulbs (Thomas Edison was on the board), and trolleys. For years, GE seemed to plod along, growing at about the same rate as the Gross Domestic Product. In fact, GE was referred to as a GDP company, meaning a com-

pany that was a solid, but not spectacular performer. The company was always highly regarded by management experts for its research and management capabilities, but looked upon by Wall Street as a defensive stock.

Everything changed in 1981 when John F. Welch was made chairman and chief executive officer. Over the past 18 years, he has taken a conservative company and turned it into one of the truly great companies in the world. The following interview details exactly how he was able to pull off one of the most remarkable transitions in American business history. In my opinion, Welch has never received the credit he deserves for the courage he showed in his early days as president of GE. Precious few people have the courage and leadership required to accomplish what Jack Welch has accomplished at GE.

Today, GE has the second largest market cap in the world. Its businesses include the following:

- Aircraft engines
- Appliances
- Capital services
- Lighting
- Medical systems
- Media (NBC)
- Plastics
- Power systems
- Electrical distribution and controls
- Industrial control systems
- Information systems
- Transportation systems

These businesses are covered more fully in the following interview.

While Jack Welch certainly receives and deserves a lot of the credit for GE's successes, he is the first one to tell you that he is backed by an incredibly capable group of outstanding managers, many of whom could be CEOs themselves. When he retires in 2000, it will mark a huge change for GE, but there are a lot of very talented people "waiting in the wings" to take GE to new heights. And even when he retires, I can't imagine that he won't be sticking his head in the shop every now and then.

Evaluation using Great Company Screens:

- *Highly Regarded by Knowledgeable Experts:* Currently, many people consider General Electric to be the best company in the world. GE ranks number one among 1,000 companies in the U.S. in wealth creation, and it is both "America's Most Admired Company" and "the World's Most Admired Company," according to *Fortune.* GE is listed as a Visionary Company in *Built to Last,* and considered by *Business Week* to have the second-best board of directors in the U.S.
- *Publicly Traded:* NYSE.
- *Headquartered in the United States:* Fairfield, CT.
- *In Business at Least 50 Years and Survived the Founder:* GE was founded in 1892.
- *Market Cap in Excess of $15 Billion:* Currently, GE's market cap is approximately $333.3 billion.
- *Global Company with at Least 40 Percent of Revenues/Profits from International Operations:* GE derives approximately 42 percent of its revenues from its international operations. The company is truly a global operator that is able to leverage its size and clout throughout the world.
- *Outstanding Shareholder Returns:* GE has delivered spectacular returns to shareholders, as shown in the following chart.

General Electric Returns vs. S&P 500
ending December 31, 1998

	5 YEARS	10 YEARS
GENERAL ELECTRIC	34.15%	28.00%
S&P 500	24.05%	19.19%

Source: S&P Compustat

- *Terrific Businesses:* GE's credo of "fix, sell, or close" bad businesses has resulted in the company being in many excellent businesses. GE has done an outstanding job of turning "OK" businesses into excellent business models. This is covered in detail in the interview.

- *Protected by Strong Barriers/The Moat Effect:* GE's motto is to be "number one or number two in market share in the world in every business we are in." GE's ability to successfully execute this strategy has resulted in the development of an enormous moat that protects its core businesses.
- *People Are the Company's Most Important Asset:* GE's commitment to developing its people may well be one of its greatest strengths. Few companies have the depth of talent throughout the world that GE does. In our interview, Jack Welch expresses satisfaction that so many GE employees have done well from the stock option program, showing that GE really does care about all of its employees, not just the executives at the top.
- *Outstanding Management Team That Keeps the Company in "Prime":* This is a company that is focused on delivering outstanding returns to shareholders. GE is the perfect example of a company in "Prime."
- *Innovation-Driven Company That Turns Changes into Opportunities:* GE has invested heavily in new technology that has allowed it to turn good businesses into great businesses.

Key Competitors: The list of competitors is huge, reflecting the breadth of GE's businesses. They include AIG, Cigna, GTE, Maytag, Toshiba, United Technologies, and Walt Disney.

Sources of Additional Information

CORPORATE PUBLICATIONS
- Annual report
- Form 10-K
- Form 10-Q

RECENT ARTICLES
- "Revealed at Last, the Secret of Jack Welch's Success." *Forbes,* January 26, 1998.
- "How Jack Welch Runs GE." *Business Week,* June 8, 1998.
- "GE Capital: Jack Welch's Secret Weapon." *Fortune,* November 10, 1997.

- "Jack's Men." *Industry Week,* July 7, 1997.
- "How GE's Welch Is Remaking His Company—Again." *Business Week,* October 28, 1996.
- "Who Will Succeed Jack Welch." *Business Week,* December 21, 1998.

BOOKS

- Tichy, Noel M. and Stratford Herman. *Control Your Destiny, Or Someone Else Will.* New York: Doubleday, 1993.
- Lowe, Janet C. *Jack Welch Speaks.* New York: John Wiley & Sons, 1998.
- Slater, Robert. *Jack Welch and the GE Way.* New York: McGraw-Hill 1998.

INTERVIEW

JOHN F. "JACK" WELCH

Chairman and CEO
General Electric Company

The Incredible Cash Machine

General Electric's corporate offices are located precisely 6.9 miles from my house. It's ironic that the Great Company that is the closest to my home came the farthest to make the list of fourteen Great Companies.

Eighteen years ago, GE was looked upon as a GDP (Gross Domestic Product) company, which meant that GE grew at about the same rate as the GDP. While management experts always viewed GE as a highly innovative company, the analysts regarded GE as a defensive stock (a stock to own when the market turns down). Looked at from the three perspectives discussed earlier in this book, GE was highly regarded by management experts but panned by analysts and regarded as a large, plodding conglomerate by CEOs.

Today, GE's market cap is $333.3 billion, the second largest in the world. If ranked independently, eight of GE's businesses would be among the *Fortune 500* companies. GE recently received *Fortune's* award as America's Most Admired Company, and was ranked first in shareholder wealth creation. *Business Week* ranks GE's Board of Directors as second best among all U.S. companies.

Today, GE operates twelve major business units:

- *Aircraft Engines.* The world's largest producer of large and small jet engines for commercial and military aircraft.
- *Appliances.* One of the largest manufacturers of major appliances in the world, producing Monogram, Profile, GE, RCA, and Hotpoint brands.
- *Capital Services.* A diversified financial services company that creates comprehensive solutions to increase client productivity and efficiency.
- *Electrical Distribution and Control.* An industry leader in the design and manufacture of products used to distribute, protect, and control electrical power and equipment.
- *Industrial Control Systems.* A leading supplier of product and service solutions for commercial and industrial applications.
- *Information Services.* A global leader in business-to-business electronic commerce solutions and manager of the world's largest electronic trading community with more than 40,000 trading partners.
- *Lighting.* A leading supplier of lighting products for global consumer, commercial, and industrial markets.
- *Medical Systems.* A world leader in medical diagnostic imaging technology.
- *NBC.* The leading U.S. television network.
- *Plastics.* A world leader in versatile, high-performance, engineered plastics used in the computer, electronics, office equipment, and automotive industries.
- *Power Systems.* A world leader in the design, manufacture, and service of gas, steam, and hydroelectric turbines and generators.
- *Transportation Systems.* Manufactures more than half the diesel freight locomotives in North America, and its locomotives operate in more than seventy-five countries worldwide.

At first glance it appears that GE is just another conglomerate composed of a variety of different businesses, but it isn't. GE is a large company that operates like a small company rather than a silo-structured conglomerate.

GE's transformation (this was not a transition) from a GDP company to one of the most dynamic companies in the world—as well as one of the largest—proves that good companies can become great companies, but it is a difficult process. GE, more than any other company that I studied, has proven that the principles on which this book are based, and the qualities of the Great Companies that we have identified, are indeed valid.

What GE has done isn't management theory or academic hype—it's very real. For GE shareholders, it means that they earned 45 percent on their investment in 1995, 40 percent in 1996, and 51 percent in 1997. Along with this outstanding performance, ongoing operating margin rose to 15.7 percent in 1997, exceeding 15 percent for the first time in GE's history.

What is really amazing is that during the course of this transformation GE continued to meet or exceed earnings expectations. It's nearly unbelievable that GE could sell over $10 billion in existing businesses and acquire over $20 billion in new businesses, establish key core values, shift from a business base that was 70 percent manufacturing to one that is 70 percent service, and introduce Six Sigma (GE's quality initiative) without skipping a beat.

Because of these successes, *USA Today* reports that the chairman's letters to shareholders in the GE annual report have become "must reads for CEOs, academics and investors looking for the sources of GE's management success. They are to management types what Warren Buffett's annual letters for Berkshire Hathaway are to stock pickers."

Preparing for my interview with John F. Welch, the chairman and CEO of GE since 1981—a man whose writings are compared to those of Warren Buffett and who is greatly admired by his fellow CEOs—reminded me of Dorothy's quest for the Wizard of Oz. You see, GE is perched on a hill overlooking the Connecticut countryside, its white façade glowing in the sun. Its fleet of helicopters darts in and out taking busy senior executives to meetings in New York, or to surrounding airports. From a distance, GE's headquarters has the mystical look of Oz. As I thought about my interview, I envisioned GE as Oz, and Jack Welch as the all-knowing wizard in charge of the city. I wondered what I might find if I got an opportunity to sneak a peek behind the curtains.

As I drove off to our interview, my car radio was tuned to Don Imus, a New York radio talk-show personality. When I heard Imus declare that over the weekend Jack Welch shot a 69 and beat Greg Norman, one of the top golfers in the world, by one stroke, my first thoughts were that Jack Welch is beyond the stuff that wizards are made of. Imagine, he runs one of the largest-market-cap companies in the world, has created enormous shareholder wealth, and shot a 69 to beat Greg Norman. . . . My Hero!

During my interview, I found out that GE is a lot more than Jack Welch. It is a collection of market-leading businesses staffed by outstanding executives who have achieved, and I believe will continue to achieve, unbelievable results. This company is so large and so complex that it almost defies definition. Jack refers to it as "a cash machine," and that's good enough for me. I added "the incredible" because the way GE throws off cash is hard to believe.

The Interview

I began my interview with Jack Welch by reviewing the charts at the conclusion of the interview (see pages 165–167). Prior to my interview I spent several days studying the GE annual reports from 1981 through 1997. From these reports, I pieced together the steps that GE had followed in its successful transformation from good company to Great Company. GE's transformation followed a well-thought-out plan that began with ensuring that the company is in good businesses that are managed by excellent managers, and concluded with Six Sigma. I found that there were three distinct phases of the transformation, as follows:

1. *Phase 1,* which lasted from 1981 to 1988, centered on achieving Welch's vision of "becoming the most competitive enterprise in the world by being number one or two in market share in the world in every business we are in." The charge was to "fix, sell, or close" any business that was not first or second in the market, or lacked global potential. Phase 1 included the divestiture of poor businesses, the acquisition of good businesses, and the creation of a climate of personal excellence. This phase formed the base on

which the *new* GE was built. During this period, GE divested businesses that brought in over $10 billion and acquired businesses valued in excess of $19 billion.

2. *Phase 2* (1989–1995) resulted in the formation of the "boundaryless organization," and the creation of GE's core values. This phase was characterized by the following quote: "The desire and ability of an organization to continually learn from any source, anywhere—and to rapidly convert this learning into action—is the ultimate competitive advantage." The boundaryless organization provided GE with the freedom and speed required to function as a responsive, entrepreneurial company. The core values ensured continuity and consistency within this boundaryless working environment. This phase enabled GE to use its huge size to its advantage. Its end result was a war on bureaucracy that continues even today, and the evolution of a corporate entity that is huge but operates like a small company. This phase made GE different from most other large companies in the U.S. For GE is not a conglomerate composed of silos and managers with uncontrollable egos, it is a company that, as Welch describes it, "operates more like a corner grocery store with a few more zeros after the revenue number."

3. *Phase 3,* which started in 1996 and is in full gear with a vision of 2000, is GE's total quality initiative, Six Sigma. The objective of Six Sigma is to reduce defects to 3.4 per million. At GE this initiative is led by quality all-stars referred to as "Master Black Belts, Black Belts, and Green Belts." These people are responsible for training people within GE and ensuring that Six Sigma objectives are achieved. If you are a GE employee, you won't be promoted or given salary increases unless you are totally dedicated to the Six Sigma initiative. This initiative focuses on fixing processes rather than products and, as Welch says, "Six Sigma defines how we work." Because of the cultural changes that GE has already made, Six Sigma is progressing faster than he originally imagined.

You should now turn to the charts at the conclusion of this section and spend time studying each phase of GE's transformation. Much of our interview focused on these three phases, and you will find it helpful to review the transformation process before reading the interview.

Books have been written about the different phases of GE's transformation including *The Boundaryless Organization* and *Control Your Destiny or Someone Else Will.* However, the series of charts at the conclusion of this section is the first overview that I have seen of GE's overall transformation process. Welch's comments regarding the charts confirmed that the process as I had studied and understood it was consistent with what actually occurred from his perspective.

As a result of these three phases, GE is a very different company today than it was in 1981, as the chart below reveals:

	1981	1998	CHANGE
MARKET CAP	$13 Billion	$333.3 Billion	2,564%
REVENUES	$28 Billion	$100.5 Billion	358.9%
OPERATING MARGIN	$2.4 Billion	$9.3 Billion	387.5%
OPERATING MARGIN PERCENT OF SALES	9.3%	16.7%	179.6%
PERCENT OF REVENUES FROM SERVICES	15%	70%	466.7%
R&D SPENDING	$643 Million	$1.48 Billion	230.1%
PERCENT OF REVENUES FROM INTERNATIONAL OPERATIONS	22%	42%	190.9%

Source: GE

Jack Welch describes the transformation process as follows: "What you have are three phases. This [Phase 1] is the hardware fix [he refers to fixing the businesses and organization structure as the hardware]. This got rid of the stuff, if you will, layers and underbrush . . . This [Phase 2] is the software [people and values] fix, which defines how we behave. This opened us up to ideas from anywhere. This phase [Phase 3] defines how we work, how we do our jobs every day. So you have structure, how we behave, and how we work. It's that simple." It might seem simple to Welch now, but as you read through the interview you will began to realize how complex and difficult the transformation has been.

Phase 1

The Beginning. I began by asking Welch how GE was able to transform itself from a GDP company into one of the largest, most dynamic companies in the world. He responded, "A lot of that is expectations of ourselves. We thought of ourselves as a company that was solid. Steady as she goes. We sort of set our sights differently." His vision was for GE to "become the most competitive enterprise in the world by being number one or two in market share in the world in every business we are in"—a radical departure from the old vision of GE as a GDP company.

Welch believes that the transformation was made easier because "We had a strong balance sheet when we started, so we weren't in trouble. It was good because we had the money and resources that we needed to do what we had to do, but bad because the organization couldn't understand why we needed to change so dramatically." He noted that "We had a lot of assets. When we sold Utah [Utah International Inc., a mining company, to BHP of Australia for $2.4 billion] we had a gain. With that gain, you can do a lot of things. We have never taken a nonrecurring gain. We have only taken restructuring charges when we had gains to offset the charge. We only fix the house when we have money. If we don't have the money to do a repair job, we don't do it."

Fix, Sell, or Close. Welch's charge to the organization during Phase 1 was to "fix, sell or, close" businesses that were not number one or two in market share, were poor businesses, or couldn't be expanded globally. Initially, the company focused its efforts on three areas: GE's core businesses, high-technology businesses, and service businesses. The challenge was "to acquire or create those businesses that either improve an existing GE business, or stand alone in a promising market in which we want to participate."

One of the really amazing achievements at GE is the way the company has "fixed" businesses. Many of these fixes have been achieved by integrating technology into the service equation. As Welch remarked, "Our corporate forefathers tried this thirty to forty years ago and it was called apparatus service shops. They took motors and rewound them. They didn't have enough technology content, had GE benefits and costs, had superstructure, and they died . . . over the last thirty years they just died. So we have a model right in front of us of what our forefathers did. So if we don't shift our resources dramatically to technology we will fail. [Today] we spend more than $200 million on service technology."

Welch went on to say, "Our whole drive in services is to become a high-technology service company. If we don't, we are the highest-priced wrench turners on the street. Our whole game is to change the customer's demand equation so that we can change his productivity and competitiveness in his industry. We want to build only those services that the customer needs in order to win in his marketplace. This allows us to take this installed base and create a whole new game. It's really the Gillette game around our installed base. It is a great business model. The fear that you have constantly is that you don't put enough technology investment into your service activity. So that you end up providing spare parts, not full solutions."

Today there is a massive shift of resources into technology services. GE's plans have called for almost doubling the amount of R&D dollars spent on technology services annually over the past two years. As Welch said, "It's where we have to go, and engineers historically didn't want to go there, because they didn't see after-market work as being very exciting. They wanted to focus on new things. Things that go higher, faster, further. That's why many of them joined the company, to work on exotic projects. Services creates exotic [projects] if you get your head straight. Because these projects are changing the investments that our customers have made. All of a sudden, you make those investments more productive through massive technology upgrades. If you have a service company that ends up not doing this, you get outrun by mom and pop shops. They have low overhead, are local, and faster. You are competing on the basis of labor, and it's over. If it's labor [rather than technology] we lose." He noted, "We have shifted the mix of R&D from new products at the frontier of technology in terms of thrust where margins are thin, to the installed base. We are pouring our best engineers into the installed base. Because if I've got 12,000 turbines out there, and I am going to ship 80 new turbines a year with a base of 12,000, why worry about trying to ship 84 turbines, when if I change the installed base, I can change the game?"

The types of services that GE can provide are impressive. Welch noted that "We have 16,000 CTs (computer-tomography scanners), X-rays, MRs (magnetic resonance systems), and ultrasound systems in service. We can do diagnostic imaging in Milwaukee for a procedure going on in Bombay. And we can do it all over the world twenty-four hours a day seven days a week." These services also include monitoring jet engines in flight, and locomotive engines in operation.

As a result of this massive infusion of technology into the service equation, he stated that in the coming year [1998], "Aircraft engines will go by the 50 percent mark in services [50 percent of revenues will come from service], and transportation, which had nothing, will go by the 50 percent mark next year. Medical is already by the 50 percent mark." Fixing these businesses has allowed GE to turn low-growth, capital-intensive businesses into high-growth businesses that require limited capital and labor, an absolutely brilliant fix.

Good Businesses. My questioning then shifted to the things that Welch looks for in a good business. I asked him what differentiates a great business from a poor business. He began by saying, "Let's look at the appliance business. It is very competitive, low growth, and nonglobal, but it has a consumer franchise, which sharpens your image to consumers and spreads your reputation. Run well, it can get a high percentage of profits in the industry. It has great cash-flow characteristics. It has quite good return on investment characteristics. But it is not a great growth business. So if you put all of those things around it, it's a pretty good business."

He went on to discuss the electrical-distribution-control business. He characterized it as a "modest industry, highly fragmented, no dominant player, small customers, and pricing is not bad. It is so diffuse that there is an opportunity for good people doing good jobs to get a disproportionate share of the profits."

"I don't like businesses where share is determined in the newspapers. The aircraft-engine business has become this way. The worst thing that has happened to Boeing and Airbus is that every year they announce someone won 55 percent of the new contracts and some-one else has the remaining share. You know the macho nature of the business on the front page of the paper dominates the brain. It's sort of like public-share fights. Those aren't good. That just means low price. That is the definition of a low price. The PC business is like that today. Everyone announces market share at the end of each quarter. The next quarter they announce 15 percent price decreases or 12 percent price decreases." Welch feels that any high-profile busi-ness where market share is measured and reported in the media be-comes much more competitive and causes management to make pricing moves that can destroy the industry's profit structure.

When I asked him about the broadcasting business (GE owns NBC) he said, "It was tough, tough, much tougher. If a show is going to be ranked in ratings, your main goal is to improve the ratings. So television is a more difficult industry. If the newspapers are declaring the victors, it's not good. For example, our people have to fight every day in the television business because for some reason the newspa-pers traditionally measured households. Households don't matter much to ratings in terms of advertisers. Advertisers want 18-to-49-year-old viewers. So if you have a lot of households, and [their mem-bers] are older than 49, you don't get paid much for the advertising spot. But every Wednesday the newspapers publish ratings by house-holds. So you have to constantly get that out of people's minds. You have got to have shows that appeal to a younger audience."

"I like businesses where strong distribution counts, where the cus-tomer base is fragmented. The silicone businesses (like caulking and sealant) are great businesses. There are two thousand to three thou-sand customers, average customer size is $12,000, margins are good, customer concentration is diffused, sales force is important. I like those sorts of businesses. 'Below the Radar' businesses I call them. Lower-profile businesses are easily the more attractive businesses because publicity doesn't surround victories or losses. So you don't get behavior determined by press, you get behavior determined by business characteristics. The lower the profile, the better the game. If people are keeping score, other than you and the competi-tion, that makes much more of a horse race out of it. And it alters behavior."

Great People. The final element of Phase 1 was to ensure that great people were in the right positions. Welch said, "I would argue that great people are our greatest strength. I have a stable of people that's off the chart, as proven by the fact that when they leave and go run other companies, they run them well." The July 1998 issue of *Industry Week* noted that "No other major U.S. company can claim GE's level of chief-executive development—not even IBM or Xerox. Indeed, as developers of executive talent, GE and Welch are without peer among the world's major companies today."

"If you look at the profit that we get out of every industry that we are in, we get a lot more profit than our share. So great people in modest industries can get more than their fair share of the profits. Great people in great industries can blow it out. I wouldn't call appliances, locomotives, or lighting great industries. But with great people you can get more than your fair share of the profits from these businesses." He did acknowledge that in terrible businesses, even great people weren't enough. He said, "in the television-receiver business, Christ couldn't get high margins." However, he noted that "When you get into more modest industries, great people can change the game . . . big time!"

Obviously, a key to recruiting and keeping great people is to compensate them fairly. At this point in the interview, he showed me a stack of at least twenty pages that listed GE employees who had recently exercised stock options. He said, "Here is the fun of it all. I don't know most of these people, but there are rows of these people, cashing in $100,000, $350,000. A total of $28 million this week, $54 million last week, and I don't even know most of the names. These options give them a taste of everything: 27,000 people have GE options and GE is changing their lives. It's not the 'fat cats' that are getting all of the money; these people are also reaping the rewards."

Phase 2

Boundaryless Behavior. During Phase 2 of the transformation process, the company established core values and began to build a boundaryless organization. "What boundaryless behavior really is, is searching for the best idea anywhere. You must look inside, outside, up, down. The idea counts, not the stripes of the person who had the idea, not NIH [Not Invented Here]. This was a major breakthrough. It is part of our values card [a small laminated card that lists GE's values]." At this point in the interview, he reached into his pocket and pulled out his values card. He said it was important "getting everyone involved and open to ideas from anywhere. It may sound like nothing, but in most big companies NIH is huge.

"I was talking to a reporter and he asked me where we got Six Sigma. I told him we got it from Motorola and from AlliedSignal. People teach us these things. That's a sense of pride for us. We don't invent much of anything. We adapt it to our culture, to our values. If you have people getting up every morning looking to find a better way, and that's all that they are thinking about, it changes the game."

I believe that the following quote about how GE envisions the future says it best: "We want GE to become a company where people come to work every day in a rush to try something they woke up thinking about the night before. We want them to go home from work wanting to talk about what they did the day before. We want factories where the whistle blows and everyone wonders where the time went, and someone wonders aloud why we need a whistle. We want a company where people find a better way every day of doing things, and where by shaping their own work experience, they make their lives *better* and your company *best*.

"Our biggest contribution is that we made a big company informal. No one really understands what making a big company informal is all about. You use notes; here is a note from a guy in Singapore outlining things that he wants to do. It's constant action. It's got more zeros than the corner grocery store, but it's got the same principles. Get the right stuff on the shelves, move the inventory, and bring in new stuff to excite the customer. We have tried like hell to make this an entrepreneurial company. We can make deals on telephones, we trust each other . . . there is enormous trust within our company.

"I would say that it took us seven years to really change the company . . . to get it where we wanted it to be. I would like to say we did it in three years, but we didn't. It takes a generation of hiring. Now everyone that is working here in a key job bought into this game to come in. When I first took over, people said that 'This wasn't what I bought into.' Many people found the new GE environment very unsettling. They wanted a more formal structure and to do things in an orderly fashion. We changed the game. We said that this is not a bridge game, it's a hockey game. You have to move faster."

Core Values. We then discussed the importance of core values. GE's core values that are printed on laminated cards and distributed to every employee include:

- Have a passion for excellence, and hate bureaucracy.
- Be open to ideas from anywhere . . . and committed to workout (GE's term for working together).
- Live Quality . . . and drive cost and speed for competitive advantage.
- Have the self-confidence to involve everyone and behave in a boundaryless fashion.
- Create a clear, simple, reality-based vision . . . and communicate it to all constituencies.
- Have enormous energy and the ability to energize others.
- Stretch . . . set aggressive goals . . . reward progress . . . yet understand accountability and commitment.
- See changes as opportunities . . . not threats.
- Have global brains . . . and build diverse global teams.

Welch said, "If you think about it, what are our values? Our values are: give individual voice to people; give them dignity wherever they are so that their voice counts; and look for a better idea every day. These are universal traits that people anywhere can buy into. We don't have a corporate culture in the classic sense. We have a series of values that we share across many businesses and many countries. And those values are just as meaningful in India as they are in China, as they are in Japan. People want dignity. People want to have their voice count. People want the best idea to win. People want a meritocracy. GE's values are adaptable to any country's culture. Human core values of dignity and integrity translate into any language and any culture."

One of GE's values is to stretch and try to achieve things that you can't imagine how you might accomplish. Welch pointed out that, in this stretch environment, "It's important not to punish people if they fall short [of their stretch goals]. That's a big twist." He noted that "In the last five years that we have been using stretch goals, people have submitted plans with more money than we needed. It's a wonderful atmosphere of people trying to reach very difficult goals."

He noted that there is a distinct difference between values and cultures. He said, "A culture of a long-cycle business is a lot different than the culture of a short-cycle business. When you go into a business with your backlog for the year in January, and you go into a business where every week you go into the next week and you have no business, those are two different games . . . culture wise. The speed, the pace, the new-product cycle is much faster, that's what I call a culture. A value system, believing in ideas like boundaryless behavior, high integrity, all of these things are values. And I think people get confused between culture and values. You can't have the same culture in NBC that we have in jet engines. We have a lot of cultures, but only one set of values. People don't often understand this. Everyone carries this card [the GE values card], but some are rewarded differently, and cycles are different. We remove leaders with great results who don't embrace the values. Values mean everything to us."

Phase 3

Six Sigma. "The quality initiative came from the employees. In March of 1995, we did an employee survey, and they said we can do so much better with quality. They said that there is too much waste. Then we had Motorola and Larry Bossidy [chairman and CEO of AlliedSignal] showing up saying there is really something here in this quality initiative. So I have a bypass operation and I'm thinking about quality and I come charging back saying that if Larry loves it and the employees are begging for it, let's try it. Then we try it, and in this learning atmosphere that we created, they started guzzling it. So instead of us leading it, we are trying to keep up with it. It makes it all easy. We are using this feedback loop to check with our employees to see how it is going. When we get it right, when we fix the tools that we bring to the party, and match the desires that our customers have . . . hallelujah!!"

GE tracks customer satisfaction through the use of what the company calls Dashboards. The customer tells GE what critical factors to measure. The Dashboards are the customers' measures of quality. He said, "We give them feedback and they give us feedback. The discussions are quantitative, not anecdotal."

The Role of the CEO

Since Welch is one of the more highly regarded CEOs in the world, I asked him about his role at GE. He said, "My job is to pick the best people, hopefully bat over 75 percent, allocate the resources to the markets and businesses where they want to grow, shift directionally like this [as we are doing in the technology service area], and transfer . . . generic ideas across businesses. That's all I do. I don't price products, and I don't design products."

He went on to discuss the changes in the role of the CEO. He said that "Years ago the title of 'Chairman and CEO' was often the coronation, it meant that you got *the* job. Today, I see people who get the job and see it as the beginning of a career. It is a change that has evolved from the '70s to the '80s to the '90s because of global competitiveness."

Investing in GE

I concluded my interview by asking Welch how people should look at GE from an investing perspective. He responded by saying, "One of the things that investors bet on in GE is good growth and consistency. We don't surprise them, and we don't take write-offs. Whenever we have a gain, we tell them in advance. They know that we will have a gain, and an offsetting restructuring. It's part of fixing the old and getting into the new. It's a constant evolution of a set of businesses that internally get refurbished."

When I asked Jack about GE's ability to build shareholder wealth (GE is number 1 in the world), he said, "Increasing shareholder value is a byproduct of the effort. It is not an objective. We drove the revenues, and we moved the operating margin bar to 16 percent [before 1990 it was less than 10 percent]. The drivers [of shareholder wealth at GE] are Six Sigma, speed, idea flow, stretch, reward systems, cash flow [which was neutral in the '80s], and capital turns. When we make improvements in businesses, we aren't necessarily thinking about shareholder value, we are thinking about getting a more efficient operation and a higher return on capital." The first time leaders at GE heard of EVA [Economic Value Added is a measure of shareholder wealth creation] was when *Fortune* magazine told them that they had one of the highest EVAs. GE has always tried to improve its return on investment; however, at GE, EVA is a result, rather than a goal.

Welch concluded the interview by saying, "What you do is get a company that is a proxy for global business. You've got revenues growing at 15 percent, service growing at 15-percent-plus, you've got operating margins expanding and double-digit earnings growth, you have cash flow of $3 to $4 billion, you have stock repurchase. Don't think about GE in its pieces. Think of it as a whole, as an engine. And this whole is moving forward—originally at 9 percent a year growth, then 10, then 11, and now 14 moving to 15. This whole is growing. If you start picking it apart, scab-picking we call it, you won't get what GE is. If you think about it as a whole you end up with a company that has been growing at these type of returns, double the S&P 500. You are investing in a business that delivers consistent, high-growth earnings.

"When problems in Asia come, you don't panic. If jet engines have a blip in the paper, don't worry about it because something else will be doing better. So you buy this thing, this blob, this conglomeration of businesses. As I tell investors, the blob is doing very well. The blob is moving forward at this rate. Go to sleep, pull the covers up . . . sleep soundly. That's why you buy GE. You don't buy GE because you are going to get a 25 percent spike one year or a collapse next year. You buy it because you are going to get dividends increasing with earnings growth. You are getting a stock buy-back of significant proportion. So you get a dividend stream, plus an investment stream. And you will get double-digit EPS [earnings per share] growth. In great times it will be close to 15, in difficult times it will be closer to 10, but that's what you've got in your pocket. Go to sleep, and sleep quietly.

"It's a blob, but it's one that grows at 14 percent a year compounded, and has returned at 25 percent a year compounded. Think

[163]

of us as a whole, count on it, trust it, we have been doing it for seventeen years, we have never disappointed you and we don't intend to. It's better than it used to be and everything is moving in the right direction. I like the word 'blob,' because I want people to think of us as amorphous. You're not buying *Seinfeld* at 9 P.M., you aren't buying a motor business that just lost an order, you're not buying the jet engine company that just lost an order to Rolls Royce, you are not buying any of those things. You are buying a team of people that can deliver with this set of world-class businesses."

As he hurried off to a conference call with his board, I was sorry that the interview had ended. Before he left, I asked him how much of his personal wealth was in GE stock. True to form, he said "It's all I've got. If it doesn't work, it's all over."

As I reflected on our time together, I never once thought of Jack Welch as the Wizard of GE. He is a warm, personable, enthusiastic, energetic leader who takes great pride in his people. In fact, he takes much more pride in the accomplishments of his people than in his own personal achievements. Together, he and his colleagues at GE have built a Great Company that will endure long after he retires from GE in 2000. At the conclusion of our interview, I doubled my position in GE stock.

Market-Leading, Terrific Businesses (Phase 1 1981–1988)

"Become the most competitive enterprise in the world by being number one or two in market share in the world in every business we are in."

FOCUS ON MARKET-LEADING, TERRIFIC BUSINESSES	CREATE A CLIMATE OF PERSONAL EXCELLENCE	BUILD PROTECTIVE BARRIERS AROUND THE BUSINESSES	REDESIGN BUSINESSES—FOCUS ON GROWTH TO IMPROVE REVENUES AND PROFITS	MAKE STRATEGIC ACQUISITIONS AND ESTABLISH ALLIANCES

• Clear out the underbrush
• Businesses should be number one or two in the market.
• Fix, close or sell those that aren't.
• Focus in three areas:
  1. GE's core businesses
  2. High technology
  3. Service businesses
	• Strongly cohesive
	• Sense of urgency
	• Pare hierarchy
	• Reward those who dare
		• Low-cost producer
		• Worldwide businesses
		• Highest quality
		• Technological edge
		• Clear advantage in a 'niche' business
		• Dominant market position
			• Sources of growth
			  1. Quality
			  2. Globalization
			  3. Service
			  4. Information
			  5. Technology
			  6. Consumer savings
				• Acquire or create those businesses that either improve an existing GE business or stand alone in a promising market in which we want to participate.
				• Growth fueled by innovative transitional alliances, where each partner's unique assets are shared in return for greater world market access.

The Boundaryless Company (Phase 2 1989–1995)

"The desire and ability of an organization to continually learn from any source, anywhere—and to rapidly convert this learning into action—is the ultimate competitive advantage."

EMBRACE THE BOUNDARYLESS COMPANY CONCEPT	ESTABLISH AND COMMUNICATE CORE VALUES	FOSTER THE DEVELOPMENT OF A LEARNING ORGANIZATION
• Boundaryless behavior is our number one value. You must be open to an idea from anywhere—inside, outside, up, down. The only thing that counts is the quality of the idea, not the rank of the person originating it.	• *Values have made the company more high-spirited, but more adaptable, more agile than companies even a fiftieth of our size.*	• At the heart of this culture is an understanding that an organization's ability to learn, and translate that learning into action rapidly, is the ultimate competitive advantage.
• Remove barriers among the functions.	• Have a passion for excellence, and hate bureaucracy.	• Use the organization's size and diversity to generate new ideas for improving other businesses, thereby turning size and diversity into advantages.
• Recognize no distinction between "domestic" and "foreign" operations.	• Be open to ideas from anywhere . . . and comitted to workout.	
• Ignore or erase labels like "management," "salaried," etc.	• Live Quality . . . and drive cost and speed for competitive advantage.	• Raise the bar of excellence.
• Level the external walls, reaching out to key suppliers to satisfy customers.	• Have the self-confidence to involve everyone and behave in a boundaryless fashion.	• Build self-confidence.
• Increase speed.	• Create a clear, simple, reality-based vision . . . and communicate it to all constituencies.	• Remove the egregious manifestations of bureaucracy.
• Appoint leaders who can energize at every level.	• Have enormous energy and the ability to energize others.	
• Stretch—use dreams to set business targets with no real idea of how to get there.	• Stretch . . . set aggressive goals . . . reward progress . . . yet understand accountability and commitment.	
	• See changes as opportunities . . . not threat.	
	• Have global brains . . . and build diverse and global teams.	

Make Six Sigma a Reality (Phase 3 1996–)

"Six Sigma quality means the virtual elimination of defects from every product, process, and transaction this company engages in every day around the globe."

ESTABLISH QUALITY AS AN ALL-ENCOMPASSING PASSION	EXTENSIVE TRAINING OF THE ENTIRE ORGANIZATION	FOCUS ON IMPROVING PROCESSES	MEASURE RESULTS
• Every cultural change we've made over the past couple of decades positions us to take on this exciting challenge.	• Enormous training efforts supported by: 1. Masters 2. Black Belts 3. Green Belts • Identify the CTQs, Critical to Quality: 1. Define 2. Measure 3. Analyze 4. Improve 5. Control	• Change the paradigm from fixing *products* so that they are perfect to fixing *processes* so that they *produce nothing but* perfection or close to it. • Six Sigma defines how we work.	• Customer satisfaction • Cost of poor quality • Supplier quality • Internal performance • Design for manufacturability • Achieve Six Sigma by the year 2000

The Gillette Company

CORPORATE PROFILE

———※———

Address: Prudential Tower Building
800 Boylston Street
Boston, MA 02199
Ticker Symbol: G
Stock Exchange: NYSE
Phone Number: (617) 421-7000
Fax Number: (617) 421-7123
Website: http://www.gillette.com

History and Business Background

King C. Gillette founded the company in 1901 in Boston, Massachusetts. His goal was to build a company based on a razor with disposable blades, a revolutionary idea at a time when straight razors were the norm. The idea of introducing revolutionary new products is as much a part of the Gillette Company's culture today as it was in 1901.

Today, Gillette is the world leader in male grooming, a category that includes blades, razors, and shaving preparations. Gillette also holds the number one position worldwide in selected female grooming products, such as wet shaving products and hair epilation devices. Gillette is the world's top seller of writing instruments and correction products, toothbrushes, oral care appliances, and alkaline batteries.

Gillette groups its businesses into the following core categories:

- Male grooming products, including blades and razors, electric shavers, shaving preparations, and deodorants and antiperspirants.
- Selected female grooming products, including wet shaving, hair removal, hair care appliances, and deodorants and antiperspirants.
- Writing instruments and correction products, including the brand names Paper Mate, Parker, Waterman, and Liquid Paper.
- Certain areas of the oral care market, including Oral-B toothbrushes and Braun Oral-B oral care appliances.
- Selected areas of the high-quality small household appliance

business, including coffeemakers and food preparation products, sold under the Braun brand.

- Consumer batteries, sold under the Duracell brand name, the world leader in alkaline batteries.

Evaluation using Great Company Screens:

- *Highly Regarded by Knowledgeable Experts:* Gillette was included among the twenty-five companies that were classed as All-Stars in *Fortune*'s "The World's Most Admired Companies." Gillette ranks among *Fortune*'s top fifteen wealth-creating companies and is ranked number one in the Soaps and Cosmetics category in *Fortune*'s "America's Most Admired Companies" study.
- *Publicly Traded:* NYSE.
- *Headquartered in the United States:* Boston, MA.
- *In Business at Least 50 Years and Survived the Founder:* Gillette was founded in 1901.
- *Market Cap in Excess of $15 Billion:* Gillette's market cap is currently $53 billion.
- *Global Company with at Least 40 Percent of Revenues/Profits from International Operations:* Gillette sells and distributes its products in over 200 countries and territories, and approximately 63 percent of sales are generated overseas. Every day 1.2 billion people around the world use one or more Gillette products. Gillette's global manufacturing facilities are closely linked, making Gillette a truly global company capable of competing and winning anywhere in the world.
- *Outstanding Shareholder Returns:* Results versus the S&P 500 are shown in the chart below.

Gillette Returns vs. S&P 500
ending December 31, 1998

	5 YEARS	10 YEARS
GILLETTE	27.72%	29.52%
S&P 500	24.05%	19.19%

Source: S&P Compustat

- *Terrific Businesses:* Gillette has one of the best business models in American business today. As a result of Gillette's outstanding business model, 1997 operating margins reached 23.1 percent of sales.
- *Protected by Strong Barriers/The Moat Effect:* In 1997, 74 percent of Gillette's sales came from product categories where Gillette holds the worldwide leadership position.
- *People Are the Company's Most Important Asset:* Senior management is highly involved in developing people within Gillette. The following interview with Al Zeien reveals that the company is highly committed to its people.
- *Outstanding Management Team That Keeps the Company in "Prime":* This is a company that is focused. Gillette has developed a wonderful worldwide sales and distribution capability and is now adding great products, like Duracell batteries, to this world-class distribution system.
- *Innovation-Driven Company That Turns Changes into Opportunities:* Approximately 49 percent of Gillette's 1997 sales came from products that did not exist five years ago. The company has an R&D capability that compares quite favorably with those of the best high-tech companies. Gillette is committed to developing new and improved products, and spent $212 million on Research and Development in 1997.

Peer Group Companies: Colgate-Palmolive Company, Johnson & Johnson, Newell Co., Philips Electronics N.V., Procter and Gamble Company, Ralston Purina Company, Unilever PLC, and Warner-Lambert Company.

Key Competitors: Blades and razors: Bic, Warner-Lambert
Toiletries: S.C. Johnson and Son, Unilever, Procter and Gamble, Colgate
Duracell: Ralston Purina, Philips, Matsushita
Braun: Moulinex/Krups, Philips, Remington
Oral-B: Colgate, Johnson & Johnson, Procter and Gamble
Stationery products: Bic, Newell, A.T. Cross, Mont Blanc

Sources of Additional Information

CORPORATE PUBLICATIONS

- Annual report
- Form 10-K
- Form 10-Q

RECENT ARTICLES

- "Gillette's Edge." *Business Week,* January 19, 1998.
- "Would You Spend $1.50 for a Razor Blade?" *Business Week,* April 27, 1998.
- "Nick of Time?" *Barron's,* July 13, 1998.
- "It Cuts Both Ways." *Worth,* September 1998.

BOOK

- Adams, Russell B., Jr. *King C. Gillette, The Man and His Wonderful Shaving Device.* Boston: Little Brown, 1978.

INTERVIEW

ALFRED M. ZEIEN

Chairman and CEO
The Gillette Company

World-Class Brands, Products, and People

The Gillette Company is headquartered in the Prudential Tower in Boston, Massachusetts. I have consulted for Gillette for over twelve years and, during the course of my assignments, I have had an opportunity to meet and get to know a number of the company's senior managers. I have always respected the quality of Gillette's management team. The Gillette executives I have worked with were professional and highly ethical business people who were always seeking ways to improve their operations. As a result of my relationship with Gillette over the years, I thought I had a solid understanding of the strengths and weaknesses of the company. I was wrong.

My interview with Alfred M. Zeien, chairman and CEO of Gillette, gave me a whole new perspective on the company. Throughout my years in business and consulting I have found that the brightest people are the ones who can make something that has the potential to be very complicated quite simple. The not-so-smart managers take a business that is somewhat complex and make it extremely complex. If you buy into this premise, then you will conclude, as I did, that Al Zeien, the chairman and CEO of Gillette, may be one of the most intelligent people in business today.

Perhaps Al Zeien's greatest achievement is that he has taken a $10 billion company that markets products in six key categories in virtually every country in the world and turned it into a simple business in which Gillette is a leader in nearly every category in which it competes. He has simplified the business in a variety of ways:

- *Sold twenty-two companies, which were either too small or in bad businesses.* This enabled Gillette to focus on great core businesses.
- *Focused the company on six categories, which were selected because they have a worldwide presence and lend themselves to continuous product improvement.*
- *Sells the same product all over the world.* The product that is sold in the U.S. is the same product that is sold in other countries, thereby simplifying production, distribution, inventory, and pricing.
- *Develops all worldwide advertising at headquarters.* The Gillette message, like its products, is the same all over the world.
- *Utilizes the same production processes and machinery all over the world.* This makes production and training much more interchangeable and simplifies management.
- *Reduced the number of plants.* Once again, this simplified operations.

While simplifying the business, Gillette has delivered consistent shareholder returns with double-digit increases in earnings per share for the past thirty quarters, generated almost 50 percent of its sales from products not in existence five years ago, pulled off a major acquisition (Duracell), and established a truly outstanding global business platform on which to build. During his tenure at Gillette, Zeien has built Gillette into one of the Great Companies of America, and one of the truly Great Companies of the world.

The Interview

Al Zeien began his tenure as chairman and CEO by crafting the following Gillette Mission Statement: "Our mission is to achieve or enhance clear leadership, worldwide, in the existing or new core consumer product categories in which we choose to compete." In pursuing this mission Zeien has limited noncore categories to less than 10 percent of total revenues. Today, 81 percent of Gillette's sales are from product categories in which the company holds the world leadership position. These categories include:

PRODUCT CATEGORIES	BRAND NAME
1. Blades and razors	Primarily Gillette
2. Alkaline batteries	Duracell
3. Writing instruments	Paper Mate, Parker, and Waterman
4. Men's electric razors	Braun
5. Toothbrushes	Oral-B
6. Oral care appliances	Braun Oral-B Plaque Remover
7. Shaving preparations	Gillette Series, Foamy, and others
8. Ear thermometers	Braun Thermoscan
9. Hair epilators	Braun Silk-epil
10. Correction products	Liquid Paper
11. Hair-styling appliances	Braun
12. Pistol-grip hair dryers	Braun
13. Hand blenders	Braun

Significant accomplishments have been made in each category:

- Gillette is the world leader in male grooming products.
- Sensor is the world's largest-selling blade and razor.
- Gillette disposable razors are the world's top sellers.
- Gillette is the world leader in shaving preparations.
- Gillette/Duracell is the world leader in the alkaline battery category.

- Gillette is the world leader in writing instruments and correction products.
- Braun is the world leader in men's electric razors, oral care appliances, infrared ear thermometers, hair epilators, hair dryers, styling appliances, and hand blenders.
- Oral-B is the world leader in toothbrushes.

Amazingly enough, within these categories, Zeien estimated that 50 percent of 1997's sales volume will come from products that did not exist five years ago. The chart below shows how successful Gillette has been in driving revenues from new products.

The Gillette Company
Percent of Sales from Products
Introduced in Previous Five Years

YEAR	PERCENT OF REVENUES
1996	47
1995	42
1994	45
1993	37
1992	35

Source: Gillette

Core Strategies

Why has Gillette become such an outstanding company? For the answers to this question, we need to understand the company's beliefs and core strategies.

Product is King, Innovation is Key. Gillette management believes that the company is only as good as the products it markets. Herein lies one of Gillette's greatest strength—product innovation. Gillette management has developed rather mundane products into brands and products that are treasured by their consumers. For example, Zeien will tell you that the ancient Egyptians were the first people to use a toothbrush. The toothbrushes that the Egyptians used had wooden handles with bristles sticking out of them. In many ways, they were quite similar in design to today's toothbrush. Yet Gillette has established Oral-B as the world leader in toothbrushes, is coming out with a new toothbrush this summer, and will continue to develop improved toothbrushes for the foreseeable future. Gillette has followed the same approach with razor blades and the other products that the company markets in virtually all the categories in which it competes. Growth through product innovation is one of the company's core competencies.

Gillette is able to develop and successfully market new and improved products as a result of the way the company structures its research and development efforts. First, it totally separates research from the development function, both physically (they are in different buildings) and organizationally (they have different structures). Gillette does not do "pure" research, and knows full well that its researchers are not going to win a Nobel Prize. However, Gillette's research and the products that result from this effort do win millions of consumers all over the world. I am sure most Gillette shareholders prefer that Gillette focus on winning loyal consumers rather than awards or prizes.

Gillette structures its R&D efforts into the following four areas:

1. *Basic research:* Here researchers seek to understand how all the technological innovations that are taking shape around the world could possibly affect Gillette's products and processes. Each document coming from research begins with the words "Did you know that . . . ?" This phase of the R&D effort is not about experimentation as much as understanding new phenomena and technology. Basic research requires an aggressive research effort, since only three of approximately fifteen research projects make it to the next level. Those projects that don't progress aren't cancelled, they are simply delayed. This approach encourages researchers to continue to innovate. There are no bad new ideas at Gillette, just more immediate priorities.

2. *Applied research:* During this phase, Gillette researchers experiment with the process or new technology to determine the feasibility of including it in a new or existing product or process.

3. *Product development:* Once the innovation passes applied research, it moves into the product-development phase, which is linked to a profit center. For example the Razor Division controls the management of the product development process for razor blades. At one time product development was a centralized structure, but this was abandoned in favor of the profit center approach. During this phase of the new-product development cycle, emerging technologies or processes are built into new or existing products.

4. *Engineering:* One of the real powerhouses of Gillette is its engineering group. Unlike most consumer products companies, Gillette designs its own processes and builds much of the equipment that is used in its plants throughout the world. This engineering effort enables Gillette to develop "captive" processes and equipment, making it very difficult for Gillette's competitors to replicate the company's new product innovations. In its efforts to develop its own machinery and processes, Gillette is more like a manufacturing company than a consumer products company. Senior management believes that this engineering clout is a key competitive advantage.

Gillette's R&D organization has been able to deliver twenty successful new products a year and, as demonstrated earlier, has allowed Gillette to reach its objective of generating 50 percent of its revenues from products that did not exist five years ago. In this regard, Gillette's research efforts are more like those of a pharmaceutical or high-tech company that focuses on new product growth through innovation, than a consumer products company that seeks growth by launching new brands or sizes.

It becomes obvious that because Zeien is a student of business, he has been able to identify and incorporate within Gillette key attributes of unrelated industries (e.g., engineering from manufacturing companies, or new product development from pharmaceutical and high-technology companies) that will provide Gillette with a strategic advantage in the consumer products sector. As a result, Gillette is neither structured nor managed like a traditional consumer products company, but rather a hybrid of what works best in various industries.

A Truly Global Company. Al Zeien believes that companies that sell products outside the United States can be classified into three categories:

1. *International Companies:* Companies in this category are primarily exporters. They transport their business outside of the country, are geographically structured, are divided into subsidiaries, and utilize country general managers. Their products are typically sold in a fairly limited geographic area like South America or Europe.
2. *Multinational Companies:* They grow and define their business on a worldwide basis but continue to allocate resources among national or regional areas so as to maximize the total. These multinationals typically market different products throughout the world under a variety of brand names.
3. *Global Companies:* These companies treat the world as though it were one great big country. Zeien likes to think of the world as the U.S. with 500 states rather than 50. He realizes that the male shaver in Minnesota has different needs than the male shaver in Louisiana, but also knows that the shaver in Louisiana may be more like a shaver in Mexico than the person in Minnesota. Gillette is far more focused on consumers than geographies.

In order to qualify as a truly global company, a corporation like Gillette must meet the following criteria:

- *Worldwide standardized products.* Consumers purchase the same razor on Boylston Street in Boston as they do at a store on Main Street in Bangladesh.
- *World sourcing.* The company uses suppliers that can meet their needs throughout the world.
- *Integrated world production.* Plants are located all over the world and all plants are technologically connected. Manufacturing processes and equipment are the same throughout the world.
- *Consistent advertising message.* Most of Gillette's shaving and toiletry ads and commercials are produced in the United States, and then voiceovers are dubbed in for other countries.

- *Consistent pricing approach.* The pricing approach is the same throughout the world.

This global approach has allowed Gillette to achieve one of its most stunning victories. Today, Gillette leads the dry-shave category in Japan, one of the largest dry-shave markets in the world. It has achieved this share leadership despite the fact that stores representing 50 percent of the retail sales volume in Japan are owned by its competitors, world-class electronics firms like Sanyo, Hitachi, and Sony.

Gillette's global presence provides the company with a number of key strategic advantages:

- *Allocating funds for new product development and product improvement.* Braun Germany spends 20 percent of its German sales revenues on research and development. This represents a huge percentage of Braun's core business in Germany, but only 3 percent of Braun's worldwide sales. Likewise, in the U.S. Gillette invests almost 18 percent of its razor sales on R&D, but, like Braun, only 3 percent of its worldwide revenues. Competitors without this worldwide business base are at a distinct disadvantage when it comes to investing significant funds in R&D and battling Gillette for product superiority. These competitors are unable to compete effectively with Gillette in the new-products arena, and this enables Gillette to strengthen its grip on global markets.
- *Optimizing manufacturing costs.* Because Gillette's manufacturing processes and equipment are fully integrated and standardized throughout the world, the company can produce one product element in one plant at the lowest worldwide cost, another element in another plant, and so on.
- *Engineering efficiencies.* Gillette's worldwide business base makes amortizing the costs of developing new machinery much more attractive, and makes it difficult for competitors to match Gillette's new products, technologies, and processes.

Gillette's focus on global operations has resulted in an increased foreign business base, as the following chart demonstrates:

The Gillette Company
Domestic vs. Foreign Sales

YEAR	PERCENT FOREIGN SALES
1996	62*
1995	72
1994	70
1993	71
1992	70
1991	69

*Includes Duracell with 55% U.S. sales
Sources: Gillette

Leadership Position. Every budget presentation at Gillette begins with an overview of the worldwide market for the category, a statement of Gillette's market share, and a statement of how Gillette will capture the leadership position in the category within five years, if the company does not already have it today. Gillette's management isn't satisfied with increasing share; they want to be the worldwide market leader.

Consumer products companies like Gillette measure their success by tracking their share of the market over time, based on both unit and dollar sales. The strength of Gillette's share leadership is clearly demonstrated in the chart below.

The Gillette Company
Unit and Dollar U.S. Market Share
Razors/Blades, Food, Drug, & Mass Merchandising

YEAR	52-WEEK UNIT SHARE	52-WEEK DOLLAR SHARE
1996	48.4	67.0
1995	48.5	66.5
1994	49.5	66.4
1993	50.0	66.4
1992	49.8	65.6

Source: Gillette, A. C. Nielsen

The chart reveals that Gillette has a dominant share of the razor/blade category with a unit share in the 48–50 range. This means that if 10,000 razors/blades were sold in the U.S., between 4,800 and 5,000 would carry the Gillette brand name. Gillette's closest competitor has an 11.0 share. What's even more impressive is that Gillette controls around 67 percent of the category's dollar volume. Dollar volume is calculated by multiplying the unit share times the selling price of the unit, and dividing that number by total dollar category sales. The fact that Gillette's dollar share is about 38 percent higher than the company's unit share means that Gillette is able to charge a premium price for its products relative to the competition. Gillette's ability to maintain this market share and pricing margin translates into huge profits for Gillette shareholders.

Capture Consumers and Trade Them Up. Gillette seeks to build a "consumer capturing" machine that:

1. *Captures the consumer initially.* Because frequency of purchase is so high among consumers shopping its categories, the company wants to capture as many new consumers as possible. From the previous chart, we can see that this machine is working well.
2. *Moves the consumer up the ladder.* Gillette wants to trade its consumers up to better and better products, thereby increasing its margin per consumer while building brand loyalty.
3. *Encourages the consumer to buy other Gillette products.* Braun Germany's initial consumers purchase on average four or five other Braun products because they are so confident that Braun products will meet their needs. Gillette wants to expand this model throughout the organization.

This approach allows the company to:

- Look at advertising differently.
- Spend more money on promotion.
- Sample potential new consumers.
- Offer temporary loss leaders.

This marketing strategy has allowed Gillette to grow market share in virtually every category.

Outstanding Management. The first responsibility of management is to ensure that Gillette is in businesses that meet Gillette's criteria for a good business. Between 1975 and 1983 Gillette divested itself of twenty-two companies that were not a good fit. Many of these businesses were small and would never become major worldwide businesses. These divestitures simplified the business and allowed the company to focus on its core businesses.

Another key responsibility of management is to develop people within the organization. To that end, Gillette has implemented a system of "diagonal" promotions. This means that people may be transferred among divisions, countries, and functions. As a result, only 10 percent of the promotions come from situations where individuals replace their boss. The benefits of this "diagonal" promotional system are powerful:

- *People within the company aren't so focused on pleasing only their boss. They want to know and please other people in the company since they don't know where their next promotion might come from.*
- *This approach builds well-rounded managers who have experience with all of the company's various products. They are truly interchangeable.*
- *The approach builds teamwork throughout the company.*
- *The system builds morale, since the opportunities for promotion are dramatically expanded.*

The Gillette bonus plan is built around three elements:

1. *Sales growth.* Zeien places much more emphasis on expanding sales than on cutting costs, because sales growth produces repetitive benefits, unlike the one-time benefit of cutting costs.
2. *Profit from operations.* Sales growth without profits is of little benefit.
3. *Return on assets.* Finally, the company wants its managers to be aware of increasing their return on assets.

While Gillette doesn't use EVA (Economic Value Added) to manage its business on a daily basis, the company does use the elements of EVA to motivate and focus its employees.

Gillette, the Future. During Al Zeien's tenure as chairman, Gillette has been transformed from a "Nifty Fifty" also-ran to one of the Great Companies of America. Today, Gillette is poised for incredible global growth in all of its businesses. Al Zeien has a world-class global organization in place and humming along. All the company needs is more new products and acquisitions to continue to barrel ahead. Personally, I think Gillette is just getting started.(Note: Al Zeien announced he would retire from Gillette in April 1999.)

JOHNSON & JOHNSON

CORPORATE PROFILE

Address: One Johnson & Johnson Plaza
New Brunswick, NJ 08933
Ticker Symbol: JNJ
Stock Exchange: NYSE
Phone Number: (732) 524-0400
Website: http://www.jnj.com

History and Business Background

Johnson & Johnson was founded in 1886 in New Brunswick, New Jersey, when Robert Wood Johnson developed a surgical dressing that was ready made, sterile, and wrapped and sealed in individual packages. The company began operations with fourteen employees on the fourth floor of a small building. The first products produced were medicinal plasters, but these were quickly followed by surgical dressings. J & J became a leader in the development of antiseptic surgical procedures in patient care, and by 1910 it was an established leader in the health-care field. The company stepped up its efforts to diversify by establishing Band-Aid Brand Adhesive Bandages in 1921.

Today, Johnson & Johnson's businesses comprise some twenty-seven different operations in the U.S., grouped into three major segments: Consumer, Professional, and Pharmaceutical. Consumer brands (which represent 33 percent of sales) include Neutrogena, Tylenol, Band-Aid, Mylanta, and Johnson's Baby Shampoo. Professional products (37.3 percent of sales) include Acuvue contact lenses, Cidex disinfecting solution, and Palmaz-Schatz stents. Pharmaceutical products (33.3 percent of revenues) include Propulsid, Sporanox, and Floxin. Today, J & J is the largest medical-device manufacturer in the world.

Perhaps J & J's most outstanding quality is the way the company's various businesses are organized. Ralph Larsen has noted in *Forbes* magazine: "It's tough to grow an $18 billion company. But we don't view ourselves as a big company. We view ourselves as 160 small companies. So we have some companies in tough business growing 3 percent, 4 percent, 5 percent a year, but we have others that are growing 30 percent and 40 percent and 50 percent a year." Having consulted with J & J on numerous occasions, I can assure you that each person who is leading a J & J business unit realizes that he or she is part of the corporation, but the individual company is managed as if it were a separate operating entity. It is indeed a unique and very successful culture.

Johnson & Johnson is a highly successful, very well-managed company staffed by quality people who make every effort to do things the "right way." I have tremendous respect for what J & J has accomplished, and how highly regarded the company is by its customers all over the world.

Evaluation using Great Company Screens:

- *Highly Regarded by Knowledgeable Experts:* Johnson & Johnson is one of the elite group of Great Companies that was recognized as a "visionary" company by *Built to Last*, and an "exemplar" by *In Search of Excellence*. J & J is included in the Top 10 of *Fortune's* "America's Most Admired Companies." The company is ranked fourteenth by *Fortune* among the Best Companies in the World, and included in the top twenty-five companies with the best boards of directors in America by *Business Week*. Finally, J & J is viewed as one of the top wealth creators in America. The company was ranked by *R&D Directions* as having one of the ten best pipelines in the pharmaceutical industry. J & J is truly an outstanding company.

- *Publicly Traded:* NYSE.
- *Headquartered in the United States:* New Brunswick, NJ.
- *In Business at Least 50 Years and Survived the Founder:* J & J was founded in 1886.
- *Market Cap in Excess of $15 Billion:* Johnson & Johnson's current market cap is approximately $112.8 billion.
- *Global Company with at Least 40 Percent of Revenues/Profits from International Operations:* Approximately 50 percent of J & J's revenues are derived from the company's international operations.
- *Outstanding Shareholder Returns:* J & J has consistently outperformed the S&P 500 index.

Johnson & Johnson Returns vs. S&P 500
ending December 31, 1998

	5 YEARS	10 YEARS
J & J	32.41%	25.25%
S&P 500	24.05%	19.19%

Source: S&P Compustat

- *Terrific Businesses:* The combination of a wonderful consumer franchise and a growing pharmaceutical business makes for an outstanding business model.
- *Protected by Strong Barriers/The Moat Effect:* J & J is a big believer in R&D and spent $2.3 billion in 1998 to develop new products and improve existing products. The company ranked 13th last year in advertising dollars spent, reflecting a corporate commitment to strengthening its powerful brands.
- *People Are the Company's Most Important Asset:* Johnson & Johnson has extremely capable people and invests heavily to develop these people. The following excerpt from J & J's corporate credo sets the tone: "We are responsible to our employees, the men and women who work with us throughout the world. Everyone must be con-

sidered as an individual. We must respect their dignity and recognize their merit. They must have a sense of security in their jobs . . ." The credo is something that the employees of J & J live by each day.

- *Outstanding Management Team That Keeps the Company in "Prime":* This is a company that is focused and is clearly on top of its game. J & J will continue to prosper for years to come.
- *Innovation-Driven Company That Turns Changes into Opportunities:* The cover of the 1997 annual report features the following quote: "Innovation begins with a question . . ." The company's report to shareholders goes on to note that "We have made a vigorous commitment to create an environment in which innovation flourishes throughout our companies around the world." In addressing shareholders, Chairman Larsen said, "Based on our conviction that healthy top-line growth is the foundation upon which you build a strong company that delivers superior returns to shareowners . . . we set out as our first priority . . . to accelerate our sales growth through introduction of a steady stream of knowledge-based . . . research-based . . . value-added . . . new products." This is a company that is truly driven by innovation.

Key Competitors: Abbott Labs, Amgen, Bausch & Lomb, Bayer AG, Bristol-Myers Squibb, Dial, Medtronic, Pfizer, Procter and Gamble, SmithKline Beecham, United States Surgical.

Sources of Additional Information

CORPORATE PUBLICATIONS
- Annual Report
- Form 10-K
- Form 10-Q
- Fact books are published for each year.
- Brief History of Johnson & Johnson

RECENT ARTICLE
- "One Hundred Sixty Companies for the Price of One." *Forbes,* February 26, 1997.

MEDTRONIC, INC.

CORPORATE PROFILE

━━━◀◉▶━━━

Address: 7000 Central Avenue NE
Minneapolis, MN 55432-3576
Ticker Symbol: MDT
Stock Exchange: NYSE
Phone Number: (612) 514-4000
Fax Number: (612) 514-4879
Website: http://www.medtronic.com

History and Business Background

Medtronic is the youngest of all of the Great Companies. Celebrating its fiftieth birthday in April 1999, the company just makes it under the wire of our fifty-years-in-business screen. Medtronic was founded by Earl Bakken and Palmer Hermundslie in a garage in Minneapolis to service and repair electronic hospital equipment. As the repair business began to grow, Medtronic received requests from doctors and nurses to modify or design new equipment that they needed. This led Medtronic into the manufacturing business and the company produced a variety of custom products. In the mid-1950s Medtronic researchers became involved in working with the University of Minnesota Medical School on pacemakers. This led to the development of a wearable, external, battery-powered pacemaker and the beginning of Medtronic as we know it today.

Today, Medtronic is the world's leading medical technology company specializing in implantable and interventional therapies. The company divides its business into four areas:

1. *Cardiac Rhythm Management:* Medtronic is uniquely positioned to succeed in this area. The company builds on current market leadership by developing adaptive therapies and diagnostic systems to treat and monitor bradycardia (too-slow heartbeat), tachyarrhythmia (too-fast heartbeat), atrial fibrillation (rapid, uncontrolled heartbeats in the upper chambers), and heart failure (the inability of the heart to maintain its workload of pumping blood to the body).

2. *Cardiac Surgery:* Medtronic is the overall market leader in conventional cardiac surgery, and is also well positioned to be a leader in minimally invasive cardiac surgery.
3. *Vascular:* Medtronic's goal is to work with physicians as partners to help them closely match new and innovative products with their patients' needs. As a result, the company is constantly developing new vascular products.
4. *Neurological:* Here the focus is on chronic pain, movement disorders, and other significant neurological disorders. The company has made enormous strides in helping improve the quality of life of patients with Parkinson's disease.

During 1998, Medtronic aggressively expanded its business via mergers and acquisitions including Physio-Control International; AVECOR Cardiovascular, Inc.; Midas Rex; L. P. Sofamor Danek Group, Inc.; and Arterial Vascular Engineering, Inc.

Evaluation using Great Company Screens:

- *Highly Regarded by Knowledgeable Experts:* Medtronic's CEO, Bill George, was recognized as one of *Business Week's* Top 25 Managers in 1998. Medtronic was ranked second in its category (Scientific, Photo, Control Equipment) in *Fortune's* "America's Most Admired Companies" Survey. Medtronic was also ranked fiftieth of 1,000 companies in wealth creation.
- *Publicly Traded:* NYSE.
- *Headquartered in the United States:* Minneapolis, MN.
- *In Business at Least 50 Years and Survived the Founder:* Founded 1949.
- *Market Cap in Excess of $15 Billion:* Market cap is currently $36.3 billion.
- *Global Company with at Least 40 Percent of Revenues/Profits from International Operations:* Approximately 43 percent of revenues come from international operations. The company operates as a global enterprise in over 120 countries throughout the world.
- *Outstanding Shareholder Returns:* Medtronic's spectacular returns are shown in the chart that follows:

Medtronic Returns vs. S&P 500
ending December 31, 1998

	5 YEARS	10 YEARS
MEDTRONIC	49.44%	41.87%
S&P 500	24.05%	19.19%

Source: S&P Compustat

- *Terrific Businesses:* Medtronic is the dominant leader in a terrific business.
- *Protected by Strong Barriers/The Moat Effect:* The company's outstanding R&D efforts, combined with its style of working with doctors to develop new solutions, have provided Medtronic with a strong barrier.
- *People Are the Company's Most Important Asset:* Medtronic ranked 47th in *Fortune*'s report on "The 100 Best Companies to Work for in America." Medtronic believes that its people are the reason for the company's tremendous success.
- *Outstanding Management Team That Keeps the Company in "Prime":* Medtronic's focus on its core businesses has resulted in spectacular returns for shareholders.
- *Innovation-Driven Company That Turns Changes into Opportunities:* Approximately 50 percent of Medtronic's revenues come from products that the company has developed in the past twelve months. Medtronic takes innovation to a whole new level.

Key Competitors: Abbott Labs, Guidant, Johnson & Johnson, Pfizer, St. Jude Medical.

Sources of Additional Information
CORPORATE PUBLICATIONS
- Annual report
- Form 10-K
- Form 10-Q

RECENT ARTICLES
- "A Chance to Live." *Time*, August 4, 1997.

• "The 100 Best Companies to Work For in America." *Fortune*, January 12, 1998.

MERCK AND COMPANY, INC.

CORPORATE PROFILE

———◆———

Address: One Merck Drive
            Whitehouse Station, NJ 08889-0100
Ticker Symbol: MRK
Stock Exchange: NYSE
Phone Number: (908) 423-1000
Fax Number: (908) 594-4459
Website: http://www.merck.com

History and Business Background

In 1891, George Merck opened a branch office in New York to sell his family firm's chemicals. He guided the company through difficult times and enhanced the company's reputation for high-quality products. The first plant opened in Rahway, New Jersey, in 1903 to produce alkaloids. The first research laboratory, which was opened in 1933, was a pioneer in developing vitamin B-12 and steroids.

Today, Merck is a leading pharmaceutical giant that turns out exciting new products every year. Merck groups its products into the following categories:

• *Cardiovascular:* Products include Aggrastat, Aldomet, Zocor, Cozaar, Hyzaar, and Vasotec
• *Endocrinology:* Fosamax, Proscar, and Propecia
• *Gastrointestinal:* Led by Pepcid with sales in excess of $1 billion
• *Infection:* Crixivan for treatment of HIV infection. Other products include Mefoxin, Noroxin, and Primaxin
• *Inflammation:* Clinoril, Dolobid, and Indocin
• *Neurological:* Maxalt
• *Ophthalmic:* Includes Trusopt, the leading treatment for glaucoma, and Timoptic-XE

- *Respiratory:* Singulair for asthma
- *Vaccines:* Includes the established M-M-R II, Vaqta, Comvax, and PedvaxHIB
- *Animal Health and Crop Protection:* Abamectin, Enacard, Ivermectin (via joint ventures)

Obviously, it takes an outstanding research and development effort to keep the pipeline full of new products, and in 1998 Merck had budgeted some $1.9 billion on R&D, an increase of 12 percent. Since 1995, the company has launched fourteen new products, an indication that its research is paying big dividends. Merck also operates its Merck-Medco division, which provides pharmaceutical management services for approximately 50 million Americans.

Evaluation using Great Company Screens:

- *Highly Regarded by Knowledgeable Experts:* Merck has been ranked by *Fortune* among the Top 10 of "America's Most Admired Companies" for ten of fifteen years, 12th among the "World's Most Admired Companies," and 4th behind GE, Coca-Cola, and Microsoft in wealth creation.
- *Publicly Traded:* NYSE.
- *Headquartered in the United States:* Whitehouse Station, NJ.
- *In Business at Least 50 Years and Survived the Founder:* Merck was founded in 1887.
- *Market Cap in Excess of $15 Billion:* Merck's current market cap is approximately $174.2 billion.
- *Global Company with at Least 40 Percent of Revenues/Profits from International Operations:* Approximately 43 Percent of Merck's revenues were derived from international operations.
- *Outstanding Shareholder Returns:* Merck has outperformed the S&P 500 as shown in the following chart:

Merck Returns vs. S&P 500
ending December 31, 1998

	5 YEARS	10 YEARS
MERCK	36.88%	25.47%
S&P 500	24.05%	19.19%

Source: S&P Compustat

- *Terrific Businesses:* The pharmaceutical business is an excellent business. It will be interesting to see how Medco fits in over the coming years.
- *Protected by Strong Barriers / The Moat Effect:* Merck's powerful research and development operations, combined with its strong sales and distribution system, provide solid protection for the company.
- *People Are the Company's Most Important Asset:* The 1997 annual report clearly spells out the importance of people at Merck: "Merck has long believed that employees are the company's most powerful asset. Through their talent and teamwork, medicines like Crixivan are possible."
- *Outstanding Management Team That Keeps the Company in "Prime":* Merck is focused on its key business, the development of new pharmaceutical products. With patents expiring on several key products, including Mevacor and Vasotec, it is more important than ever to focus on R&D, and that is precisely what the senior management at Merck is doing.
- *Innovation-Driven Company That Turns Changes into Opportunities:* Merck has long been an innovative leader in the pharmaceutical industry.

Key Competitors: Abbott Labs, Amgen, Bayer AG, Bristol-Myers Squibb, Eli Lilly, Express Scripts, Pfizer, Procter and Gamble, Smith-Kline Beecham, Warner-Lambert.

Sources of Additional Information
CORPORATE PUBLICATIONS
- Annual report

- Form 10-K
- Form 10-Q

RECENT ARTICLES
- "Merck vs. the Biotech Industry." *Fortune*, March 31, 1997.
- "The Pipeline to Profits in Drug Stocks." *Worth*, April, 1997.
- "Merck Takes Some Growth Pills." *Business Week*, October 12, 1998.

MERRILL LYNCH AND COMPANY, INC.

CORPORATE PROFILE

Address: 250 Vesey Street
New York, NY 10281-1334
Ticker Symbol: MER
Stock Exchange: NYSE
Phone Number: (212) 449-1000
Fax Number: (212) 449-7461
Website: http://www.ml.com

History and Business Background

Charles Merrill opened an underwriting firm in New York in 1919. Shortly thereafter, Merrill brought in a partner, Edmund Lynch, and the company that we know as Merrill Lynch had its start. Initially, the company focused its efforts on individual investors—it is often referred to as "The Company that brought Wall Street to Main Street."

Over the years Merrill Lynch has grown primarily through acquisitions and geographic and business services expansion. With total assets of more than $1 trillion Merrill Lynch is the undisputed leader in planning-based financial advice and management for individuals and small businesses. As an investment bank, the company has been the top global underwriter ten years running. Merrill Lynch and Company, Inc., is a holding company that through its subsidiaries and affiliates provides investment, financing, advisory, insurance, and related services on a global basis. These services include:

- Securities brokerage, trading, and underwriting.
- Investment banking, strategic services, and other corporate finance advisory activities, including loan syndication.
- Asset management and other investment advisory and record-keeping services.
- Trading and brokerage of swaps, options, forwards, futures, and other derivatives.
- Securities clearance services.
- Banking, trust, and lending services, including mortgage lending and related services.
- Insurance sales and underwriting services.

The company is organized into four major segments that reflect the manner in which services are provided to clients:

1. *Corporate and Institutional Client.* Representing approximately 42 percent of revenues, this group provides a broad array of financial services including securities trading, investment banking, and advisory services to financial institutions, corporations, and governments worldwide.
2. *U.S. Private Client.* This sector provides a wide range of financial services and products, advice, and execution to individuals, small businesses, and employee-benefit programs, accounting for approximately 45 percent of corporate revenues.
3. *International Private Client.* Approximately 6 percent of revenues are represented by this group, which provides financial planning, private banking, and trust and investment services to individuals outside the U.S. through a network of 3,000 private bankers and other specialists in more than thirty countries worldwide.
4. *Asset Management.* This sector represents 7 percent of revenues and provides investment advisory and portfolio management services to clients.

Merrill Lynch is aggressively expanding its worldwide presence and is well positioned to be a dominant player across all business segments in the global financial services marketplace for years to come.

Evaluation using Great Company Screens:

- *Highly Regarded by Knowledgeable Experts:* Merrill Lynch ranks 18th among the Top 25 All-Stars in *Fortune*'s "World's Most Admired Companies" survey. The company is ranked as the number one securities firm in *Fortune*'s survey of "America's Most Admired Companies." *Smart Money* magazine ranks Merrill Lynch as the Best Full-Service Broker in America. Among top wealth creators, Merrill Lynch is ranked 62nd of 1,000 companies studied. Merrill Lynch is ranked 98th in *Fortune*'s survey of the 100 Best Companies to Work for in America. Merrill Lynch was ranked first in *Institutional Investor* magazine's annual "All-America Research Team" poll of institutional investors.
- *Publicly Traded:* NYSE.
- *Headquartered in the United States:* New York, NY.
- *In Business at Least 50 Years and Survived the Founder:* The company was founded in 1914.
- *Market Cap in Excess of $15 Billion:* Market cap is currently $23.9 billion.
- *Global Company with at Least 40 Percent of Revenues/Profits from International Operations:* The company has had a global presence for over forty-six years, and approximately 47 percent of revenues are derived from international operations. Outside of the U.S. the company is organized into five international regions:
    1. Europe, Middle East, and Africa
    2. Asia and Pacific
    3. Australia and New Zealand
    4. Japan
    5. Latin America and Canada
- *Outstanding Shareholder Returns:* Merrill Lynch's returns are as follows:

Merrill Lynch Returns vs. S&P 500
ending December 31, 1998

	5 YEARS	10 YEARS
MERRILL LYNCH	28.22%	30.22%
S&P 500	24.05%	19.19%

Source: S&P Compustat

- *Terrific Businesses:* Merrill Lynch's business meets our criteria for a terrific business.
- *Protected by Strong Barriers/The Moat Effect:* The combination of the company's size, geographic diversity, quality of services delivered, diversity of services, and position in the marketplace provide it with great barriers.
- *People Are the Company's Most Important Asset:* One of the company's core principles, "Respect for the Individual," combined with its ranking among the 100 Best Companies to Work for in America, shows the value that management places on its people.
- *Outstanding Management Team That Keeps the Company in "Prime":* Merrill Lynch's aggressive plans for expansion and its focus on strengthening its market position will keep the company in "Prime."
- *Innovation-Driven Company That Turns Changes into Opportunities:* The company is clearly a leader in this area.

Key Competitors: A. G. Edwards, Banker's Trust, Bear Stearns, Charles Schwab, Deutsche Bank, Equitable Companies, Goldman Sachs, J. P. Morgan, Mellon Bank, PaineWebber, Raymond James Financial, Union Bank of Switzerland.

Sources of Additional Information
CORPORATE PUBLICATIONS
- Annual report
- Form 10-K
- Form 10-Q
- Numerous speeches are available on the website.

RECENT ARTICLES
- "Merrill Lynch Takes Over." *Fortune,* April 27, 1998.
- "Bear on the Loose at Merrill." *Business Week,* February 8, 1999.

PFIZER, INC.

CORPORATE PROFILE

———◦———

Address: 235 E. 42nd Street
        New York, NY 10017
Ticker Symbol: PFE
Stock Exchange: NYSE
Phone Number: (212) 573-2323
Fax Number: (212) 573-7851
Website: http://www.pfizer.com

History and Business Background

Pfizer, Inc. was founded in Brooklyn, New York, by German immigrant cousins, Charles Pfizer and Charles Erhart in 1849. Pfizer was incorporated in 1900 as Charles Pfizer & Co., and celebrates its 150th birthday in 1999. Charles Pfizer had apprenticed with an apothecary, and his cousin was a confectioner. Their company's first product, which combined those skills, was santonin, a bitter antiparasitic which the cousins formulated into a candy cone. Later products included fine chemicals such as camphor and iodine. But it was the company's success at fermenting citric acid in deep tanks that led to its entry into the pharmaceuticals business. Pfizer continued to grow by producing polio vaccines, making strategic acquisitions and, in the 1960s, moving into consumer products.

Today the company's direction is clearly set. In a recent communication to Pfizer employees, Bill Steere, chairman and CEO, stated that Pfizer's mission is as follows: "Over the next five years, we will achieve and sustain our place as the world's premier research-based health care company. Our continuing success as a business will benefit patients and our customers, our shareholders, our families, and the communities in which we operate." The keys to achieving this mission are the company's research and development efforts and innovative marketing programs.

Pfizer has received a lot of publicity about its noteworthy new product, Viagra. Let me assure you that Pfizer is much more than Viagra. As the following interview reveals, Pfizer is a company that is investing over $2 billion annually in research and is developing new products at an unbelievable pace. Pfizer is focused and just beginning to hit its stride. This is a company that is 150 years young.

Evaluation using Great Company Screens:

- *Highly Regarded by Knowledgeable Experts: R&D Directions* in its annual report on the "Best Pipelines" (pharmaceutical talk for the newest products waiting to be introduced to the public) ranked Pfizer as having the best pipeline in the pharmaceutical industry. Pfizer is ranked seventh among *Fortune*'s twenty-five All-Stars in the "World's Most Admired Companies" survey. Pfizer ranks eighth in value creation, and is a close second to Merck in *Fortune*'s "America's Most Admired Companies" report. Pfizer is a great company in wonderful businesses.
- *Publicly Traded:* NYSE.
- *Headquartered in the United States:* New York, NY.
- *In Business at Least 50 Years and Survived the Founder:* Pfizer was founded in 1849.
- *Market Cap in Excess of $15 Billion:* Market cap is approximately $162.2 billion.
- *Global Company with at Least 40 Percent of Revenues/Profits from International Operations:* Approximately 47 percent of revenues come from international operations.
- *Outstanding Shareholder Returns:* Pfizer has produced unbelievable returns, as the chart shows.

Pfizer Returns vs. S&P 500
ending December 31, 1998

	5 YEARS	10 YEARS
PFIZER	51.19%	35.94%
S&P 500	24.05%	19.19%

Source: S&P Compustat

- *Terrific Businesses:* Pfizer is in two excellent businesses, consumer products and pharmaceuticals. The company has systematically reduced its presence in unattractive businesses.
- *Protected by Strong Barriers/The Moat Effect:* Pfizer's research and development capabilities, combined with its aggressive marketing effort, will continue to protect the company's core businesses.
- *People Are the Company's Most Important Asset:* The following quote from Pfizer's Vision Statement says it all: "We recognize that people are the cornerstone of Pfizer's success. We come from many different countries and cultures, and we speak many languages. We value our diversity as a source of strength. We are proud of Pfizer's history of treating employees with respect and dignity and are committed to building upon this tradition."
- *Outstanding Management Team That Keeps the Company in "Prime":* Steere and his team have done an outstanding job of focusing Pfizer's efforts on the things that count. Pfizer is clearly focused on its mission of becoming the "world's premier research-based health care company."
- *Innovation-Driven Company That Turns Changes into Opportunities:* Again referring to Pfizer's Vision Statement, we quote, "Innovation is the key to improving health and sustaining Pfizer growth and profitability. The quest for innovative solutions should invigorate all of our core businesses and pervade the Pfizer community worldwide." Pfizer is indeed a company committed to innovation.

Key Competitors: Abbott Labs, Amgen, Baxter, Bayer AG, DuPont, Glaxo Wellcome, Hoechst AG, Merck, Novartis, Schering-Plough, Warner-Lambert.

Sources of Additional Information

CORPORATE PUBLICATIONS

- Annual report
- Form 10-K
- Form 10-Q
- Other publications include: *Pfizer Education Initiative, The Role of Prescription Medicine in Healthcare, Pfizer Philanthropy, Pfizer in Brooklyn*

RECENT ARTICLES

- "The Best Pipelines." *R&D Directions,* January/February 1997.
- "Pfizer Versus Merck." *Forbes,* April 6, 1998.
- "Why Pfizer Is So Hot." *Fortune,* May 11, 1998.
- "Viagra, The New Era of Lifestyle Drugs." *Business Week,* May 11, 1998.
- "Beyond Viagra, Taking Stock." *Barron's,* June 8, 1998.

INTERVIEW

WILLIAM C. STEERE, JR.

Chairman and CEO
Pfizer Inc.

Focused Innovators

As I began to prepare for my interview with William C. Steere, Jr., chairman and chief executive officer of Pfizer, Inc., I realized that the people of Pfizer had a lot to be proud of. Recently the company had been recognized as follows:

- Pfizer was cited by *Forbes* as the Company of the Year in the January 11, 1999 issue.
- Pfizer was cited the number one pharmaceutical company in the world in *Fortune's* 1997 survey of "The World's Most Admired Companies."

- Pfizer was ranked eighth among the companies included in *Fortune*'s 1997 survey of "America's Most Admired Companies."
- *R & D Directions*, a journal that specializes in pharmaceutical research, noted in its 1997 issue that Pfizer has "the richest pipeline in the pharmaceutical industry." A pipeline, in pharmaceutical jargon, is the source of all new products. Because the developmental time for new drugs is so long, pharmaceutical companies look at their new products at various stages of development, or different positions within the pipeline.
- Bill Steere was included among *Business Week*'s "Top 25 Managers of the Year" in 1996.
- Pfizer's board of directors was ranked by *Business Week* as one of "The Top 25 Boards of Directors" in 1997. *Business Week* went on to note that the companies with the best twenty-five boards "boasted annual shareholder returns of 27.6 percent over the past five years, far outperforming the annual gains of 19.8 percent for the S&P 500 index . . ."
- *Fortune*'s 1997 survey of "America's Greatest Wealth Creators" ranked Pfizer as 11th out of 1,000 companies studied.

In an industry where well-managed companies abound and innovation is key, Pfizer has risen to the top. I wondered how the company had achieved such heights. What was Pfizer doing that was so different from the other companies in the pharmaceutical industry? Perhaps Pfizer had made a number of acquisitions.

I found that while Pfizer had acquired its animal health business from SmithKline Beecham several years ago, it had not made any other notable acquisitions. In fact, it had neither made major biotechnology acquisitions, nor had it purchased a pharmacy benefit management company like several of its competitors. Rather than make huge acquisitions, the company had actually divested itself of a number of businesses. The more I searched for the mysterious secret to Pfizer's success, the more I realized that the answer was on the front page of the Pfizer annual report. Who would ever think to look there? In bold letters it states, "Innovation is the value driving Pfizer's success. By innovating in all we do, we are helping millions of people around the world live healthier and happier lives." In the pharmaceutical industry, new drug innovation is the engine that drives the company. In this regard, the money invested in developing new drugs is as vital to a pharmaceutical company's success as the advertising dollars spent by huge consumer products companies like Coke or Procter and Gamble.

In the pharmaceutical industry research emerges from three sources:

1. Government-funded basic research
2. Privately funded basic research
3. Applied research sponsored by research-based pharmaceutical companies

In total, some $29 billion will be spent on pharmaceutical research in the U.S. Over half of this amount will be funded by large U.S. pharmaceutical companies.

In this industry size and financial strength are important advantages in two areas:

1. *Small biotech firms might raise enough capital to focus on only one idea.* If their focus is wrong, or the research doesn't pan out, the company is acquired or closed. On the other hand, a large company like Pfizer has the resources to pursue potential cures across a broad spectrum of diseases.
2. *It costs between $400 and $600 million and takes an average of fifteen years to bring a product to market.* Companies need both resources and financial staying power to succeed.

The costs and risks associated with the business have driven, and will continue to drive, consolidation within the pharmaceutical industry. However, mergers bring on a whole different set of challenges. Pfizer intends to remain an independent entity for the foreseeable future. The success of new products like Viagra will help preserve Pfizer's independence.

Pfizer will celebrate its 150th year in business in 1999. During that time, Pfizer has had only ten chairmen. This continuity among leaders is important and has enabled Bill Steere to lead the company in new and exciting directions. At 150 years of age, Pfizer is in "Prime." The company is as dynamic and successful as any company in the industry. The people resources and the pipeline that Pfizer has built will ensure its success for years to come.

The Interview

Bill Steere is a quietly confident man who came up through the marketing ranks at Pfizer. He is known within the company as an outstanding leader who is focused on building Pfizer's pharmaceutical business. Therefore I was not surprised when he begin by saying, "We are focused on our core business, which is to discover, develop, and bring to market innovative pharmaceuticals that either improve the quality of life or cure serious diseases in either humans or animals." In order to understand the significance of this statement, you must examine six different but key elements that define Pfizer: focus, discovery, innovation, quality of life, serious diseases, humans and animals.

Focus. Steere noted that "It was pretty clear what our strengths were when I took over. I just cleaned out a lot of the 'underbrush.'" He went on to say, "The businesses that we sold were businesses that we didn't do very well. They were taking a lot of management time, they required a fairly high level of investment, and weren't making much money for the shareholders. Since we weren't the market leader, we decided to divest those businesses."

He offered his experience with the chemical business as an example of the importance of being focused on what Pfizer does well. The person who ran Pfizer's chemical business had continually suggested opportunities for Pfizer to invest more money in that area. These included both acquisitions and potential new businesses that the division should enter. While the strategies and suggestions were a perfect fit for the chemicals business, they required that Pfizer invest money outside the health-care business. Steere advised the general manager that these investments would eventually make the chemicals business more attractive to someone else than it was to Pfizer. When the chemicals business became more attractive to someone else, he sold it.

In another interview, he had mentioned the talc mines that the company once owned. He said, "We had talc mines in Montana. What do you do with a talc mine? We had environmental issues to deal with. The management of the company was being consumed by a talc mine in Montana where we made no money. Why were we even in that business?" Like the chemicals business, he sold the talc mines. He explained, "We are not in the generics business, the distribution business, the chemical business, or some of the other businesses that we were once in. We have decided to focus on our core business, and the things that we do well." By adhering to this strategy of focusing on pharmaceuticals, Pfizer is doing what all great companies do, making sure that it is in terrific businesses, and that its resources are focused on these businesses.

Discovery. Pfizer spends billions of dollars searching for new drugs to fill the pipeline. The process begins with discovery scientists exploring the molecular basis of a disease. The discovery scientists seek to understand how a disease works inside the human body at the molecular level. They try to understand why, when, and where a disease occurs. This is time-consuming, highly sophisticated, scientific research. If the scientists are able to re-create the disease, they are able to test various compounds to determine their effect on it. At this phase of the research process, the scientists run a variety of different tests. If the results of the tests are encouraging, and the compound appears to work, the drug is next tested in healthy humans.

There are three levels of human trial:

1. *Phase 1, Clinical Trials.* These focus on the safety and side effects of the drug in healthy humans.
2. *Phase 2, Small-Scale Efficacy Studies.* The drug is tested on a small group of humans who have the disease. Here the focus is on the compound's effectiveness against the illness it was originally designed to treat.
3. *Phase 3, Wide-Scale Studies on Large Populations.* During this phase, researchers aim to confirm the results of earlier tests in a large, worldwide patient population. This may involve case studies on as many as 10,000 to 12,000 patients.

If it looks like the drug might work out, Pfizer establishes teams composed of scientists and marketers, bringing research and marketing together early in the process. This eliminates "silos" where marketing goes one way and research goes in another direction. Pfizer does a lot of matrix management. Steere believes that if you bring the researchers and marketers together early on, the product gets developed with input on how it's going to be marketed. In a matrix organization, you get around a lot of the bureaucracy and hierarchies. As a result, things get done faster, better, and occasionally even cheaper.

These teams determine the steps required to develop the drug, which may include conducting large broad-based studies to determine its effects; developing economic studies that detail the costs of developing it; and conducting studies that compare the drug to those of competitors. These tests take time and money. In fact, the period from human trial to launch takes approximately six years. The teams of Pfizer employees change during this six-year period, depending on the progress of the drug and the skills required at different phases of development. Since the attrition rates for new products are very high, these teams come and go. On the other hand, if the product makes it through the process, the team stays with the product the entire way.

Few people realize how difficult it is to bring a new product through the testing phase all the way to market. For example, for every new Pfizer product that makes it to launch, around 5,000 molecules were synthesized. Those products that have potential move into toxicology tests that are successfully passed by only one new product in 400. The new products that pass these tests are then moved into Phase 1 human trials. Only one out of every fifty new drugs passes the human trial tests. Next, a new drug application is filed, and only 50 percent of the new products will be approved.

The closer a new drug gets to market launch, the lower the attrition rate. However, the high failure rate throughout the research process means that it is critical for Pfizer to maintain a really aggressive and successful research effort in order to keep the pipeline filled with potential new products. Pfizer refers to these new products as "shots on goal." This is hockey lingo for shooting the hockey puck at the net. The theory is that the more shots a hockey team takes at its opponent's goal, the more likely the team is to fire the puck into the net and score. Therefore, Pfizer's strategy for dealing with the probability that most products won't make it to market is to aggressively spend on research and develop a lot of new products. Steere noted that the research group even has a budget for "shots on goal." This year Pfizer's research budget will be "in excess of $2 billion, one of the highest spend rates in the industry." The enormous investment in research by Pfizer produces a lot of "shots on goal."

In order to increase its success rate for new products, the company does not bring a new drug forward unless it is best in class or first in class. Pfizer has taken this approach because it feels that if you bring a "me too" product to market, the only way you can sell it is by reducing price, and that's not Pfizer's business. Steere remarked that "Today we are stopping development of products that ten years ago we would have killed for because it was easier to put products on the market. Now with the fierce competition that exists, unless you have demonstrable advantages, these 'me too' products won't succeed."

The fact that so few drugs ever make it to market presents Pfizer management with an interesting challenge—motivating their research scientists. Steere noted, "We have five to six thousand researchers, and only a few hundred will ever work on a commercial success. They soldier on for their entire careers, but [some] have never worked on a product that was introduced into the market. Even though they have done terrific science their whole career—and we have a number of outstanding M.D.'s and Ph.D.'s involved in our research efforts—they may never be associated with a commercial success. So they must be motivated through the science that they do rather than through a commercial success." He said, "A very small percentage will ever have their name on a patent. If people are working on a 'dead end' project, we have to take them off that project and put them on another project that has more potential." These research scientists who spend their careers developing and improving the science are the unsung heroes of Pfizer.

He went on to state, "People are our most important asset. You can characterize the company any way you want, but in the end it's the people," noting that "Respect for people is one of our core values." Because of the company's appreciation for the great job these people do, Pfizer has very little turnover.

In order to keep the "shots on goal" coming at a record pace, Pfizer is expanding its discovery labs by 30 percent. Pfizer has three major research campuses around the world, located in the U.S., England, and Japan. Discovery research is expensive, but not as expensive as development. The reason the research budget is so high this year is because Pfizer has a number of products in the development part of the pipeline. That's good news for Pfizer shareholders.

Innovation

Steere remarked that "Innovation drives the company. Innovation drives the way we develop drugs, our regulatory strategies, and how we market the drugs. We see innovation in our legal department and our tax group. For example, four years ago we had a 33 percent tax rate, we now have a 28 percent tax rate."

As a result of this focus on innovation, he noted, "We let the science go where the science goes." For example the impotence drug, Viagra, started out as a product for angina. Pfizer researchers found that the product caused healthy males in Phase 1 trials to became sexually aroused, so they decided to develop the drug to treat male impotence. Viagra had one of the most successful launches of any new pharmaceutical ever introduced, and continues to rack up huge revenues and profits for Pfizer and its shareholders. Pfizer is flexible and ready to go where innovation leads. In line with its strategy of going where the science goes, Pfizer doesn't try to restrict its researchers to a limited area of science. The company is stronger in anti-infective, cardiovascular, and central nervous system drugs, but Pfizer researchers don't avoid any area.

Pfizer builds barriers around its business by securing patents on its new products. Steere said, "When the patent expires we will lose 80 to 90 percent of the revenues in the first year to generics." Therefore Pfizer needs a constant stream of innovation. The penalty for not innovating in the new products area is severe. "Companies whose patents have not been replaced in a timely way are the ones who have had to search for partners [to merge with]." He went on to add, "You must continue to reinvent yourself, because every time a patent expires, something must be coming in behind the product to replace the lost revenues and profits. You can't sustain the business on old products." As a result, he estimated that "about 80 percent of Pfizer's revenues come from products that were not around five years ago."

The company has developed several strategies for protecting its patented products:

- *The first strategy is to modify patented products before they go off patent.* For example, Procardia (a cardiovascular drug) was designed to be taken three times per day. As the patient took the pills, blood levels of the drug rose and fell with each tablet that was taken. Shortly before Procardia went off patent, Pfizer placed it in a sophisticated, patented delivery system that was developed by one of Pfizer's alliance partners. The new delivery system provided the patient with a sustained blood level of Procardia during the day. This resulted in Procardia XL, the same basic drug with a new patented delivery system. This change in the delivery system allowed Pfizer to continue to successfully sell and market Procardia for the next five to seven years.

- *Another strategy that Pfizer is following is to speed up the process from patent approval to introduction into the marketplace.* By shortening the time it takes to develop a new product, Pfizer will enjoy additional years under the protection of the patent laws. Steere noted, "With patents, the faster you get the product to market, and the faster you get the new drug commercialized, the more money you make. The last year of the patent is when you are making the most money, and it's followed by the biggest decline in sales. You need more good years under patent protection, so speed is critical."

- *A third strategy is to expand the U.S. model of patent legislation throughout the world.* He noted that "The U.S. is the industrial model that the rest of the world should follow. In the U.S. there is a premium for innovation, and as a result you get a lot more innovation in the U.S. than other countries." He pointed out that "America has been more successful than any country in providing the right mix of incentives to keep our research moving forward. Today nearly half of the world-class drugs introduced over the past two decades come from the laboratories of American pharmaceutical companies. No other country even comes close."

Pfizer prefers to operate in markets where innovation is rewarded. For example, Pfizer would like to get the U.S. model installed throughout Europe. Europe has low prices for innovators and high prices for generics. Steere noted that there is only about a 10 percent price gap between innovative products and generics. This situation exists because in Europe there are a large number of small family-owned pharmaceutical companies whose efforts at innovation have failed. As a result, these small firms are now making a living from generics. The European situation is also different from ours in that the government is the single purchaser of pharmaceuticals. Government regulators dictate the price, and sometimes the price they offer isn't high enough for Pfizer to even sell the product in the marketplace. Since Pfizer officials won't destroy world pricing by selling to a market that won't give them a fair return, Pfizer marketers must either convince the central purchasing organizations of the value of their products, or withdraw the product from the market.

If Europe implements a model like that of the U.S., some of the smaller, family-owned pharmaceutical companies might not survive, and this is a concern to European legislators. However, the U.S. model would no doubt result in improved health care. The good news is that there is increased European interest in installing the American model.

Pfizer encounters different market situations around the world. In Japan, they talk about reimbursement problems, and regulatory issues for new claims. In the U.S. the focus is on distribution and competition. There are no patent laws in India, so generics come out at the same time that Pfizer's new drugs are introduced. Likewise, Argentina does not have patent laws. Because legislation concerning patent protection varies around the world, Pfizer is continually fighting to protect intellectual property rights. As Steere noted, "Pfizer products are products of the mind. It costs very little to make the product. The intellectual input is what drives the business. Without intellectual property protection, Pfizer is doomed." Therefore, Pfizer, along with the rest of the pharmaceutical industry, is aggressively pursuing patent issues throughout the world—in the U.S., India, Egypt, Argentina, and elsewhere. The pharmaceutical industry has enjoyed some recent successes: Brazil just implemented new patent legislation, and Korea and China now have reasonable patent protection.

Quality of Life and Serious Diseases. Pfizer places special emphasis on diseases that impact the quality of life. Today, quality-of-life drugs represent about 30 percent of Pfizer's product portfolio. This portfolio includes drugs for impotence, hair loss, obesity, and aging skin. These are not life-threatening diseases, but they do impact the quality of life. With an aging population, the quality-of-life market segment has become huge. Nevertheless, a larger percentage of Pfizer's drugs are still focused on diseases that are life threatening. These include cancer, osteoporosis, cardiovascular disease, and asthma.

The company also has a consumer products business that is a part of the pharmaceutical business. Pfizer has brands like Ben Gay that are over 100 years old. The principal rationale for the business is to provide a platform for Rx-to-OTC (prescription to over-the-counter) switches. Pfizer has done the Rx-to-OTC switch quite a number of times in Europe, but has not done it as much in the U.S. because of regulatory constraints. At $500 million, the consumer products business is a nice, profitable business and a good platform for the switches.

The company's animal health business will total approximately $1.4 billion in 1998. The demographic trends suggest long-term growth in demand for livestock, poultry, and companion products. The hospital products business is also profitable and growing. Sales revenues are approximately $1.5 billion. The division is composed of several independent businesses that are pursuing opportunities in four major markets: musculoskeletal, interventional, urology, and surgical instrumentation.

Alliances. One of the unique features of Pfizer is the company's corporation-wide use of alliances with other companies. In central research, Pfizer has developed and implemented a portfolio strategy. Steere believes that "This is the golden age of science, and science is moving so fast that you can't put all of your eggs in one basket. Furthermore, you can't build your own research staff quickly enough to keep up with all of the changes that are occurring in all of the different branches of science." Rather than acquire companies, Pfizer makes equity investments and/or signs licensing agreements with a variety of companies in businesses that are of interest to Pfizer's scientists. Since Pfizer's scientists are the developers of the portfolio, this is a bottom-up approach to alliances.

If the science that Pfizer invests in via the alliance structure peters out, reaches a dead end, or proves that the hypothesis was wrong, Pfizer simply drops the companies from the portfolio and replaces them with other companies. Some of these alliances have been very productive, and Pfizer has frequently either renewed the alliance or increased its equity stake in the company. Pfizer has become a "partner of choice" for people in the industry who are launching new products and want marketing help. Pfizer will also co-promote with companies like Warner-Lambert's Parke-Davis Research Division on the introduction of drugs like Lipitor (a cholesterol-reducing drug, and one of the most successful introductions in the history of the industry).

There is no one set format that Pfizer follows for all alliances. The alliance structures vary from purchasing a piece of a company to signing a contract to provide services to help launch a new product. In cases where Pfizer provides sales and marketing support, it gets a piece of the profits. Alliances give Pfizer an opportunity to explore areas of science where the company has no expertise.

This is a very different strategy from making an acquisition. An acquisition often involves bringing two very divergent corporate cultures together. In an environment where the research capabilities of the acquired company are so important to the success of the acquisition and the scientists are very independent, if the scientists in the acquired company decide to leave, you have bought nothing. In fact, the acquiring company can find itself forced to write off the acquisition.

Pfizer has made acquisitions in the past. For example, Pfizer bought the SmithKline Beecham animal health business. As Steere noted, it took a year to integrate the business into Pfizer's operations. The company had to reassign some senior Pfizer managers and lost some senior SmithKline managers in the process. He noted that while "this was a very good acquisition, we lost about a year in the transition. If we did that today it would really hurt our momentum." He is very much aware that "If you bet the ranch on one piece of science in today's age, you are probably going to miss. Because science is so broad based today, new things are happening all of the time. Pfizer has taken the approach of spreading our risks. If we see a new [scientific advance] coming out then we will try to get in there and get a piece of it in order to understand it." His approach of strategically using alliances makes a lot of sense.

Global Company. Pfizer is a global company and markets "the same products everywhere." It has over $1 billion in sales in Japan, a plant in China, and major research facilities in England and Japan. Approximately half of Pfizer's sales come from outside the U.S. The company is fully integrated from a research, marketing, and product perspective.

Changing Customer Base. The company's customer base is changing. "Many of the people making purchase decisions today are not health-care professionals, they are in managed care." Where Pfizer had a very simple universe of customers ten to fifteen years ago, today they have as many as fifty different types of customers. Pfizer's customers include:

- The FDA
- Managed-care companies
- Pharmacists
- Consumers, who are getting much more involved in making purchase decisions
- HMOs
- State medicaid groups

Some customers are covered by sales reps in the field, some are covered by interdisciplinary specialists calling on universities, while others sell to managed-care groups. Every sale requires a different customer solution. The company classifies its customers by need and then determines how best to sell to them, using a mass customization selling approach to meet the needs of its diverse customers.

Consolidation/Merger. We concluded our conversation by discussing risks. Steere noted, "This business is high risk. If your research lets you down, then you are searching for a partner. As a result, you see a lot of consolidation in this industry. We have been approached by almost everyone about a merger. I am not opposed to a merger—it just has to do something to enhance our position." He went on to state, "I have seen a lot of consolidation within the industry, but I have elected not to put Pfizer through a merger right now because it would just slow our growth. There are very few large-cap pharmaceutical companies that are growing as fast as we are, and anyone that merged with us would just slow us down."

His biggest concern is maintaining and even building the company's speed. As Pfizer grows, he doesn't want people to get bogged down in bureaucracy. "If you aren't careful, the bureaucrats get into the new innovative ideas and they get bogged down. In a company where speed is critical, this can be very damaging. Speed is important and things have to be done faster. Competition is fierce and you must be fast to stay ahead of it. We must constantly look at how we can get rid of these impediments to speed."

Before we closed I asked Steere what percentage of his personal net worth was in Pfizer stock. He responded, "The only stock I really own is Pfizer. I think it's a good company and returns have been good." His financial advisor says that he ought to diversify his holdings and invest in other stocks. Steere asks, "What do you move into that is as good as Pfizer?" A good question.

THE PROCTER AND GAMBLE COMPANY
CORPORATE PROFILE

Address: One Procter and Gamble Plaza
    Cincinnati, OH 45202
Ticker Symbol: PG
Stock Exchange: NYSE
Phone Number: (513) 983-1100
Fax Number: (513) 983-9369
Website: http://www.pg.com

History and Business Background

Established in 1837, the Procter and Gamble Company (P&G) began as a small, family-operated soap and candle company in Cincinnati, Ohio. From that modest beginning, P&G has grown into a world company, which today markets more than 300 brands to nearly 5 billion consumers in over 140 countries with on-the-ground operations in more than 70 countries. In the fiscal year ending June 30, 1998, P&G had worldwide sales of over $37.1 billion. The company's strengths lie in its commitment to:

- Providing products of superior quality and value that improve the lives of the world's consumers.
- Being a world leader in relevant scientific research and technology.
- Maintaining economic success based on P&G's experience in managing the business with excellence and training and developing people to build it.

P&G is a recognized leader in the development, manufacture, and marketing of a broad range of superior quality laundry and cleaning, paper, personal care, food and beverage, and health-care products, including prescription pharmaceuticals, and a variety of products for business and industry. These brands include Tide, Downey, Pampers, Always, Bounty, Pringles, Crisco, Crest, Vicks, Pantene, Jif, Cascade, and others.

Innovative research and development at P&G provides the superior products on which its commercial success is based. This involves creating new products and technologies such as Dryel and Febreze, as well as the continuing improvement of existing products.

P&G employs over 110,000 people worldwide. The company's historic policy of promoting employees from within ensures that its managers fully understand P&G principles and have the experience to move the company ahead.

P&G's corporate tradition, spanning 161 years, is rooted in the principles of personal integrity, doing what's right for the long term, respect for the individual, and being the best at what it does.

I had the privilege of working for P&G when I graduated from college. I am proud of my affiliation with P&G, and have enjoyed watching the company evolve into a global market leader.

Evaluation using Great Company Screens:

- *Highly Regarded by Knowledgeable Experts:* P&G was one of the few companies to be mentioned in both *Built To Last* and *In Search of Excellence. Fortune* ranked it 6th among 1,000 companies in wealth creation, and 15th among the "World's Most Admired Companies." *Business Week* ranks P&G's board of directors 24th among the best 25 boards in America. P&G ranked 19th in *Fortune's* "100 Best Companies in America to Work For." Within the consumer products industry, P&G is generally regarded as the number one company.
- *Publicly Traded:* NYSE.
- *Headquartered in the United States:* Cincinnati, OH.
- *In Business at Least 50 Years and Survived the Founder:* P&G was founded in 1837.
- *Market Cap in Excess of $15 Billion:* P&G's current market cap is approximately $138.5 billion.
- *Global Company with at Least 40 Percent of Revenues/Profits from International Operations:* Approximately 50 percent of P&G revenues are generated by the company's international operations.
- *Outstanding Shareholder Returns:* P&G's returns are as follows:

Procter and Gamble Returns vs. S&P 500
ending December 31, 1998

	5 YEARS	10YEARS
P & G	28.52%	26.39%
S&P 500	24.05%	19.19%

Source: S&P Compustat

- *Terrific Businesses:* P&G's consumer businesses are characterized by market-leading brand shares and highly consumable products with strong household penetration, all of which make for an excellent business.
- *Protected by Strong Barriers/The Moat Effect:* P&G's tremendous market shares and highly developed brands provide a wonderful moat, which is being strengthened by the company's use of new and emerging technology.

- *People Are the Company's Most Important Asset:* P&G's base, on which all of its brand franchises are built, is "great people." P&G is one of the best recruiters of talent in the world. P&G people are aggressively recruited by other companies in all industries that are trying to build consumer franchises.
- *Outstanding Management Team That Keeps the Company in "Prime":* P&G is a highly disciplined company that focuses on the things that make a difference. It continually seeks ways to improve its operations and enhance its industry leadership position.
- *Innovation-Driven Company That Turns Changes into Opportunities:* P&G has one of the best R&D organizations in the world, and perhaps *the* best in consumer products. The company's annual expenditures for research and development exceed $1 billion. P&G and its subsidiaries operate seventeen major R&D facilities around the world. P&G won the U.S. National Medal of Technology in 1995. Developing new products and categories and improving existing ones are key elements of P&G's success.

Key Competitors: Alberto-Culver, Carter-Wallace, Clorox, Colgate-Palmolive, Dial, Gillette, Nestlé, S. C. Johnson, Unilever.

Sources of Additional Information

CORPORATE PUBLICATIONS
- Annual report
- Form 10-K
- Form 10-Q

RECENT ARTICLES
- "Where P&G's Brawn Doesn't Help Much." *Business Week,* November 10, 1997.
- "Inside P&G, A Pitch to Keep Women Employees." *Wall Street Journal,* September 9, 1998.

BOOKS
- Decker, Charles L. *Winning with the P&G 99.* New York: Pocket Books, 1998.
- Schisgall, Oscar. *Eyes on Tomorrow.* New York: Doubleday, 1981.

OTHER

- Andrew Shore, an analyst with PaineWebber, publishes research reports on P&G that are very well written.

SCHERING-PLOUGH CORPORATION

CORPORATE PROFILE

Address: One Giralda Farms
Madison, NJ 07940-1000
Ticker Symbol: SGP
Stock Exchange: NYSE
Phone Number: (973) 822-7000
Fax Number: (973) 822-7048
Website: http://www.schering-plough.com

History and Business Background

Established in the late 1800s as the American subsidiary of the German-based pharmaceutical and chemical company Schering A.G., Schering Corporation was nationalized by the U.S. government during World Wars I and II. Following World War II, the Company was overseen by the government until ownership passed to the private sector in 1952. In 1971, Schering Corporation, which had evolved into a global, research-based, pharmaceutical firm, merged with Plough Inc., a Memphis, Tennessee-based manufacturer of consumer products that had grown from modest beginnings in 1908 into a worldwide company.

The company manufactures and markets prescription pharmaceuticals, generic drugs, and animal health products through its Schering-Plough Pharmaceuticals operating unit, which accounts for more than 90 percent of total company sales. Additionally, Schering-Plough manufactures and markets leading foot care, sun care, and over-the-counter pharmaceutical products through its Schering-Plough HealthCare Products unit.

Today, Schering-Plough is a worldwide pharmaceutical company committed to discovering and marketing new therapies and treatments that can improve people's health and save lives. One of the early investors in biotechnology, Schering-Plough is a recognized leader in biotechnology, genomics, and gene therapy. The company's businesses may be grouped into two categories:

1. *Pharmaceuticals.* Approximately 90 percent of 1998 revenues were in pharmaceuticals. Major sectors within the pharmaceutical business include:
   - *Allergy and Respiratory (42.0%).* Key brand is Claritin (nonsedating antihistamine).
   - *Anti-infective and anticancer (16.0%).* Key brand is Intron A (anticancer/antiviral agent).
   - *Dermatological (8.0%).* The leading brand is Elocon (a topical steroid).
   - *Cardiovascular (9.0%).* Imdur (angina) is the company's key offering.
   - *Other Pharmaceutical (8.0%).*
   - *Animal Health (8%).*
2. *HealthCare Products.* These products represent 9 percent of 1998 corporate sales and include the following:
   - *Foot Care (4%).* Dr. Scholl's is the key brand, but the category also includes Lotrimin AF and Tinactin.
   - *Sun Care (2%).* Coppertone is the U.S. leader in sun care with approximately 33% of the market.
   - *OTC (3.0%).* Key brands are Correctol (laxative) and Afrin (nasal spray).
   - *Other HealthCare (2%).*

Evaluation using Great Company Screens:

- *Highly Regarded by Knowledgeable Experts:* Schering-Plough was ranked twenty-third in wealth creation by *Fortune,* which also gave it a 6.6 ranking in the "America's Most Admired Companies" survey.
- *Publicly Traded:* NYSE.

- *Headquartered in the United States:* Madison, NJ.
- *In Business at Least 50 Years and Survived the Founder:* The company was founded in 1864.
- *Market Cap in Excess of $15 Billion:* Schering-Plough's market cap is currently $81.2 billion.
- *Global Company with at Least 40 Percent of Revenues/Profits from International Operations:* Approximately 50 percent of Schering-Plough's revenues come from its international operations. The company functions as a global pharmaceutical company.
- *Outstanding Shareholder Returns:* Schering-Plough's returns have been impressive:

Schering-Plough Returns vs. S&P 500
ending December 31, 1998

	5 YEARS	10 YEARS
SCHERING-PLOUGH	48.18%	34.66%
S&P 500	24.05%	19.19%

Source: S&P Compustat

- *Terrific Businesses:* The combination of a strong pharmaceutical business and a consumer products business built on leading brands is a powerful business model.
- *Protected by Strong Barriers/The Moat Effect:* The company's strong R&D capabilities coupled with leading market shares form a solid protective barrier.
- *People Are the Company's Most Important Asset:* The company appears to do a relatively good job of developing its people.
- *Outstanding Management Team That Keeps the Company in "Prime":* As you look at returns over time, it is clear that management is focused on the core business, and as a result is delivering outstanding returns to shareholders.
- *Innovation-Driven Company That Turns Changes into Opportunities:* The company's ability to continue developing industry-leading pharmaceuticals and stay on the leading edge of biotechnology is clear evidence of its innovative spirit.

Key Competitors: Abbott Labs, Amgen, Astra, Chiron, Eli Lilly, Genentech, Merck, Pfizer, Rhône-Poulenc.

Sources of Additional Information

CORPORATE PUBLICATIONS
- Annual report
- Form 10-K
- Form 10-Q

Chapter 5

APPLYING THE STRATEGY TO IPOS, INTERNATIONAL COMPANIES, AND GREAT COMPANIES OF THE FUTURE

 The Great Companies investing strategy has a variety of applications that can be used in the following ways:

- *To develop portfolios of stocks that are consistent with the Great Companies approach but differ from the stocks in our original Great Companies of America portfolio.* By altering a few of the twelve screens, investors can produce portfolios that contain totally different sets of companies.
- *To screen IPOs (Initial Public Offerings) for investing.* While IPOs tend to have profiles that are exactly the opposite of Great Companies in many ways, the screens that focus on what makes for a terrific business and which protective barriers surround the company can be used to evaluate IPOs.
- *To hedge the portfolios that were developed using the Great Companies strategy and screens, sophisticated investors who want to sell short in order to cover their long positions might select companies with exactly the opposite profile from that of the Great Companies.* The shorting strategy involves purchasing stocks that are overvalued and that the investor believes will decline in value. Some sophisticated investors use this strategy to cover their long positions (good

stocks they own that they think will increase in value). The idea is to short poorly managed companies that are overvalued, in bad businesses, and without protective barriers, and own the stocks of good companies that will increase in value. Some investors believe that this is an effective strategy for minimizing market risks.

- *Finally, the twelve traits can be used by executives to evaluate how their companies measure up to the qualities of the Great Companies identified in this book.* By identifying their own companies' strengths and weaknesses relative to the traits of the Great Companies and making the necessary changes, leaders of companies that did not clear our screens might well improve shareholder returns.

DEVELOPING PORTFOLIOS CONSISTENT WITH THE GREAT COMPANIES INVESTING STRATEGY

You can apply the strategy used to identify the Great Companies to create a totally different set of stock portfolios. Here are the hurdles a company must clear to be considered a Great Company of America:

1. The company must be highly regarded by knowledgeable industry experts.
2. Each company must be headquartered in the United States.
3. Each company must have been in business at least fifty years and survived the founder.
4. The company's market cap must exceed $15 billion.
5. The company must be a global company, not just multinational or international, with at least 40 percent of revenues derived from international operations.
6. Each Great Company has provided outstanding shareholder returns.
7. The company is in terrific businesses.
8. The Great Company has powerful franchises that protect it from competitors.
9. The management of these companies strongly believes that people are the company's most valuable asset.

10. Innovation is a critical element of the Great Company.
11. The Great Company has an outstanding management team that keeps the company in Prime.
12. The company's stock must be publicly traded.

THE GREAT TECHNOLOGY COMPANIES™

The screens that were used to create our Great Companies of America™ portfolio did in fact produce a group of outstanding companies that have delivered long-term index-beating returns. However, as I considered the significance of the three business revolutions that we have experienced in the United States (the agricultural revolution, the industrial revolution, and now the technology revolution), it became quite evident that a number of excellent technology companies were omitted from the GCA portfolio. For example, Microsoft, an incredibly successful company, has not been in business for fifty years, and has not survived its famous founder, Bill Gates. Sun Microsystems, Intel, Cisco, and a number of other outstanding companies that are leading the technology revolution have been in business less than fifty years and were also excluded.

I believe that technology will continue to play an important role in the development of the global economy. I also believe that a number of the technology companies have excellent business models and are well managed. While I believe that the technology sector will continue to be more volatile than our Great Companies America™ portfolio, I believe that most investors should invest a portion of their assets in the technology sector.

We used the Great Companies America™ screens as our base to select the Great Companies Technology™ portfolio because we wanted to identify technology companies that will be great for years to come. Whenever a sector "takes off" like the technology sector, a number of companies rush into the market in an effort to grab sales and profits. Many of these companies are poorly managed, based upon flawed business models, and fail to survive the initial sector shakeout that always comes. For example, when automobiles were first introduced in the United States, over 2,000 automobile companies were started to capture a share of this potentially huge market. Today, only a handful of automobile companies remain in business. The same phenomena occurred when commercial airlines were first launched. Some 500 optimistic businessmen launched airlines to take advantage of the enormous opportunities created by air travel. Today, there are less than 20 viable airlines serving air passengers in the United States. I am confident that twenty years from now, the technology landscape will look quite different than it does today, and that many of the "hot stocks" of today will be long gone.

However, by applying the Great Companies America™ screens to the technology sector, we are using the same discipline that created a portfolio of companies that have, on average, been in business over 103 years. While I would never suggest that all of our Great Companies in the technology portfolio will be in business for 100 years, I do feel comfortable that each of the companies in the Great Companies Technology™ portfolio has passed virtually the same criteria as the companies in our GCA™ portfolio.

In order to identify the Great Companies Technology, we made minor modifications to our Great Companies America™ screens as follows:

The company must be in business at least fifteen years (The Great Companies of America Screen is fifty years in business and survived the founder.)

The company must be a global company with at least 30 percent of revenues derived from international operations (The GCA screen is 40 percent. We reduced the percentage of international revenues from 40 percent to 30 percent because technology is underdeveloped in many countries, and several of these companies are still in their developmental stages,)

The company is in terrific technology businesses (The GCA screen is in the company is in terrific businesses.)

Outstanding shareholder returns vs. the NASDAQ (We compared the performance of the technology stocks in our Great Companies Technology™ portfolio to the NASDAQ. While many NASDAQ listed securities are not in technology businesses, we felt that this was a more relevant comparison than the S&P 500.

We used the S&P 500 index for the Great Companies of America™.

Since companies must report a profit in order to generate an intrinsic value, unprofitable companies were automatically deleted from consideration. A partial list of companies that passed these screens includes, but is not limited to, the following:

- *Applied Materials, Inc.*—The number-one maker of equipment used in semiconductor factories.
- *Cisco Corporation*—Supplies approximately three-fourths of the products that are used to link computer networks.
- *EMC Corporation*—The acknowledged leader in data storage technology.
- *Intel Corporation*—The world's number-one chip maker.
- *Microsoft Corporation*—Known for its Windows products, Microsoft is a global software leader that is always searching for new opportunities.
- *Motorola, Inc.*—A global leader in a variety of new and emerging technologies.
- *Oracle Corporation*—The leader in database management software.
- *Sun Microsystems, Inc.*—A leader in UNIX-based workstations, storage systems, and servers.

GREAT COMPANIES VERSUS INDEXING

When Jack Bogle, the Chairman Emeritus of Vanguard and the "Father of Indexing" (he developed the concept of indexing as part of his college thesis), read *Great Companies, Great Returns*, he sent me a personalized note stating that "I loved Great Companies . . . I think we need mutual funds that buy companies (not stocks) and hold them well, 'forever.' Index funds are very close, but can be improved upon." As I reviewed Jack's note I began to think about how investors could use the two portfolios to create a concentrated index.

When you analyze the performance of the top-performing stocks in the S&P 500, you find that a very few stocks contribute the majority of the returns. For example, in 1998 the top 25 companies in the S&P 500 accounted for approximately 63 percent of the returns. The numbers change slightly for 1999 with the top 25 companies representing 53.6 percent of the returns of the total S&P. The obvious question is why would anyone purchase the other 475 companies in the index if only 5 percent of the companies are producing between 50 percent and 60 percent of the returns.

Whenever you examine virtually any index in depth, you realize that you are investing in a hodgepodge of companies. Some of the companies in the index are in great businesses, while others are in very difficult businesses. Likewise, you will find that some of the companies in the index are led by great managers, while others are led by incompetents. Your analysis will reveal that some of the companies in the composite are dramatically overvalued, while others are extremely undervalued. Furthermore, some of the companies have strong protective barriers, while others have virtually none. I believe that this enormous variance in the quality of companies within an index accounts for a very few companies driving a disproportionate share of the index's returns.

Therefore, rather than invest in an index fund or exchange-traded funds, you could invest in the two Great Companies portfolios, Great Companies America™ and Great Companies Technology™, in the same ratio as the index. For example, at the beginning of 1999, approximately 80 percent of the market cap of the S&P 500 index was represented by nontechnology stocks, while technology stocks accounted for approximately 20 percent of the index. By the end of the year, technology stocks had soared and represented approximately 30 percent of the S&P 500 index. If you owned an equal weighted portfolio of GCA and GCT stocks at the beginning of 1999 that was split 80 percent GCA and 20 percent GCT you would have enjoyed returns of 31.3 percent. This compares to the S&P 500 that was up approximately 21.4 percent during 1999.

An analysis of the importance of the Great Companies to the S&P 500 index reveals that as of June 1, 2000, the $4.9 trillion market cap of the two Great Companies portfolios represents approximately 39 percent of the $12.4 trillion market cap of the index. Further analysis shows that the GCA portfolio represents approximately 15 percent of the index and 22 percent of the nontechnology companies. The GCA portfolio, on the other hand, represents 24 percent of the S&P 500 and 78 percent of the technology companies in the index.

The Chart below summarizes the differences between investing in an index fund and investing in the Great Companies portfolios:

S&P 500 Index	*Combined Great Companies Portfolios*
Own 500 companies	Invest in 31 companies*
Invest in a variety of businesses and sectors	Invest only in terrific businesses
Invest in some companies with Protective barriers and some without	Invest only in companies with strong protective barriers
Market cap determines portfolio Weighting	Intrinsic value determines weighting
Seek index average returns	Seek index beating returns
Seek tax efficient returns	Seek tax efficient returns

After considering the advantages of investing in the two Great Companies portfolios, you may want to reconsider the traditional approach to indexing.

GREAT COMPANIES INTERNATIONAL™

The screens that we used to identify the fourteen Great Companies America™ and the Great Companies Technology™ portfolios excluded companies headquartered outside of the United States. As an investor seeking diversification, we realized that you might want to invest in Great Companies located outside of the United States. Therefore, we modified the GCA and GCT screens as follows:

The company must be publicly traded as either an ADR or U.S. listed security (This screen replaces the screen of publicly traded on a major U.S. exchange.) For those who do not know, ADR is short for

American Depository Receipt. Companies that are headquartered outside of the United States can have their stocks trade on a U.S. exchange by filing for ADR status. ADR registration places certain financial reporting requirements on a firm, but we think this is a plus for investors.

The company must be headquartered outside of the United States (Our earlier screens required that "Each company must be headquartered outside of the United States.")

Outstanding shareholder returns versus the MSCI World Index (This is an index developed by Morgan Stanley and is commonly used to monitor returns of international companies.) We used the S&P 500 index for the Great Companies of America, but switched to the MSCI because it is more relevant to the performance of the companies in the Great Companies International portfolio.

The company cannot be controlled by a foreign government (This is a new screen). I included this screen as a result of my past consulting experiences. As I mentioned earlier, for years I led a very successful consulting firm that consulted with clients in the United States and overseas. During one of our consulting assignments, we were consulting with a food company that was owned by the Italian government. This firm had struggled for years until our client, the current CEO, took over. The CEO was a very capable leader and was doing all of the right things to build the company's brands, bolster its managerial ranks, and expand into global markets. One day there was a change in the Italian government, and the next day the CEO and his entire staff were terminated. The CEO was replaced by a political appointee who had no idea how to run a branded foods company. This same scenario was repeated throughout Italy, as the new government installed its political appointees in a variety of companies owned by the Italian government. While not an issue for U.S.-based companies, and certainly not limited to Italy, governmental interference is a very real problem in many government owned companies. While many of these companies receive special treatment from the governments that own them, in my opinion these advantages do not outweigh the limitations posed by governmental ownership. This screen will force us to exclude some profitable companies; however, I have no interest in being a long-term investor in a company that is owned by any government.

We then applied the screens used for Great Companies America™ to the nontechnology companies in our database, and the Great Companies Technology™ screens to the technology companies. Our screens generated a group of truly outstanding international companies, including, but not limited to, the following:

NONTECHNOLOGY

- *AEGON*—A global financial services firm with a strong U.S. presence that is headquartered in The Hague in the Netherlands.
- *AstraZeneca*—A pharmaceutical powerhouse that ranks fourth in 1999 global pharmaceutical sales.
- *Barclay's*—Founded in 1736, this innovative financial services firm is headquartered in the U.K.
- *Glaxo SmithKline*—Ranked second in global pharmaceutical sales.
- *ING Group*—Headquartered in the Netherlands, this company continues to build its presence around the world.
- *L O'real*—A French company that is a leader in the global cosmetics industry.
- *Nestlé*—A truly global consumer products company headquartered in Switzerland.
- *Reuters*—An information provider headquartered in the U.K.
- *Sony Corporation*—A major player in the global consumer electronics market.

TECHNOLOGY

- *Infineon Technologies*—Europe's number-one chip producer.
- *Kyocera*—A leader in semiconductor packaging and electronic components.
- *Nokia*—The global leader in wireless handsets.
- *Nortel Networks Corporation*—A Canadian-based leader in communications.
- *Vodaphone AirTouch, PLC*—The company that has the most mobile phone subscribers in the world.

While this is only a partial listing of the Great Companies International™, it provides the reader with a sense for the type of companies that are included in this portfolio. Interestingly, most of these companies easily passed our fifty years in business screen for the nontechnology companies and the fifteen-year technology screens. Of note are companies that have been in business over 150 years, like Barclay's, founded in 1736; Nestlé, 1843; and Reuters, 1849. Although these companies have been in business for years, they are still dynamic, growth-oriented companies. We believe that their ability to grow and change as the business environment changes will ensure that years from now these companies will still be in business and delivering great returns to shareholders.

ANALYZING IPOs

A third application of the Great Company strategy is to use the screens to assess IPOs (Initial Public Offerings). IPOs are the stocks of companies that for a variety of reasons have decided to sell stock in their companies to the investing public, and have filed and been approved to have their stock listed on an exchange. The Securities and Exchange Commission has established a comprehensive filing process for the listing of new securities. This process has been developed to protect the investing public from fraud or improper financial accounting by the company. All new issues must adhere to this process. The various stock exchanges have also developed listing requirements. Before a stock can be listed on an exchange, it must conform to the standards of the exchange.

While steps have been taken to protect investors from fraud, the investor must realize that IPOs are still risky investments. In most cases the IPOs are relatively young companies that are seeking capital for a variety of reasons. Furthermore, the investor must realize that it is very difficult for an individual investor to purchase the stock of a "hot" IPO. Frequently, the stocks of the best IPOs are sold to large institutional investors or favored clients of a brokerage firm, and the small investor does not have an opportunity to purchase these stocks until the price has dramatically increased. Studies have shown that purchasing an IPO shortly after it goes public can be dangerous, for many IPOs often underperform the market after the initial pricing euphoria subsides.

With these caveats in mind, as an investor you might still want to purchase IPOs. If you find yourself in this category, you should

use our Great Companies investing screen to analyze IPOs, as follows:

> *The company must be highly regarded by knowledgeable industry ex-
> perts and/or its customers.* Since the company may be virtually un-
> known to most analysts or investing experts, you should try to
> speak with some of the company's customers to learn what they
> think about the company. Is this a good company that is highly
> thought of by key customers, or is it a case of management want-
> ing to go public so they can cash in on their successes?
>
> *Each company must be headquartered in the United States.* At least
> you will be sure that steps have been taken to ensure that the
> company's filings are accurate.
>
> *Each Great IPO has a track record of outstanding growth and profits.*
> Many of the "hot" technology IPOs have never been profitable. I
> frankly don't know how to calculate the intrinsic value of a
> company that has never generated a profit. If the IPO doesn't
> have a track record of profit, you need to be aware that you are
> about to make an incredibly high-risk investment. If you are
> wondering just how much you can lose by investing in a stock
> that trades for $2, the answer is that you can lose all of your
> money. If you invest $10,000 in a $2 stock, you can lose
> $10,000. The optimism that surrounds IPOs can cost you all of
> your investment.
>
> *The company is in terrific businesses.* This is an absolutely critical
> screen. You must understand the business of the IPO and assess
> it using our list of qualities of a terrific business. If it doesn't mea-
> sure up, don't invest.
>
> *The Great IPO has powerful franchises that protect the company from
> competitors.* With an IPO you will need protection on all fronts. A
> successful IPO will have already established barriers. If there are
> no strong barriers, don't invest.
>
> *The management of these companies strongly believes that people are
> the company's most valuable asset.* Since the defection of key peo-
> ple can mean disaster for the IPO, you need to make sure that
> the management of the company is focused on its key people.
> This includes offering them stock options to ensure that they
> stay after the company goes public.

Innovation is a critical element of the Great IPO. This often determines the success of IPOs, so don't overlook this in your analysis.

An outstanding management team. Look for a team of managers who have been successful in other companies. If they have been successful in other companies that are in similar businesses, perhaps they can transfer that success to the IPO.

I am not against investing in IPOs. I merely want to caution you that IPOs bring a much higher level of risk than Great Companies do and therefore require in-depth analysis before investing. Don't purchase the IPO simply on the recommendation of your broker. *Do your homework before you invest.* Remember, your broker has a vested interest in selling you the IPO. Typically he is given a quota of IPOs to sell and is paid a significant commission for selling them. The odds are that if you are a small, individual investor and are being offered an IPO, it's not a Great IPO. Remember, never invest more in an IPO than you can afford to lose.

SHORTING BAD COMPANIES

Another application for the Great Companies screens is to use them in a way that is exactly the opposite of how they were intended to be used. A friend who is a very sophisticated investor uses the screens to locate bad companies that are overpriced. He screens for companies in bad businesses with no barriers that are trading at relatively high PE ratios. He then shorts these companies, waits until the price of the stock collapses, and sells them at a profit.

Warning! Shorting Stocks Could Be Hazardous to Your Wealth!!! Only the most sophisticated investors with the data and time required to develop these analyses should use the screens in this manner, and even these people should realize that this is a high-risk approach to investing that flies in the face of the Great Companies investing strategy. Therefore, I cannot endorse this approach, but felt it should be mentioned for those sophisticated investors who can tolerate risks associated with shorting stocks.

MANAGERS MAY USE THE SCREENS TO
EVALUATE THEIR OWN COMPANIES

While this book was never intended as a business management book, the screens can be used by managers to evaluate their companies from an investing perspective. Since starting the book, I have been asked by a number of friends and associates how their companies measure up to the Great Companies profile. After explaining the screens and the concept of Great Companies to them, I have helped several of them develop analyses of their companies. For many people, it's the first time they have really understood the strengths and weaknesses of the businesses they manage. While some have walked away depressed, most have been encouraged and developed an action plan for the future. I would suggest that you use the original screens to make this comparison. You can download a form from our website, http://www.greatcompanies.com, to use for your analysis.

One thing you should realize is that all the leaders of Great Companies that I interviewed followed a similar process after they took over the company. The first thing they did was get their management team in place; then they got rid of their bad businesses and focused their resources on building the good ones.

———

The Great Companies investing strategy has a number of different applications. The screens can be altered to produce an infinite number of portfolios based on your investing needs. As you adjust these screens, remember that your portfolio's risks will also change. Please note, the companies mentioned in this chapter have not been thoroughly analyzed and evaluated. Therefore, I cannot recommend them for purchase at this time. I am in the process of developing a Great Companies of the Future portfolio which should be finalized during 1999.

C h a p t e r 6

ALLOCATING YOUR FUNDS INTO A GREAT COMPANIES PORTFOLIO

———=◉=———

You have decided that investing in Great Companies makes sense. You plan to either add to your current position in Great Companies, convert a portion of your current portfolio into Great Companies or, if you are a new investor, begin by investing in Great Companies. Where should you start? How much should you invest in Great Companies?

In order to transfer some or all of your current portfolio into Great Companies or start a brand new Great Companies portfolio, you should follow this five-step process:

1. Determine the portfolio structure that meets your needs.
2. Classify your current holdings by management style.
3. Understand the importance of core investing strategies.
4. Analyze the funds and stocks that you own.
5. Develop an action plan for converting some portion of your portfolio to holdings in Great Companies.

STEP 1: DETERMINE THE PORTFOLIO STRUCTURE THAT BEST SUITS YOUR NEEDS

Thousands of individual plans have been developed, numerous articles have been written, hundreds of books published, and a variety of software programs developed that specialize in asset allocation. These individual investment plans recommend how to allocate your funds among stocks, bonds, cash, treasuries, etc. Normally, they recommend that older investors invest more of their assets in bonds and treasuries, and that younger investors allocate more to stocks. If you need help developing a financial plan or allocating your assets, I suggest that you see a financial planner, or conduct your own research. Once you have decided how much money you have to invest in stocks, you can follow the model presented in this section to implement the Great Companies allocation plan.

Traditional approaches to allocating the stock/equities portion of your portfolio suggest that you allocate your funds based on the following factors:

1. *Your investing mindset, or level of investing aggressiveness.* Some investors are comfortable holding a large percentage of their portfolios in higher risk, more aggressive stocks while others feel more comfortable following a more conservative style of investing. Individual preferences are driven by a variety of factors including age, income, years to retirement, expected returns, market conditions, and net worth.
2. *Diversification.* Traditional investment theories suggest that investors should diversify their holdings in an effort to minimize their risks. Since investing styles go in and out of favor, and it is impossible to predict when this shift will occur, traditional theories recommended that individuals invest some portion of their equities portfolio in all five investing styles: large-cap value, large-cap growth, small-cap value, small-cap growth, and international.

Under the traditional approach, a broker or financial planner might recommend that investors allocate the equities portion of their investments as follows:

Allocating Your Funds into a Great Companies Portfolio

	CONSERVATIVE	MODERATE	AGGRESSIVE
LARGE-CAP GROWTH (INCLUDES INDEX FUNDS)	25%	30%	40%
LARGE-CAP VALUE	60%	40%	15%
SMALL-CAP GROWTH	5%	10%	20%
SMALL-CAP VALUE	5%	10%	10%
INTERNATIONAL	5%	10%	15%
TOTAL	100%	100%	100%

This allocation model is pretty straightforward. Once you have identified the level of risk that you are comfortable with, you then allocate your holdings accordingly, realizing that some styles carry higher risks than others. The problem with this approach is that investing styles go in and out of favor. During 1996, 1997, and 1998, both large-cap growth and large-cap aggressive growth were in favor. Had you allocated your funds among all five styles, you would have underperformed the market in four of the five styles over the last three years.

Frankly, I believe that investors should adopt a plan that meets four criteria:

1. *Long Term.* The most successful investors that I have studied are long-term investors who don't enter and exit the market. Frankly, I have no idea, nor do I really care, what the market does during the next six or twelve months. If I knew that the market was going down 5 percent tomorrow, I wouldn't sell any of my holdings. I am confident that over the next ten years, the stock market will outperform all other investing options, and I want to fully participate in that rise.

2. *Conservative.* I believe in practicing what I call "sleep-at-night investing." I don't want to wake up at three o'clock in the morning wondering what my Internet stock, which is down 20 percent in the last two weeks, will do tomorrow. I want to go to sleep at night knowing that I own the stocks of the best companies in the world, and that while I am sleeping, the terrific managers in these companies who are located all over the world are doing

everything in their power to increase the value of their companies.

3. *Simplistic.* Forget about all of the complex strategies and computer models. The long-term investors who win will follow a simple, straightforward approach to investing.

4. *Proven.* I want my money invested in a strategy that has been proven over time, and that performs well in a variety of market conditions. I believe that one of the advantages of the Great Companies strategy is its reliance upon all three traditional investing strategies: growth, value, and indexing. This helps ensure that the strategy performs well across a wide variety of market conditions.

A recent study sponsored by Charles Schwab & Co. suggested that investors should invest a portion of their net worth in index funds. The study also suggested that investors place a portion of their net worth in managed funds. The authors note that "there are specific blends of index funds and so-called actively managed funds that have the best chance of accomplishing a goal held by many investors: maximizing the risk of lagging behind the market, while increasing the probability of outperforming it."

For many investors indexing with the Great Companies portfolios will provide the balance they seek. Others may want to invest in index funds as well as the Great Companies portfolios. Investors may participate in indexing via mutual funds or through stocks offered by the American Stock Exchange. Mutual index funds operate like traditional mutual funds, since you purchase shares in a fund that tracks the index of your choice. The stocks offered by the American Stock Exchange, SPDRs, ticker SPY (which tracks S&P 500 index), and DJIA Diamonds, ticker DIA (which mirrors the Dow Jones Industrial Average), trade like stocks. Investors can place stop limit orders, buy shares on margin, and short these stocks as a hedge. Since there are advantages and disadvantages to both index funds and stocks, investors should consider both options before investing.

Structuring your portfolio around indexing and Great Companies should meet the investing objectives of most investors. Aggressive investors should allocate more money to Great Companies and less to indexing and should allocate more to the Great Companies Technology, a more aggressive portfolio, than Great Companies of America, a more conservative portfolio.

This model should serve as a guide as you begin to plan your portfolio. You may need to change the ratios slightly so that they fit your unique and specific needs, but don't get too creative. Remember, your goal is to keep investing simple.

STEP 2: UNDERSTAND WHAT YOU OWN, CLASSIFY YOUR CURRENT PORTFOLIO BY MANAGEMENT STYLE

Investors who own stocks, mutual funds, or hedge funds should begin the Great Companies conversion process by classifying their current holdings by management style.

A study presented by William Sharpe in the *Journal of Portfolio Management* in 1992 revealed that the fund universe can be divided into six basic styles of investing. Funds include:

1. *Small-cap growth*—invest in the stocks of small-cap companies that are expected to grow faster than the industry average and the overall market.
2. *Small-cap value*—consist of stocks of small-cap companies that are trading at a discount relative to their value.
3. *Large-cap growth*—hold the stocks of large companies that are expected to outgrow the industry average.
4. *Large-cap value*—are composed of stocks of large companies that are trading below their perceived values.
5. *Foreign funds*—invest in stocks of companies that are headquartered outside the United States.
6. *Fixed-income funds*—typically invest in bonds or money-market funds that generate income.
7. *Index funds*—these funds are really growth funds, but because of the popularity of index funds, and the tremendous share of the investing dollars now allocated to them, I have allowed for a separate classification.

Some mutual fund companies combine styles to produce hybrid funds. For example, by combining the stocks of companies that pay high dividends with those that are growth oriented, a growth-and-income fund is produced.

As a first step, you need to group the funds that you own into six of these categories (we have not included the fixed-income fund classification since our focus is on stocks rather than bonds). Be aware that this classification may not be as straightforward as it appears.

Classifying mutual funds and managed accounts is complicated by the following factors:

- *Some fund companies mislabel funds.* Knowing that investors measure a fund against its peers in a category, the fund company might label a growth fund a growth-and-income fund in hopes that it will outperform all other growth-and-income-funds during a particular time period. *Worth* magazine noted in March 1995 that "In 1994 Warburg Pincus's Growth and Income fund was the fourth best performer among the 387 growth and income funds tracked by Morningstar, Inc. Investors received a handsome 7.6 percent total return in a year that saw the average growth and income fund decline 1.4 percent in value. What's more, Warburg Pincus returned 17.18 percent on average in each of the last three years—good enough to place second in its category over that period. The only flaw in this apparently flawless investment was revealed in an interesting qualification from a Morningstar analyst in Morningstar's annual rankings. The Warburg Pincus fund, said analyst Adam Wright, wasn't a staid growth and income operation at all, but rather an 'aggressive-growth fund in disguise.' In fact, the fund achieved its impressive record by investing in low-dividend, high-risk stocks . . ." The article goes on to state that two major research studies "concluded that more than half of all mutual funds are misclassified in performance rankings. And more than one out of ten is listed inaccurately enough that investors could be misled about [its] true nature . . ." Fund companies misclassify funds because high-performing funds within a classification attract huge cash inflows from investors, and this translates into profits for the mutual fund company. It reminds me of the old Wall Street axiom "The best way to win a contest for the largest tomato is to paint a cantaloupe red."

- *It's difficult to know how a fund really operates.* Since funds are required to report their holdings only twice a year, you get a snapshot of a fund's holdings on only two out of 365 days. It is virtually impossible for even knowledgeable investors to determine how a fund operates with such limited information.
- *Funds often change over time.* I have observed numerous examples of high-performing, successful small-cap funds that attracted so much new money from investors that the nature of the fund changed. Frequently, the managers of successful small-cap funds begin investing in more mid-cap and large-cap stocks because there are not enough small-cap companies in which to invest.

You can began to differentiate funds that are growth oriented from those that are value oriented by examining the stocks that they hold. Typically, growth-oriented funds will own stocks of companies that are in growing industries, have strong market positions, are growing faster than the industry, and have strong management. On the other hand, value-oriented funds own stocks of companies that have low price-earnings ratios, have been neglected or frequently criticized, and have not kept pace with their industry. The "Dogs of the Dow" is an example of a large-cap value strategy.

You can also utilize software developed by Advisors Software to classify funds into investing styles. You can look up the investing style of a number of funds at no cost by connecting to the following website: http://www.advisorsw.com.

Once you have completed your style analysis, you can use the following worksheet to classify the mutual funds that you own.

Mutual Funds

| MUTUAL FUNDS | U.S. SMALL-CAP | | U.S. LARGE-CAP | | FOREIGN | INDEX |
	GROWTH	VALUE	GROWTH	VALUE	FUNDS	FUNDS
_____	$____	$____	$____	$____	$____	$____
_____	____	____	____	____	____	____
_____	____	____	____	____	____	____
Totals	$____	$____	$____	$____	$____	$____

Next, you need to classify stocks that you hold in the same manner that you classified mutual funds. Use the following guidelines to classify the stocks in your portfolio.

- *Growth Stocks.* These include companies that are in growing industries, have strong market positions, are growing faster than the industry, and have strong management. Companies like Coca-Cola, General Electric, Gillette, Microsoft, and Cisco Systems are classified as growth stocks.
- *Value Stocks.* These stocks include companies that have low price-earnings ratios, have been neglected or frequently criticized, and may not have kept pace with their industry. At this writing this would include stocks like Phillip Morris (typically undervalued because of its exposure in tobacco), General Motors, and International Paper.
- *Market Caps.* This is determined by multiplying the shares outstanding by the closing price. Number of shares outstanding can be obtained from annual reports, America Online, a broker, or any number of other sources. Generally, stocks with market caps over $5 billion are considered to be large-cap stocks. For our analysis, stocks with market caps below $5 billion will be considered small-cap stocks.

Stocks

STOCKS	U.S. SMALL-CAP GROWTH	VALUE	U.S. LARGE-CAP GROWTH	VALUE	FOREIGN	TOTAL
_____	$____	$____	$____	$____	$____	$____
_____	____	____	____	____	____	____
_____	____	____	____	____	____	____
Totals	$____	$____	$____	$____	$____	$____

Using the previous two forms, complete the following form to determine your total stock portfolio holdings.

Total Portfolio

	U.S. SMALL-CAP GROWTH	VALUE	U.S. LARGE-CAP GROWTH	VALUE	FOREIGN HOLDINGS	INDEX HOLDINGS	TOTAL
TOTAL	$____	$____	$____	$____	$____	$____	$____
PERCENT OF TOTAL	____%	____%	____%	____%	____%		100%

You have now completed the first step of the transition process.

STEP 3: UNDERSTAND THE IMPORTANCE OF CORE INVESTING STRATEGIES

Traditional asset allocation models tend to overlook the importance of an investing strategy. The implication of these models is that if you are invested in large-cap stocks and small-cap stocks, you have sufficiently diversified your portfolio and are therefore minimizing your risks. While diversification among stocks of various market caps is important, it's not enough. It is vitally important that investors also diversify among core investing strategies. Having two core strategies provides a level of diversification that is adequate for most investors.

Core strategies should form the basis on which your wealth is built. They differ from non-core investing strategies because they exhibit certain very important qualities:

- *Proven over time.* Most importantly, a core strategy is time tested. You should examine portfolio performance over at least a five- and ten-year period. Don't fall for the "newest" strategy or the "hottest" money manager. Seek out core strategies that have endured the test of time across a variety of market cycles.
- *Consistent.* The best core strategies are based on screens/criteria that are consistent. While these screens may be occasionally fine tuned for subtle market changes, they should endure over time. This ensures a consistent investing approach, a key for long-term investing success.
- *Low risk.* While the core strategy should outperform the indexes, it should also protect your capital. Remember that your core strategy will represent a significant portion of your net worth, and you want to use a strategy that effectively manages risks. You can determine risk by measuring the standard deviation of the portfolio.
- *Understandable.* You must be able to understand the core strategy. If you don't understand it, don't use the strategy. Also, don't use "black box" investing strategies that sound sophisticated and are being used by "everyone" for a core strategy. Likewise, if a money manager won't take the time to explain a core strategy to you in detail, don't use the manager.
- *Logical.* If the core strategy doesn't sound right to you—if it doesn't make sense—stay away from it. Whenever I have encountered a money manager with a complex strategy that doesn't hang together, I have found over time that the manager is using a flawed strategy.
- *Diversification.* Core strategies should provide diversification among the stocks in the portfolio. The Great Companies portfolio includes stocks from four different industry sectors that move in different ways.
- *Tax efficient.* Core strategies should deliver index-beating, tax-efficient returns. The key measure of performance is how much money you have left over after taxes.

Additionally, you might consider the following criteria:

- *Socially responsible.* More and more investors are not purchasing the stocks of companies that produce tobacco or alcohol or pollute the environment. You might want to add this criterion to your core strategy.
- *International exposure.* Many investors seek to hold stocks of American companies that generate overseas revenues in their core portfolios. Owning these stocks allows the investor to purchase U.S. stocks, but participate in the growth of international markets.

The Great Companies strategy meets the criteria of a core investing strategy. Strategies that fail to meet these criteria are not core investing strategies. I believe that you should invest a large portion of your actively traded portfolio in stocks or funds that meet the criteria of proven core investing strategies.

To help you envision your strategic allocation plan for your portfolio, I have developed the following model:

In this particular model, the Great Companies Strategy is shown as a core investing strategy and includes the three different portfolios that were detailed in chapter 5—the Great Companies of America, the Great Companies Technology, and the Great Companies International. As we discussed in chapter 5, these three portfolios are based on the Great Companies investing strategy but consist of the stocks of different companies. These strategies are classified as follows:

- *Great Companies America*—Large-Cap Domestic Growth
- *Great Companies Technology*—Large-Cap Aggressive Domestic Growth
- *Great Companies International*—Large-Cap Growth

Ideally, the investor should identify at least one other core strategy that meets the core strategy criteria. Since the Great Companies strategy is growth oriented, the investor might want to consider a core strategy that is value oriented. I am developing a Great Business, Great Value Strategy. The key is to build the bulk of your stock portfolio on these core strategies.

STEP 4: ANALYZE THE MUTUAL FUNDS AND THE INDIVIDUAL STOCKS THAT YOU OWN

Mutual Fund Analysis

Once you have classified your funds by management style and defined your core strategies, you need to understand the investing strategy of each manager who manages funds in your portfolio. During this phase of your analysis, you should consider the following:

1. *What is the fund manager's investing strategy?* You may find that the strategy you thought the manager was following is not being used. You might also be surprised to find that the manager has a difficult time clearly articulating the fund's investing strategy. In answering this question, you need to determine:
   - If the manager really has an investing strategy or operates as a "stock picker" (stock pickers simply pick stocks that they believe will outperform the market without a particular strategy as a guide).

- If the manager is disciplined and follows the strategy over time.
- If the manager is focused on sound investing strategies or tries all the latest fads.
- If the manager times the market (sells if she believes the market will drop).
- If the manager relies on one strategy or uses a combination of strategies.

2. *What is the manager's stock selection process?* Specifically, you need to understand the specific screens that the manager uses before purchasing a particular stock (his version of the twelve screens that we used in evaluating Great Companies). By understanding the manager's investment process, you can determine if the manager is buying companies or simply purchasing stocks.

3. *What is the process that the manager follows when selling a stock?* The manager should follow a disciplined process when either buying or selling a stock. This process should be understandable and logical. Don't fall for a "black box" discussion that centers around a computer and a bunch of formulas or calculations that make absolutely no sense to you.

4. *Has the strategy been proven over time in a variety of market cycles?* You should examine how the fund performed in both up and down market cycles. A sound core strategy will perform well in virtually any market situation.

5. *How tax efficient is the fund?* Total returns less taxes paid equals tax-adjusted returns. Tax-adjusted returns are important, because this is the real rate of return that goes into your pocket. Investors can calculate tax-adjusted returns by dividing tax-adjusted returns by total returns to determine tax efficiency. For example, a $20,000 investment in a mutual fund increases 20 percent during the year for a gain of $4,000. However, you must pay $2,000 in taxes on your fund. If you subtract the $2,000 in taxes from the total return of $4,000, the tax-adjusted return is $2,000. If you divide the tax-adjusted return of $2,000 by the total return, you realize that 50 percent of your gains must be paid in taxes. Obviously, this is not a tax-efficient fund. Since mutual-fund companies earn fees based on funds under management, and since it is difficult to determine how tax efficient a fund really is, there is

no incentive for a manager to manage a tax-efficient fund. The manager is driven to produce high returns, since high total returns, not tax-adjusted returns, are what most investors consider when investing in a mutual fund. Since the Great Companies strategy holds stocks for the long term and is composed of growth-oriented stocks that pay relatively low dividends, it is highly tax efficient.

6. *What is the risk-and-return level of the fund?* Funds with high standard deviations don't always produce above-average results. In fact, what you are seeking is a fund with a low standard deviation and a high rate of return. Morningstar reports standard deviations for funds. You should examine the standard deviation at the same time you look at returns.

Once you have addressed these questions, you can determine if the fund's strategy is compatible with your core investing strategies.

Obtaining answers to these questions won't be easy. You may need to search a number of places including the prospectuses of mutual funds, Morningstar reports, *Mutual Funds* magazine, *Money* magazine, *Worth*, and other publications to find answers to your questions. You might also consult *Investment Gurus* by Peter J. Tanous. This book consists of interviews with money managers and focuses on the investing strategies used by these managers. The book provides interesting insights into the world of money management, and may offer up some ideas on other core investing strategies that you should consider.

Ultimately, you will also need to contact the mutual fund directly. It's important to take the time to understand how the manager operates, for this is key to your financial future. It amazes me that people seem to spend more time analyzing TV sets before purchasing one than they do when investing in stocks and mutual funds.

The following form should be used to classify the mutual funds that you own. For each criterion, you should fill in a score ranging from one to ten, with ten being excellent and one being poor.

MUTUAL FUND	SCORE 1-10

Proven Over Time   _____
   1 Never beaten the relevant index
   10 Outperforms in a variety of market conditions

Consistent Performance   _____
   1 Up and down performance
   10 Consistently outperforms the market

Low Risk   _____
   1 High standard deviation
   10 Low standard deviation

Comprehensible investing strategy   _____
   1 Complex and confusing
   10 Easily understood

Logical approach   _____
   1 Doesn't make sense
   10 The logic is sound

Diversification   _____
   1 The stocks are concentrated in one sector or industry
   10 The stocks represent at least three industries that
      don't move in tandem

Tax efficient   _____
   1 At the end of the year over 40% of my gains are taxable
   10 Taxable gains are below 10%

Cost effective   _____
   1 Management expenses are above 2%
   10 Management expenses are below 1%

Socially responsible (optional)   _____
   1 The fund holds stocks of tobacco companies,
      alcoholic beverage companies, etc.
   10 The fund owns stocks of socially responsible companies

Total score (add totals from each line and divide by 9)   _____

Please note that we have marked "socially responsible" as optional. Some investors feel that socially responsible investing is very important, while others don't. Funds that score below 6 should be considered for liquidation.

Individual Stocks

For individual stocks that you hold in your portfolio, you should address the following questions:

1. *What does the company do?* If you don't know, you shouldn't own the stock. I believe that one of the most important factors in evaluating a company is the types of businesses in which the company is engaged. If the company is in a bad business, you shouldn't own the stock. The qualities of a good business are discussed in detail in chapter 3.

2. *Why do I own the stock?* If you can't answer this question in one simple paragraph, you need to rethink your position in the stock. Remember, you should be investing in companies, not stocks. If you can't explain in some detail why a stock represents a good company that you should own, you shouldn't purchase the stock.

3. *Does the company fit with my core investing strategies?* By now you have determined the core investing strategies that you will be following. If this stock doesn't fit with those strategies, you should consider selling the stock. The more disciplined you become in your stock selection process, the better your returns will be.

You can further assess the large-cap growth stocks you own against the screens in chapter 5. For assessing domestic large-cap growth stocks against the Great Companies use the first screens on page 221. For companies in your portfolio that have been in business less than fifty years, use the Great Companies Technology screens found on page 223. International stocks you own should be measured against the screens for Great Companies International on page 226. Large-cap stocks that don't meet the criteria and other stocks you own that no longer fit with your investing strategies should be considered for liquidation.

Once you have completed your analysis of the funds and stocks in your portfolio, you should complete the following worksheet.

	U.S. SMALL-CAP		U.S. LARGE-CAP				
	GROWTH	VALUE	GROWTH	VALUE	FOREIGN	INDEX	TOTAL
Mutual Funds to Keep	$ _____	$ _____	$ _____	$ _____	$ _____	$ _____	$ _____
Stocks to Keep	_____	_____	_____	_____	_____	_____	_____
Subtotal	_____	_____	_____	_____	_____	_____	_____
Mutual Funds to Sell	_____	_____	_____	_____	_____	_____	_____
Stocks to Sell	_____	_____	_____	_____	_____	_____	_____
Subtotal	_____	_____	_____	_____	_____	_____	_____
Totals	_____	_____	_____	_____	_____	_____	_____

STEP 5: DEVELOP AN ACTION PLAN

During this phase of the transition process you should develop an action plan for modifying your current portfolio structure and converting your existing portfolio into one that includes the Great Companies investing strategy. Use the following form to develop your personal transition plan.

Great Companies Transition Plan

Funds to Invest in Stocks $_____

	PORTFOLIO ALLOCATION	FUNDS TO INVEST BY STYLE	STOCKS/FUNDS TO KEEP	ADDITIONAL INVESTMENT
INDEX FUNDS				
S&P 500	_____%	$_____	– $ _____	= $ _____
NASDAQ	_____%	$_____	– $ _____	= $ _____
INTERNATIONAL	_____%	$_____	– $ _____	= $ _____
LARGE-CAP GROWTH				
GREAT COMPANIES (AMERICA)	_____%	$_____	– $ _____	= $ _____

GREAT COMPANIES (FUTURE)	____%	$_____	– $ _____	= $_____
LARGE-CAP VALUE GREAT BUSINESS, GREAT VALUE	____%	$_____	– $ _____	= $_____
SMALL-CAP GROWTH	____%	$_____	– $ _____	= $_____
SMALL-CAP VALUE	____%	$_____	– $ _____	= $_____
INTERNATIONAL GREAT COMPANIES (INTERNATIONAL)	____%	$_____	– $ _____	= $_____
TOTAL	____%	$_____	– $ _____	= $_____

At the top of the form, insert the amount of money that you plan to invest in stocks and mutual funds. Next enter the percentage of your portfolio to be allocated to each style under the column titled Portfolio Allocation. Now multiply the percentage to be allocated within each style times the money that you plan to invest in equities. For example, if you have $50,000 to invest in stocks, and your index fund allocation is 20 percent, you would enter $10,000 in the column titled "Funds to Invest by Style" ($50,000 × 20% = $10,000). Next, enter the stocks and funds that you own and plan to keep in your portfolio by style segment. For example, if you own SPDRs (Standard & Poor's Depository Receipts) or an index fund worth $5,000, you should enter the $5,000 in the column titled "Stocks/Funds to Keep." Finally, subtract the total of the stock funds to keep from the funds to invest and enter that amount in the column titled "Additional Investment." Keeping with our example, you would subtract $5,000 (stocks/funds to keep) from $10,000 (funds to invest by style). This results in an additional $5,000 that needs to be invested in index funds. Upon completing this form, you will know how much money you need to invest altogether in each style, how much money is already invested, and how much new money needs to be invested in order to achieve your plan.

You should now begin developing a plan for liquidating the funds and stocks you own that no longer fit your needs. As you begin to liquidate your current holdings, you should keep the following in mind.

- *You may owe taxes on some of the funds or stocks that you sell.* Be sure to consider how much you owe before you begin reinvesting. This will ensure that you have enough money to pay taxes and don't have to sell stocks to come up with the cash.
- *A number of mutual funds make dividend payments during the October–November period.* If you purchase any of these funds during this time period, you may well have to pay taxes on them.
- *You are implementing a long-term investment plan.* Try not to become distracted by short-term events that are occurring in the market.

———

By completing the steps outlined in this chapter, you have developed a transition plan for investing some or all of your portfolio in Great Companies. The next chapter will present various investing alternatives.

Chapter 7

Do I Need a Broker?
Five Investing Options
for a Great Companies
Portfolio

———«◦»———

In chapter 6 you developed your portfolio allocation plan and evaluated your current stock and mutual-fund holdings. You now know which stocks or mutual funds you should sell and which ones you should keep. The next step is to begin investing so that the Great Companies portfolios are aligned with your allocation plan. In some cases, your investment in Great Companies will be made in a lump sum, while in other cases you will add to your position over time. There are five options to choose from when investing in stocks. First, I will provide an overview of the five options, then provide guidelines for investing in the Great Companies. I have arranged these investing options by minimum investment required:

OPTIONS	INVESTMENT MINIMUMS*
Direct Purchase	$50–$1,000
Broker	$500
Mutual Fund	$2,000–$5,000
Managed Account	$100,000–$250,000
Hedge Fund	$250,000–$500,000

*Note: In certain cases investment minimums may be much higher for a specific fund or stock. For example, the minimum investment in Long Term Capital was $10 million, and Brandywine Fund, a mutual fund, has a $25,000 minimum. The investment minimums shown in the chart are representative of the option, but specific requirements may be higher.

We will now examine each of these investing options in detail.

DIRECT PURCHASE

Increasingly, investors who want to manage their own portfolios, and who want to purchase stocks at the lowest possible cost, are considering direct-purchase programs, which allow investors to buy shares of a company's stock in much the same way that a no-load mutual fund is purchased. The investor contacts the company (or transfer agent) and requests an application form and prospectus. Enrollment forms may also be obtained at websites including www.netstockdirect.com, www.noloadstocks.com, and www.enrolldirect.com. The initial investment is made by returning the completed form or registering online and sending payment directly to the company. After making an initial purchase, the investor can make additional purchases directly from the company. Fees are quite low and normally include a one-time enrollment fee for new investors, which typically ranges from five to ten dollars. Nominal fees are also charged for purchasing and selling the stock.

Direct-purchase plans have increased in popularity, rising from only 52 companies offering direct-purchase plans at the end of 1994 to over 500 companies in 1998. Direct-purchase plans are definitely the least expensive way to buy stocks, but they are not offered by all companies. In fact, at the close of 1998 only three of the fourteen Great Companies offered a direct stock-purchase program:

COMPANY	PHONE	NEW INVESTOR MINIMUM
General Electric	(800) 786-2543	$250
Gillette	(888) 218-2841	$1,000
Merck	(800) 831-8248	$350

Since it is impossible to purchase the shares of all Great Companies on a direct basis, you will need to choose from among several other investing alternatives. If you are interested in direct-stock purchases, you might want to read the book *Buying Stock Without a Broker* by Charles Carlson.

STOCKBROKERS

The term "broker" is simply another name for a dealer or agent who functions as a go-between in the buying and selling of stocks and bonds. Brokers receive fees in the form of commissions for the services that they provide. Over the years, three different classifications have emerged for stockbrokers, based on the services they provide and their fee structures:

1. Traditional, full-service brokers
2. Discount brokers
3. Deep discount/Internet brokers

Until the 1970s traditional, full-service, full-commission stockbrokers were the only type of broker in existence. They recommended stocks to clients, provided personal investing advice, and earned commissions based on buying and selling securities for their clients. Today, full-service brokers like PaineWebber, Shearson Lehman Brothers, Prudential-Bache, and Merrill Lynch also conduct research studies on companies, host investment seminars for clients, offer financial-planning services, and even provide tax consulting services in addition to issuing buy and sell recommendations.

Over the last few years, a new breed of full-service broker has emerged, the managed-accounts broker. These brokers select money managers for investors and earn their commissions based on "wrap fees." The wrap fee is a flat fee that is calculated as a percentage of the portfolio value. For example, if you had $200,000 in your account and a 1.5% wrap fee, you would pay $3,000 per year ($200,000 × 1.5% = $3,000) regardless of the number of trades your account had during the course of the year. The wrap fee ensures the investor that commissions will not exceed a certain percentage of the portfolio value. Managed-accounts brokers seek to find unique investing approaches for their clients that outperform mutual funds. Typically, these brokers also sell mutual funds, bonds, and other financial instruments.

Discount brokers like Jack White and Charles Schwab are relative newcomers to the brokerage scene. These firms offer limited advice but do provide various services including checking accounts, credit cards, and individual retirement accounts. They also place buy and sell orders twenty-four hours per day, and charge lower fees than the traditional, full-service broker. They will execute stock trades, sell bonds, provide monthly client statements, trade mutual funds, and provide other services. *Smart Money* magazine annually evaluates the services performed by a number of discount brokers in its annual review. If you don't have a discount broker, or are unhappy with the one you are using, you should read *Smart Money*'s review. The July 1998 issue ranked the top five discount brokers as follows:

How the Discount Brokers Stack Up

OVERALL RANK	BROKER	TOLL-FREE NUMBER
1	Waterhouse Securities	(800) 934-4410
2	Jack White	(800) 233-3411
3	Muriel Siebert	(800) 872-0666
4	Charles Schwab	(800) 435-4000
5	Quick & Reilly	(800) 262-2688

Source: *Smart Money*, July 1998, p. 89.

With the growth of the Internet, a new breed of broker referred to as the online, Internet, or web broker, has emerged. Most online brokers have only been in business since 1995 or 1996, but this service is experiencing explosive growth. Online brokers provide limited services like real-time quotes, real-time account information, a variety of investment products online, and a wide range of research links. Their low commission structures—some companies charge less than $10 per trade—are especially attractive to active investors. Investors must have access to a computer in order to use these services, for Internet brokers provide virtually no personal contact. *Smart Money* ranked the top online brokers in its February 1998 issue:

Online Broker Ratings

OVERALL RANK	FIRM	WEBSITE ADDRESS
1	Discover Brokerage Direct	www.discoverbrokerage.com
2	Datek Online	www.datek.online
3	Waterhouse Securities	www.waterhouse.com
4	Charles Schwab	www.schwab.com
5	Fidelity	www.fidelity.com

Source: *Smart Money*, February 1998, p. 116

I would strongly encourage you to read each *Smart Money* issue in which discount and online brokers are ranked. The articles provide a wealth of information about these firms.

As with anything, there are pros and cons to the various types of brokers. Investors who want regular access to investment professionals should consider full-service brokers; however, it is important to realize that the broker is really a salesperson whose income depends on commissions. Full-service brokers may discourage investors from placing their funds in buy-and-hold strategies like the Great Companies since the portfolio seldom trades and, as a result, the strategy does not generate significant commissions for the broker. Rather than tell you that they don't like buy-and-hold strategies because these strategies reduce their commissions, they will say that buy-and-hold strategies never work.

Investors who know which stocks they want to own, who do not need outside advice, and who want to manage their own portfolios often turn to either discount or online brokers. These investors feel that they don't need the counsel of brokers because they make their own buy and sell decisions. Increasingly, many of them have one full-service broker and one discount broker that they trade with. This dual structure gives investors access to research data and market insight but also enables them to execute trades at low costs.

MUTUAL FUNDS

Many investors who want an investment professional to manage their holdings in stocks and bonds have turned to mutual funds. Mutual funds own the stocks of other companies and charge investors a fee for investing their money in stocks or bonds. A mutual fund is a state-chartered public corporation that invests in a portfolio of assets. Like any corporation, it has a board of directors and shareholders who own the assets of the company. When you invest in a mutual fund, you are buying shares in a company.

There are two types of mutual funds. Open-end funds sell shares throughout the life of the company and are the most popular funds with investors. Closed-end funds issue a fixed number of shares and are typically sold at a discount. Funds may be further categorized as active or passive. Index funds, which are designed to mirror stock indexes like the S&P 500 or the Dow Jones Industrial Average, are passively managed funds. Index fund managers do not make decisions on which individual stocks to buy and sell. The fund manager simply mirrors the changes in the relevant index. Conversely, the managers of actively managed funds decide which stocks to buy and sell, when to trade, and how the portfolio should be structured. They are actively involved in the management of the fund.

Funds are subject to very rigid control by the federal Securities and Exchange Commission. Additionally, every state where the fund is sold has regulations with which the fund must comply. The fund's prospectus reveals many of its features, including the objective of the fund, its expenses, relevant performance data, and the names of its managers, and in general explains how the fund operates. The prospectus should be carefully studied before investing in a fund.

Mutual funds may be further classified as either load funds (a fee is charged to purchase the fund) or no-load funds (there is no fee). Load fees may be charged at the time the fund is purchased or at the time it is sold. Load funds are sold by brokers who receive a commission (all or part of the load) for selling the fund to investors. If you were to buy $10,000 in a fund with a 4 percent front-end load, this would mean a payment of $400 in fees ($10,000 × 4% = $400). A 10 percent rise in the fund during the first year would amount to a $1,000 paper profit, but your actual return would be only $600 (6%) after you deduct the $400 load. The American Association of Individual Investors reports that funds with loads, on average, consistently underperform no-load funds when the load is taken into consideration in performance calculations *(Individual Investor's Guide to Low-Load Mutual Funds)*. I believe that investors are much better off researching funds on their own and purchasing no-load funds that meet their investment needs than buying load funds.

Mutual funds charge investors a fee for managing the fund. This fee is normally expressed as a percent of funds under management and ranges from a low of 0.3 percent on index funds to over 2 percent on actively managed funds. Additionally, some funds have 12b-1 plans which allow the fund manager to use the fund's assets to pay expenses like advertising and brokers' commissions. The combination of front-end loads, high management fees, and 12b-1 plans may have a significant impact on an investor's returns. The more progressive funds are aware that investors consider fee expenses during the fund-selection process and closely monitor the fees they charge.

The value of a mutual fund, calculated at the end of each trading day, is composed of the assets held less expenses and liabilities. The fund's value is quoted as its NAV (Net Asset Value) and represents the price of one share of the fund. This is the figure that you see quoted in the financial pages.

No-load mutual funds may be purchased either directly from the fund or from a mutual fund "supermarket." The American Association of Individual Investors published a list of mutual fund supermarkets in its September 1998 journal [members of AAII receive this journal at no extra charge (800) 428-2244]. According to the study, fund supermarkets offering the greatest number of no-transaction-fee funds were as follows:

Individual Investor's Guide to
Mutual Fund Supermarkets

BROKER	NO. OF NO-LOAD NO-TRANSACTION-FEE FUNDS OFFERED	PHONE NUMBER
Charles Schwab	1,452	(800) 435-4000
Jack White & Company	1,312	(800) 233-3411
Bush Burns Securities	1,020	(800) 821-4803
Waterhouse Securities	1,010	(800) 934-4443
Muriel Siebert	1,001	(800) 872-0666

Source: American Association of Individual Investors, September 1998

Investors who are making large purchases in a fund may prefer using a broker who offers a fund supermarket, since the broker provides the investor with a monthly statement of the fund's value as well as a number of funds to choose from, and makes it easy to sell the fund.

Mutual funds come in virtually every "flavor" imaginable. There are aggressive-growth funds, growth funds, small-company funds, international funds, fixed-income funds, money-market funds, equity-income funds, index funds, funds of funds (composed of several mutual funds), short-term bond funds, municipal bond funds, and international bond funds. The variety of funds available allows investors to diversify their portfolios.

Huge mutual-fund companies have emerged that manage and market a broad variety of mutual funds. Companies like Fidelity, Franklin Resources, and Vanguard manage billions of dollars for investors. These fund families have come to dominate the mutual-fund landscape.

The advantages of mutual funds for the investor include:

- *Low costs.* Mutual funds offer investors the opportunity to have a professional manage their investments at relatively low cost.
- *Variety of investment approaches.* There are literally thousands of mutual funds in which to invest, ranging from micro-cap domestic funds using a value approach to large-cap foreign funds using a growth strategy. Some of the funds are managed by individuals,

while others are managed by investment teams. Some funds offer concentrated portfolios, while index funds hold hundreds of stocks.

- *Diversification.* Many mutual funds own a broad group of securities, which provide the diversification that only a large portfolio can offer.
- *Regulated.* Since mutual funds are tightly regulated, they offer the investor some degree of protection from fraud.
- *Liquidation.* It is easy to liquidate your holdings in mutual funds. A simple phone call to the broker or to the fund is all that is required.
- *Performance tracking.* It is easy to track the progress of mutual funds you own. All financial journals and many daily newspapers list the NAV for many mutual funds each trading day.
- *Low minimum investment.* Since most funds require a low minimum investment, they are readily available to many investors. With an initial investment of as little as $2,000, an investor can own a broad portfolio of stocks.

The primary negatives of mutual funds are as follows:

- *Dilution.* As highly successful funds establish a successful track record, huge sums of money are invested in them. Typically this hurts fund performance and often changes the nature of the fund. This is especially a problem in small-cap and mid-cap funds.
- *Awareness of holdings.* The investor has no control over which stocks are purchased and often does not know what stocks are owned by the fund. Since mutual funds are required to publish their holdings only twice each year, and many funds turn their portfolios two to three times each year, investors may not know which stocks the fund owns at a given point in time.
- *Redemptions.* Other investors who sell their shares of the fund during market declines can negatively impact the fund's performance. Fund managers may have to sell some of the fund's stocks to raise the cash needed to redeem shares of the fund that other investors want to sell. Most fund managers try to maintain an adequate cash

balance for redeeming shares, but during steep market declines and mass redemptions, the cash held by the fund may not be sufficient to meet redemption requirements.

The mutual fund industry has grown dramatically over the past few years, and today mutual funds play an important role in the portfolios of many investors. Since the mutual fund business has become so complex and dynamic, we have only covered it from a top-line standpoint. If you want to know more about mutual funds, I suggest that you read the book *Building Wealth With Mutual Funds* by John H. Taylor. This book contains a wealth of information about investing in mutual funds. Additionally, Morningstar, a mutual fund research company (800-735-0700), provides potential investors with mutual fund performance ratings. *The Individual Investor's Guide to Low-Load Mutual Funds*, published by the American Association of Individual Investors, also contains information about the performance of specific mutual funds. This directory is updated annually (800-428-2244).

At this time, I am not offering a mutual fund of the Great Companies of America because of the restrictions placed on a concentrated mutual fund. We do offer an individually managed portfolio which I believe offers investors a number of advantages not found in mutual funds. Please check our website at http://www.greatcompanies.com for details.

INDIVIDUALLY MANAGED ACCOUNTS

If you have over $100,000 to invest, you might consider investing in an individually managed account. These are accounts that are established in the investor's name and held by a brokerage firm. The buy and sell decisions for the account are managed by a professional money manager rather than a stockbroker.

Individually managed accounts utilize a hybrid structure that is a cross between a brokerage account and a mutual fund. The investor's funds are placed in a brokerage account; however, a professional money manager (like a mutual fund's portfolio manager), rather than the broker, decides which stocks to buy and which stocks to sell. The money manager directs the broker on how to trade the account, and the broker executes the orders.

Individually managed accounts tend to function as follows:

1. An investor appoints a money manager and places money in an account with a stockbroker.
2. The money manager tells the broker which stocks, and how many shares, to purchase. The broker then executes the orders.
3. The investor receives a monthly statement from the broker listing the account's holdings, the value of the holdings, and trades that were made during the past month. Many brokers also provide a quarterly analysis of the managed account's performance relative to meaningful benchmarks.
4. The money manager typically sends investors a monthly or quarterly newsletter highlighting changes in the account and the market that may impact future investment moves. The manager may also conduct conference calls with investors, and is typically available to answer investor questions.

For this service, the investor pays a fee to the money manager based on the value of the portfolio. Typically, money managers charge 1 percent for funds under management, but this rate usually is reduced for institutional clients. Additionally, the investor pays a fee to the broker for trading the stocks in the account. The broker's fee may be calculated as a wrap fee (all trades are covered by paying the broker a fee based on funds under management) or a fee for each trade.

Investors should realize that the name "individually managed account" is something of a misnomer. While it is true that stocks may be weighted differently within each individual account, virtually all the accounts handled by a single manager using the same style tend to include the same stocks. For example, Investor A, who has $200,000 in his account with Manager B, may own $10,000 of Gillette, while Investor B, who also has $200,000 invested with Manager B, has $12,000 worth of Gillette stock. The Gillette stock has a different weight in each account, but each account owns Gillette.

Individually managed accounts provide the investor with several advantages:

- *Awareness of holdings.* The investor knows which stocks are held in the portfolio at all times. Unlike a mutual fund, where you aren't sure which stocks the fund is investing in, the investor knows exactly what is held in a managed account.
- *Customized portfolios.* Investors have some say in the account's holdings. If the money manager invests in a stock that you don't want to own, you can contact either the broker or the manager and advise them to sell the stock. Most managers will follow your requests as long as they are made infrequently; however, some managed-accounts managers resent client interference. You should explore this before you invest.
- *Personal access to the money manager.* While the access is somewhat limited, someone will answer your questions when you call.
- *Management stability.* Unlike a large mutual-fund family where managers are shifted from one fund to another or leave to start their own funds, money managers are in business for the long term.
- *Government regulation.* The operations of money management firms are rather closely regulated by the SEC. While they aren't as tightly regulated as mutual funds, they are much more closely regulated than hedge funds.

The disadvantages of managed accounts are as follows:

- *Fees and expenses.* Investor fees and expenses may be higher than those of a mutual fund. For example, if you have a managed account in which you pay the manager a 1 percent management fee and the broker charges a 1.5 percent wrap fee, your fees for the fund are 2.5 percent annually. This is much higher than the 1.41 percent average fee for all equity mutual funds.
- *Tax efficiency.* Rebalancing the portfolio costs the investor in taxes. A mutual fund or hedge fund is a pooled account where the cash

from all investors placing money in the fund is maintained in a central account. This allows the money manager to use cash inflows to adjust individual stock weightings. For example, if you invest $250,000 in a managed account, and the manager invests 5 percent of your account in GE, you have $12,500 in GE stock. If the manager wants to increase your GE holdings to $20,000, the manager sells another stock that you own (assuming you are fully invested) in order to increase your GE holdings. You then pay capital gains taxes (assuming there were gains) on the stock that was sold. In a mutual fund or hedge fund, the manager would use cash flowing into the account to add to the fund's position in GE, increasing its holdings in GE without incurring taxable gains for investors.

• *Size and resources.* Since many money management firms are relatively small, they may not have the research capabilities and resources of the larger mutual funds.

An annual publication titled *Nelson's Worlds Best Money Managers* shows the performance of money managers over time, based on their management styles. Another source for information about money manager performance is *Money Manager Review,* which tracks the performance of over 800 money managers. You can receive a free performance update for a specific manager by contacting the company's website at www.managerreview.com. We offer clients the opportunity to participate in individually managed accounts. Our minimum initial investment for an individually managed account is $150,000 and we offer investors a lower brokerage rate structure than most managed accounts.

HEDGE FUNDS

Hedge funds are virtually unregulated investment pools for high-net-worth individuals. In fact, securities laws limit participation in hedge funds to individuals who have earned in excess of $200,000 for the last two consecutive years or have a net worth in excess of $1 million.

There are believed to be between 2,200 and 4,000 hedge funds in the United States. With the global turmoil that occurred during 1998, a number of hedge funds, led by Long Term Capital Management, were thrust into the news. Long Term Capital Management lost hundreds of millions of dollars in a span of just a few weeks, but it was not the only hedge fund that suffered greatly. As a result of all the negative publicity surrounding a few large hedge funds that lost billions of dollars, many investors have the impression that all hedge funds utilize high-risk management strategies and should be avoided. The truth is that hedge fund managers are given more leeway in how they operate than mutual fund managers. As a result, some hedge fund managers use highly leveraged, exotic, and high-risk investing strategies involving foreign currencies and bonds. However, I know of many hedge fund managers who operate in a very conservative manner.

Hedge funds are similar to mutual funds in that all investors own a share of the total portfolio, a manager manages the fund, and the investor may not know which stocks are included in the portfolio. However, hedge funds differ from mutual funds in several key areas:

- *Regulation.* Hedge funds are not as tightly regulated as mutual funds; therefore, some hedge fund managers use more high-risk investment strategies than their mutual fund counterparts.
- *Liquidity.* Hedge fund investors have limited access to their money. Typically, investors can only withdraw their funds during one period of the year (some hedge funds allow for quarterly withdrawals); as a result, investors are unable to cash out whenever they desire.
- *Expenses.* Since hedge fund managers charge a fee for managing the fund, and normally also receive a performance-based bonus calculated on fund performance, hedge fund fees may be higher than those of a comparable mutual fund. However, many investors believe that if the hedge fund is really outperforming the market, the extra charge is a small price to pay.
- *High initial investment.* The minimum investment in a hedge fund is much higher than that required by most mutual funds (normally $250,000 to $500,000, versus $2,000 to $5,000).

- *Performance tracking.* Since mutual fund performance is published in most financial papers daily, it is easy to determine the value of your investment. This is not the case with hedge funds, which typically publish only quarterly statements.
- *Fewer investors.* Hedge funds are limited to only 500 investors. Mutual funds may have thousands of investors.

When considering the advantages and disadvantages of hedge funds, the following should be noted:

ADVANTAGES
- *Talented management.* Since the incentive portion of a hedge fund manager's compensation is so great, and the potential earnings so high, hedge funds often attract some of the most talented people within the industry.
- *Hedge fund managers are usually invested.* Typically, hedge fund managers have a substantial portion of their own net worth invested in the fund. I would much rather invest with a manager who is invested in the fund than someone who has nothing to lose.
- *Investing options.* Because hedge funds are not tightly regulated, the manager has a number of investing options available.

DISADVANTAGES
- *High risk.* Some hedge funds may be managed in a manner that makes them extremely risky investments, but remember, other hedge funds utilize very conservative investment styles. The management of the fund, rather than the hedge fund structure, drives the risk level of the fund.
- *High investment minimums.* Unless you have between $250,000 and $500,000 to invest, you will need to consider other investment options.
- *Liquidity.* It is difficult to cash out of a hedge fund. Most hedge funds limit redemptions to one period a year, although some do allow for quarterly redemption.
- *Knowledge of the fund's operations.* Most hedge fund investors don't know precisely which stocks are owned by the hedge fund at any point in time. Furthermore, the managers may not explain how

operating decisions are made by the fund. Hedge fund managers seem to revel in creating a mystique around their funds.
- *Performance updates.* Since hedge funds are not tracked by most financial journals, you must call the hedge fund for an update, and it may not be readily available.

Because of their minimum investing levels, restrictions on withdrawing funds, and the high-risk nature of some hedge funds, hedge funds aren't for everyone.

WHICH OPTION IS RIGHT FOR YOU?

Now that you are aware of the various investing options available to you, you need to select the option or options that best fit your needs. Your selection should be driven by four factors:

1. *How much money you have to invest.* A key driver in your decision-making process will be the amount of money that you plan to invest in Great Companies. The more money you have to invest, the more options you have to choose from. We have classified money available to invest into three groupings:
   - Less than $100,000
   - $100,000 to $249,000
   - Over $250,000
2. *Your experience and confidence in managing your own portfolio of stocks. I have grouped investors into three categories:*
   - *Novice.* This includes investors who know what the stock market is and may own a couple of mutual funds and stocks, but have little if any experience managing their portfolio and investing in stocks.
   - *Knowledgeable.* Investors in this classification read the *Wall Street Journal,* own several mutual funds, purchase a stock from time to time, probably have a broker, may watch CNBC occasionally, and have a basic understanding of the market.
   - *Experienced investors.* These investors read the *Wall Street Journal* daily, subscribe to *Barron's,* have several brokers, own several mutual funds that they monitor closely, own a number of

stocks, and trade regularly. They follow investing strategies and are very involved in managing their portfolios.

3. *The time that you are willing to spend managing your investments.* The classifications are as follows:
   - Two hours per week
   - Two to ten hours per week
   - Over ten hours per week
4. *Availability of financial data:*
   - You read the financial section of your paper and the *Wall Street Journal.*
   - You subscribe to *Barron's,* watch CNBC several hours each week, subscribe to AOL, and track your portfolio.
   - You have all the data you need at your fingertips. You have bookmarked a number of investing links on the Web. You know exactly how your stocks performed at the end of every day. You have several stocks that you are following.

The chart below is designed to help you select the investing options that are best for you based on these four factors. Since you may not fit perfectly within any one classification, use your own judgment in selecting the profile that is closest to your situation.

Investing Guidelines

INVESTING EXPERIENCE	FUNDS AVAILABLE FOR INVESTING		
	LESS THAN $50,000	$51,000-$250,000	OVER $250,000
Novice	mutual fund or newsletter	managed account	managed account
Knowledgeable	mutual fund, broker, or newsletter	managed account	managed account
Experienced	mutual fund, broker, or newsletter	managed account or broker	managed account or broker

ASSESSING FINANCIAL MANAGEMENT TALENT

Any investing option is only as good as the person you are investing with. For each of the five options described above, the quality of talent varies dramatically. Unfortunately, there are no rules that say you have to possess a great investing record to become an investment manager. Certainly there are tests that must be taken and regulations that must be followed by professional money managers, but once the basic requirements have been fulfilled virtually anyone can "hang out a shingle."

Your ability to seek out the good managers will have a huge impact on your investing success. Fortunately, the really bad managers are so bad that they seem to exit the business rather quickly, but at any point in time, there are incompetent people providing investment advice that can cost you dearly. Conversely, there are a number of very knowledgeable money managers who dispense sound advice and routinely beat the market. One of the biggest challenges you will face as an investor is separating the good managers from the bad. I discussed how investors should evaluate their holdings in the previous chapter. Now I will provide guidelines for evaluating money managers that you will invest with in the future. Building a team of high-quality money managers is critical to your future investing success.

The following guidelines are designed to help you in your search for financial advisors.

1. *Don't be intimidated.* If you are a novice investor, you are going to feel somewhat intimidated in your discussions with an individual who has built a career providing financial advice and managing investors' portfolios. You will realize that there are a lot of things you don't know and may feel "dumb" asking basic questions. You need to take the attitude that this is your money and you have every right to ask any question you want. If the manager talks down to you or ridicules your lack of knowledge, look elsewhere. You want someone who will patiently answer your questions and address your fears and concerns.

2. *Examine performance over time.* Many mutual funds or investors

have great years when everything goes right and they trounce the indexes. Typically, this is a one-year phenomenon. The manager got lucky and structured the portfolio in exactly the right way to beat the market. Funds that get lucky one year attract huge investment dollars from investors who think the manager has figured out the market and will continue this award-winning performance for years to come. Wrong! In most cases, the manager got lucky. Occasionally, you will find a manager who has an unbelievable four- or five-year streak, but this is the exception rather than the rule.

As an investor, you should look at actual returns on at least a one-, three-, and five-year basis. As you look at returns, compare year-to-year consistency, realizing that inconsistent performance spells increased risk. I would recommend you consider the following sources for analyzing returns:

- *Mutual funds.* Morningstar captures this data about most of the funds.
- *Newsletters. The Hulbert Financial Digest* tracks investing results from newsletters.
- *Money managers.* Nelson's publishes an annual report titled *America's Best Money Managers,* which looks at manager results by investing style over time. It also reveals the amount of funds under management.
- *Hedge funds.* Tass Management, Inc., in New York tracks the performance of 1,219 hedge funds that have registered with the company.

In addition to studying these sources, make sure you consider the following:

- Has the same manager been in charge for the period in which you are assessing performance?
- How has the manager done in bear markets?
- What has been the quarter-to-quarter volatility of the fund?
- Has the firm had rapid growth?
- Did the firm perform better when it was small?

Unfortunately, information regarding stockbrokers is not widely available. You will in most cases need to rely on performance data that the managers provide. If this is the only source of data available, make sure that you know how the data was developed. Questions to ask might include: Was this a mock portfolio, or the portfolio returns of a current investor? What is the risk level of this portfolio? Has an outside firm audited the returns? May I speak with several of your current investors?

While past returns provide the investor with a record of how the fund performed in the past, they are not necessarily indicative of how the fund will perform in the future. A number of changes may impact future performance, including, but not limited to, the following:

- *A change in fund managers.* Especially at mutual funds, managers don't stay in one place forever.
- *The size of the fund.* Small-cap funds that get huge inflows of investing dollars may have trouble replicating their previous performance because they are no longer able to buy the select groups of small-cap stocks they once did.
- *Changes in the market.* Few funds have a style that is great in all market conditions. For example, a fund that is highly invested in technology stocks may trounce the market average for several years. However, if the market turns and these stocks go out of favor, performance may drop dramatically.

3. *Understand the manager's investing strategy.* Some managers have what I refer to as "black box" methods of investing. They have created an investing strategy so complex that they are unable to explain it to the normal investor. These managers talk about regression models, exotic charting techniques, and a host of other tools that only they understand. *If you can't understand the manager's investing strategy, or if the strategy doesn't make sense to you, don't go with it.* Successful managers typically follow a strategy they have developed that has worked for them over the years in all types of market situations. If a manager says that he doesn't have a strategy and refers to himself as a "stock picker," be careful. In addition to understanding how the man-

ager invests, investors should seek to understand how the firm gets its investing ideas. Investors should also ask if the fund is always fully invested and seek to understand what determines the level of investment.

As we discussed in chapter 6, it is more difficult to get a feel for investing strategies when investing in mutual funds. The prospectus of the individual fund should explain the fund's investment objectives and approach. Usually, this is a fairly simple statement and does not provide a great deal of insight. It's important that the investor study this prospectus closely and call the fund with any questions.

4. *Assess the risk of the investing approach.* By analyzing annual returns over time, the investor can determine how much more— or less—volatile the fund has been than the market in general. The normal way of measuring volatility is standard deviation. This is a statistical measure that calculates the range of performance within which the total returns of a fund will fall. When a fund has a high standard deviation, there is more potential for volatility.

5. *Consider the amount of funds under management, and how rapidly the fund has grown.* Funds and managers who have great performance records attract the attention of investors, and hence the investors' cash. Sometimes funds that grow too quickly suffer performance shortfalls. This is particularly true with small-cap and micro-cap portfolios. Make sure that the fund manager is able to manage this growth without changing the fund's management style or focus.

6. *Consider portfolio turnover and tax-adjusted returns.* Remember it's what you put in your pocket, or the value of your portfolio at the end of the year, that's important, not percentage returns. You should also examine portfolio turnover (a measure of the fund's trading activity that is calculated by taking the lesser of purchases or sales and dividing by average monthly assets), for this can have a big impact on your taxable returns. A turnover rate of 20 percent would be indicative of a buy-and-hold strategy, while a rate of 200% would indicate an aggressive turnover strategy.

If you spend time in the beginning researching the portfolio managers that you select, you can assemble a really professional team that will be of immense value to you over time. Ultimately, your team may include a combination of mutual funds, money managers, newsletters, hedge funds, and brokers. You must go beyond the recommendations of others if you are to develop a first-rate team.

Chapter 8

MANAGING AND MONITORING YOUR GREAT COMPANIES PORTFOLIO

You are now ready to begin investing. Some readers will decide to purchase several of the Great Companies stocks and hold them for the long term. Others will construct their own portfolios and tinker with the stocks in the portfolio from time to time. Some will try to follow my approach in managing their Great Company portfolios. However, many readers will decide that they simply don't have the time, experience, or confidence to develop and manage their own portfolio of Great Companies, and will choose to have Great Companies, LLC, manage their portfolios. This chapter was developed for investors in all four situations.

Regardless of your investing preference, you need to have an understanding of how to monitor and manage your portfolio for optimum results. There are two basic approaches: active management and passive management.

PASSIVE MANAGEMENT

Passive management is used to describe an investment strategy that takes a minimalist approach to portfolio management. Investors who take the passive approach either make minimum changes to their portfolio over time or follow a disciplined approach that dictates the changes that will be made. Two examples of passive investing strategies that you may be familiar with are:

1. *The Dogs of the Dow,* a strategy where you rank the stocks in the Dow Jones Industrial Average based on dividend yields as a percentage of the stock's price. You then invest equally in the ten stocks in which dividends represent the highest percentage of the stock's price at the time the investment is made. This process is repeated every twelve months. This is a passive investing strategy, since nothing is done to modify the portfolio once the stocks have been purchased.
2. *Indexing.* This is a passive strategy since the only decision required is to decide which index you want to mirror (S&P 500, Dow Jones Industrial Average, etc.). Once this decision is made, stocks are purchased in a manner so that the portfolio's performance matches that of the chosen index.

I have identified two passive investing strategies that you might want to consider in managing your Great Companies portfolio. They include:

1. *Market-Weighted by Initial Market Value.* This approach requires the investor to purchase stocks for the portfolio based on the price of the stock at the time the purchase decision is made. For example, if you were building a market-weighted portfolio composed of American International Group, Bristol-Myers Squibb, Gillette, and Merck, you would purchase shares of the stocks so that each company's share of the total portfolio would be equal to the value of one share of stock relative to the price of the other three shares of stock. For example, let's say AIG's shares are trading at $85.50. The combined value of one share of AIG, BMY, G, and MRK is $369.12. Therefore, AIG represents 23.16 percent ($85.50/$369.12 = 23.16%) of the combined value of the portfolio.

TICKER SYMBOL	COMPANY	SHARE PRICE	% OF TOTAL
AIG	American International Group	$85.50	23.16%
BMY	Bristol-Myers Squibb	$108.56	29.41%
G	Gillette	$44.56	12.07%
MRK	Merck	$130.50	35.36%
	Total	$369.12	100.00%

Using this chart as an example, an investor would invest $10,000 as follows:

TICKER	% OF PORTFOLIO ×	$10,000	÷	PRICE PER SHARE	=	# SHARES PURCHASED
AIG	23.16%	$2,316		$85.50		27
BMY	29.41%	$2,941		$108.56		27
G	12.07%	$1,207		$44.56		27
MRK	35.36%	$3,536		$130.50		27
Total	100.00%	$10,000				108

In this portfolio example, the investor would purchase twenty-seven shares of each stock, and AIG would represent 23.16 percent of the portfolio's value at the time the stocks are purchased. The passive investor would simply monitor the performance of the portfolio over time.

2. *Equal-Weighted Strategy.* Using this strategy, the investor purchases shares of stocks so that each stock has the same total value as every other stock in the portfolio. For example, an investor with $10,000 to invest in the four stocks would invest $2,500 ($10,000 / 4 stocks = $2,500) in each stock.

TICKER	AMOUNT TO INVEST ÷	SHARE PRICE	=	# SHARES PURCHASED
AIG	$2,500	$85.50		29
BMY	$2,500	$108.56		23
G	$2,500	$44.56		56
MRK	$2,500	$130.50		19
Total	$10,000			127

In this example, the investor buys $2,500 of each stock in order to be equally invested in each company. Since share prices differ, the investor purchases more shares of the lower-priced stocks than of the higher-priced stocks. Then the investor simply monitors the returns of the portfolio.

It is interesting to see how these two passive strategies impact returns. Let's assume that ten years ago two investors invested an equal amount of money in the Great Companies. One investor used a market-weighted strategy, the other an equal-weighted strategy. Neither investor traded any of the stocks in the portfolio; they simply watched the portfolio grow over time.

The results may be somewhat surprising. As the chart below reveals, the equal-weighted outperformed the market-weighted portfolio on a three-, five-, and ten-year basis.

Great Companies
Total Returns

	3 YEARS	5 YEARS	10 YEARS
MARKET-WEIGHTED BY INITIAL MARKET VALUE	37.96%	34.58%	28.00%
EQUAL-WEIGHTED	38.24%	35.99%	29.86%
S&P 500	28.22%	24.05%	19.19%

Source: S&P Compustat

The accompanying graph shows that from almost the beginning, the equal-weighted portfolio outperformed the market-weighted portfolio.

ACTIVE MANAGEMENT

An active investing strategy may be characterized by any of the following management approaches:

- *Portfolio turnover.* The manager sells stocks that are expected to underperform in the future and replaces them with stocks that she believes will outperform the market. This is by far the most common of all active investing strategies. Unfortunately, this approach typically results in higher taxes and trading costs for the investor.

GREAT COMPANIES OF AMERICA
EQUAL-WEIGHTED VS. MARKET-WEIGHTED VALUES

December 31, 1988 to December 31, 1998

Dividends Reinvested

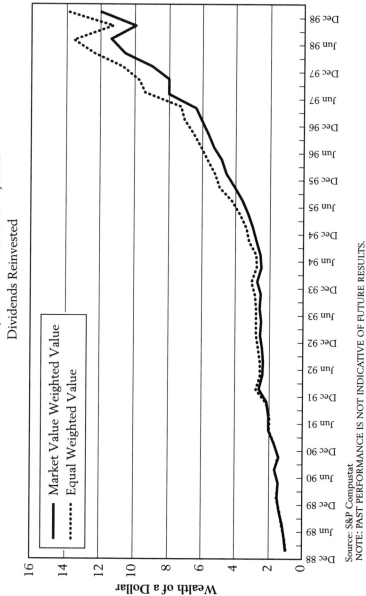

Market Value Weighted Value
.... Equal Weighted Value

Wealth of a Dollar

Source: S&P Compustat
NOTE: PAST PERFORMANCE IS NOT INDICATIVE OF FUTURE RESULTS.

- *Timing the market.* Some active managers are market timers, and will move from being fully invested in cash to being fully invested in stocks. Depending on how often the manager moves in and out of the market, the impact on taxes and expenses may be significant.
- *Sector rotation.* Other active managers move their portfolio from one sector to another based on their belief that a particular sector will outperform other sectors in the future. This strategy may also have a major impact on investor taxes and trading expenses.

There are many different approaches to active portfolio management—these three represent some of the most popular ones. Active managers normally have higher investing costs than passive managers, and their portfolios are usually less tax efficient than the portfolios of passive managers, since the stocks in the portfolio are not held for the long term and the investor is forced to pay short-term capital gains taxes. Since mutual fund returns are typically reported on a gross basis and don't reflect either expenses or taxes paid by investors, active managers are driven to produce returns that exceed those of other funds using the same management style. Most active managers are not concerned with the tax-adjusted returns of their investors.

GREAT COMPANIES MANAGEMENT

The Great Companies of America portfolio should be classified as a large-cap growth style of investing, while the Great Companies of the Future should be classified as a large-cap aggressive growth portfolio. While the investing styles differ, the management of the two portfolios is quite similar.

The approach that I use to manage the Great Companies of America is a hybrid strategy that combines both passive and active investing approaches to manage the portfolio. The approach is designed to produce excellent tax-adjusted returns while minimizing my trading expenses. My approach would be considered by most to be passive, since I seldom sell a position in a Great Company of America (more about that later). However, the strategy is active in that I adjust the weights of companies within the portfolio.

STOCKS IN GREAT COMPANIES OF AMERICA
December 31, 1988 to December 31, 1998
Equal Weighted, Dividends Reinvested

Legend:
- aig
- bmy
- c
- cl
- g
- ge
- jnj
- ko
- mdt
- mrk
- pfe
- pg
- sgp
- mer
- S&P 500 Index

X-axis: Dec 88, Jun 89, Dec 89, Jun 90, Dec 90, Jun 91, Dec 91, Jun 92, Dec 92, Jun 93, Dec 93, Jun 94, Dec 94, Jun 95, Dec 95, Jun 96, Dec 96, Jun 97, Dec 97, Jun 98, Dec 98

Y-axis: Wealth of a Dollar — 0, 5, 10, 15, 20, 25, 30, 35

Source: Standard & Poor's Compustat PC Plus, Intrinsic Value Associates, LLC
NOTE: PAST PERFORMANCE IS NOT INDICATIVE OF FUTURE RESULTS.

In reality, this management approach borrows something from each of the investing strategies. It is similar to indexing because I hold the same stocks in the portfolio over time. The management approach is reflective of a growth style of management, because I only invest in companies that are growing. Finally, it borrows from value investing because I adjust portfolio weights based on intrinsic value and intrinsic value momentum.

In essence, the strategy could be classified as "Super Indexing" because I invest in what I consider to be the fourteen greatest publicly traded companies based in America—note that Ibbotson Associates has found that over 50 percent of the S&P 500 returns are generated by the top 50 performing stocks, the other 450 companies contribute the balance—and then hold the stocks of these companies over time. However, unlike indexing, which adjusts portfolio weights based on market cap, I adjust portfolio weighting based on intrinsic value, intrinsic value momentum, EVA, and company and sector momentum.

I developed this approach after examining a chart similar to the one on the previous page showing the growth in value of the Great Companies over the past ten years. While all of the companies outperformed the S&P 500, some companies, like Pfizer, Medtronic, and Schering-Plough, grew much faster than the others. I realized that if I could identify those companies that will grow faster than the others, I could enhance the returns of the portfolio. After studying this problem for some time, I found that increases in the stock price were driven by four very important factors—changes in intrinsic value, changes in intrinsic value momentum, improvements in EVA (Economic Value Added), and, to a lesser degree, company and sector momentum.

Intrinsic Value

Warren Buffett refers to intrinsic value as "an all-important concept that offers the only logical approach to evaluating the relative attractiveness of investments and businesses. Intrinsic value can be defined simply: It is the discounted value of the cash that can be taken out of a business during its remaining life." He goes on to note that "Intrinsic value is an estimate rather than a precise figure, and it is additionally an estimate that must be changed if interest rates move or forecasts of future cash flows are revised."

Perhaps the following example will help you better understand how I use intrinsic value to manage the portfolio. I developed an intrinsic value analysis of Gillette on December 15, 1997. At the time of the analysis, Gillette was trading at the equivalent of $50 per share (adjusted for the split). My intrinsic value calculation showed that the true intrinsic value of Gillette's stock was $42.50. In essence, the market was overvaluing the stock by 17.6 percent ($50 − $42.50 ÷ $42.50 = 17.6%). The stock price subsequently climbed to $58.25 per share, an overvaluation of 37 percent. I reduced my holdings in Gillette as a percentage of the total portfolio. When the market "tanked" during the summer, Gillette's share price dropped to $35.32 per share, a wonderful buying opportunity. The day I wrote this paragraph, Gillette closed at $44.56. The most recent intrinsic valuation for Gillette (calculations were made almost sixty days ago) is $48.20. At the current price of $44.56, Gillette is slightly undervalued versus the current intrinsic value calculation.

Intrinsic values and stock prices don't always work together as well as they did in this example, but I have found that over time, stock prices correlate rather closely with intrinsic values.

Intrinsic Value Momentum

By monitoring changes in intrinsic value over twelve to eighteen months, I am able to track what I define as a company's Intrinsic Value Momentum (IVM). In essence IVM measures the rate at which a company is increasing or decreasing its intrinsic value.

As Buffett suggests, intrinsic value is an estimate that is driven by changes in interest rates, sales, cost of capital, and ultimately, free cash flow. I have found that the primary drivers of cash flow vary by company and business. Our most recent intrinsic value estimate for Gillette was $48.20. Since that value was calculated, Mach 3 sales have started to soar. No doubt the intrinsic value of Gillette today is higher than when I developed the original calculation. I refer to this growth in intrinsic value as intrinsic value momentum. It is important to purchase stocks at a price less than their intrinsic value, but in a long-term buy-and-hold strategy, the companies in which you invest must be increasing their intrinsic value. Based on my calculations, Gillette increased its intrinsic value approximately 13 percent in 1998.

Not a bad performance, but some of the Great Companies of

America increased their intrinsic values in excess of 29 percent during 1998. Since the stock market has historically grown at approximately 10 percent to 11 percent per year, companies whose intrinsic values grow faster than 10 percent per year should outperform the market over the long term. Warren Buffett seeks to invest in companies that are increasing their intrinsic values at 15 percent per annum. At the 15 percent rate, Berkshire Hathaway should over the long term outperform the market by 30 percent to 40 percent. I believe that the 15 percent rate indicates a solid performance, and I am pleased that so many of our Great Companies far exceed this target.

Companies that are dramatically increasing their intrinsic value momentum typically are more heavily weighted in our portfolio. This IVM allocation process is critical to improving Great Company portfolio returns.

EVA (Economic Value Added)

As an investor, you would like to feel that the managers and employees of the companies in which you invest are doing everything that they can to increase the market and intrinsic values of their companies. In many cases, however, they are actually destroying capital, which, over time, has a negative impact on the stock price.

In an effort to ensure that company management is aligned with investor needs, Stern Stewart and Company developed the concept of Economic Value Added (EVA). EVA is defined by Stern Stewart as "operating profits less the cost of all of the capital employed to produce those earnings. EVA will increase if operating profits can be made to grow without tying up any more capital, if new capital can be invested in projects that will earn more than the full cost of the capital, and if capital can be diverted or liquidated from business activities that do not provide adequate returns. It will be reduced if management fritters away funds on projects that earn less than the cost of capital or passes over projects likely to earn more than the cost of capital.

Several of the Great Companies utilize the EVA process, and most of those that do not certainly use elements of the concept. For example, the private companies that Hank Greenberg of AIG referred to as incentives for AIG's senior managers reward AIG managers for growing the market value of the company.

Likewise, while Gillette has not installed the EVA program, the incentive plan that Gillette uses is closely aligned with the concept of increasing EVA. If you are interested in learning more about EVA, I suggest that you read *The Quest for Value* by G. Bennett Stewart III, senior partner in Stern Stewart & Company, and review the issue of *Fortune* that ranks companies by their ability to build EVA.

I believe that it is more than a coincidence that 8 of the 14 Great Companies of America rank among the top 15 U.S. companies in wealth creation. Of the 1,000 companies covered in the *Fortune* study, The Great Companies of America are among the top 70 (the top 7 percent of all companies studied). I feel confident that companies that are successful in increasing their EVA will see their stock prices rise over time.

Momentum

To a much lesser degree, I also use company and sector momentum to weight stocks within the portfolio. I have observed that from time to time companies seem to pick up momentum, and sales and profits begin to take off. There are any number of reasons why a company can gain momentum almost overnight. Momentum changes may be driven by the success of a new product, the growth of a market the company dominates, or the successful execution of a new strategy. Whatever the reason, it happens, and if you can capitalize on this momentum in the early stages, it can provide handsome returns.

———

As you can see, my management approach is indeed a hybrid. I rarely sell a position in a company, thereby resembling a passive investor. However, I adopt an active investing style in adjusting the portfolio's weightings.

WHAT IF SOMETHING GOES WRONG WITH ONE OF THE GREAT COMPANIES?

I am frequently asked the following questions:

- "Would you ever sell the stock of one of your Great Companies?"
- "How do you know that a company will be great forever?"
- "What will it look like when a Great Company falters?"

As I mentioned earlier, these are Great Companies, not perfect companies. Quite frankly, I can't be certain that all these companies will be great one hundred years from now, or even twenty years from now. The dramatic changes that will occur in the new millennium will present enormous opportunities and challenges for all companies. I believe that the Great Companies are positioned to be the leaders in this new high-technology, global operating environment, but no one can be certain. However, I don't believe that a Great Company will fall from grace overnight. I can't imagine a circumstance where a Great Company (unlike a speculative small-cap that reports disappointing earnings) will lose 50 percent of its market cap overnight. Rather, if one of the Great Companies falters, it will decline gradually over time, much like IBM.

IBM was once hailed by management experts and analysts as the best company in America. It had an enormous market cap, was producing incredible returns for shareholders, and was clearly in "Prime." Unfortunately, the operating environment changed faster than IBM. IBM management didn't take the steps necessary to keep the company in "Prime," and shareholder returns began to suffer. As performance declined, the board became concerned about IBM. A new leader (Louis V. Gerstner, Jr.) was brought in from the outside to take the steps required to get IBM back into "Prime." While IBM has made enormous strides under Gerstner's leadership and appears to be well positioned for the future, the jury is still out on whether IBM will again reach and remain in "Prime."

I believe that if one of my Great Companies selects the wrong strategies, implements the wrong business model, or makes a bad acquisition, investors will no doubt see a decline in the market price. Don't panic and sell the stock. Give the company time to correct its mistakes. Remember—these are Great Companies. However, if the condition persists over a period of three to five years, then you should drop the company from your portfolio. Selling the stock of a Great Company should be a rare occurrence.

MONITORING YOUR PORTFOLIO

The development of the Internet and other advances in technology have made monitoring your Great Company portfolio much easier. However, since not everyone has a computer, I have organized this section into two parts. Part 1 is designed to address the investors who do not have access to a computer. Part 2 was written for those with a computer and access to the Internet.

Calculating Great Company Returns

	WORKSHEET	EXAMPLE
Beginning Value	$_____	$50,000
Ending Value	$_____	$60,000
Net Cash Inflow	$_____	$6,000
1 Beginning Value	$_____	$50,000
2 Plus 50% of Net Income	+ $_____	+ $3,000
3 Result:	= $_____	+ $53,000
4 Ending Value	$_____	$60,000
5 Minus 50% of Net Inflow	– $_____	– $3,000
6 Result:	$_____	= $57,000
7 Enter line 6	$_____	$57,000
8 Divide by line 3	$_____	$53,000
9 Result (to 4 decimals)	= $_____	= 1.0755
10 Subtract 1	−1	−1
11 Result	= _____	= 0.0755
12 Multiply by 100	× 100	× 100
13 Estimated Return*	= _____%	= 7.55%

*To figure returns over multiple periods, convert the returns for each period into decimals (divide by 100), then add 1 to each. Multiply these results by each other and then subtract 1 from the product. Multiply the result by 100 to get a percentage.

Source: American Association of Individual Investors

Part 1: Monitoring Your Portfolio

If you don't have a computer, or don't have access to the Internet, you can still monitor your portfolio easily. The combination of financial television channels, magazines, and journals provides a lot of information that is readily available at low cost.

The first thing you should monitor is your Great Companies portfolio's returns. The example was developed by the American Association of Individual Investors and provides a structure for tracking your returns.

The example on the opposite page assumes an investment valued at $50,000 at the beginning of a four-month period and valued at $60,000 at the end of that time. Taking into account both withdrawals and contributions, there was a net cash inflow of $6,000 during the period. In the example, the estimated return for the period was 7.55 percent. This should be compared to the S&P 500 returns for the same period. Investors can obtain the information required to complete this analysis from the monthly statement distributed by most brokers.

You can also use stock quotes from the *Wall Street Journal, Investor's Business Daily,* or your local newspaper to develop these calculations, though you might miss the dividends paid during the period.

The second thing you should monitor is what is happening to the stocks in your portfolio. Your potential resources include:

1. *Key journals and magazines that print stories about the companies or the industries in which they operate.* Sources include:
   Magazines:
   - *Business Week*
   - *Forbes*
   - *Fortune*
   Journals:
   - *Wall Street Journal*
   - *Investor's Business Daily*
   - *Barron's*
2. *Research reports from brokerage firms.* All the full-service brokerage firms produce research reports on companies from time to time. Clients of these firms have access to these reports.

3. *Corporate publications.* When you own stock in a company, you receive the annual report and quarterly earnings updates.
4. *Financial channels.* CNBC, Bloomberg, and others broadcast ongoing programming about developments in individual companies and the market.
5. *Great Companies of America newsletter.* I publish a newsletter that reports on key developments in the Great Companies.

Part 2: Monitoring Your Portfolio with a Computer

If you have a computer and access to the Internet, monitoring your portfolio has become easy and enjoyable. You have two options for tracking your portfolio:

1. Purchasing software for your personal use
2. Using portfolio tracking services at different websites

If you are interested in purchasing your own software, consider the Personal Record Keeper from the National Association of Individual Investors (800-428-2244) or Quicken products from Intuit, Inc. There are other software products you might also consider.

Alternatively, you can track the progress of your stocks or mutual funds using various websites. Many of these sites offer free portfolio tracking services that not only provide updates for changes in your portfolio, but also provide information about individual companies. You might consider the following websites:

- http://moneycentral.com
  This is the Microsoft website, and it's well done.
- http://cbs-marketwatch.com
  Developed and maintained by CBS, this site has a good portfolio tracker.
- http://quote.yahoo.com
  Offers links to a number of other financial sites. This is a must.
- http://stockmaster.com
  A website that links you to other financial sites.
- http://morningstar.com
  The experts in mutual fund tracking also operate a site for investors with both stocks and mutual funds.

- http://lipperweb.com
  This site also specializes in mutual funds.

I have included only a partial listing of helpful websites. If you need more information on financial websites, you should obtain the *Individual Investor's Guide to Investment Web Sites.* This document is available to all AAII members through AAII's website, http://www.aaii.com.

I believe that it is extremely important for investors to stay on top of changes in the stocks and the mutual funds that they own. The more you know, the better an investor you will be. When the stock market crashed in August of 1998, it was very comforting to know that I was invested in the best companies in the world, and that these companies were doing the things necessary to build for the long term.

REDUCING THE
WORRY FACTOR

 As a potential investor in the stock market, you face four types of risks:

1. *Market Risks:* risks associated with the upward and downward movement of the total market. You will encounter these risks as long as you are an investor in the stock market.
2. *Business/Sector Risks:* risks that exist within a given industry sector. For example, if there is an airfare war, all airlines lose market value.
3. *Individual Stock/Company Risks:* risks associated with owning stock in a particular company.
4. *Purchasing Power/"Do Nothing" Risks:* the risks of not investing in the stock market.

It is impossible to eliminate these risks, but there are steps investors can take to minimize their impact. The Great Companies strategy was designed with these risks in mind. As you will see, each element of the Great Companies strategy is structured to lessen the impact of these risks on investors' portfolios.

MARKET RISKS

I began writing this chapter on an airplane at 6 A.M. Tuesday, September 1, 1998. It seemed an appropriate time to begin this section of the book given the market situation:

- The day before, the Dow had plummeted 513 points, a decline of 6.4 percent. The Dow had lost 1,064 points during the last four days—the worst four-day drop since the 1987 crash.
- The NASDAQ, whose stocks had been battered for weeks, to the point where many said they couldn't go any lower, dropped 140 points or 8.6 percent, the biggest one-day drop ever for the NAS-DAQ. Hot performers like Yahoo, Dell, America Online, and Cisco Systems saw their market values decline by 16.9, 15.8, 14.9, and 13.5 percent, respectively.
- The Russell 2000 (small-cap index) was down 22.7 percent for the year.
- More than $2.3 trillion in market wealth had vanished since July 17, 1998. A bull market that had been up 20 percent on the year was now down 5 percent.

The only news was bad news. Russia's move to a capitalistic economic system seemed like it would collapse, costing U.S. financial companies hundreds of millions of dollars in bad debts. Asian economies, which had started the downslide, continued to falter. Japan was trapped in a horrendous depression and was not taking the steps needed to turn the situation around. There was news of major economic problems in South America. President Clinton was under investigation. Numerous highly speculative funds were widely rumored to be failing. Just when you thought the news couldn't get any worse, it did.

As I drove to the airport, that morning, the financial talk shows were trying to whip investors into a fever pitch. One "expert" likened the current economic situation to the Great Depression of 1929 but said that things would be much worse than 1929. Another "wizard" stated, with conviction, that we were headed for a global recession and the market could easily drop another 2,000 points. The most optimistic report came from a Wall Street trader who simply felt the market was "testing new lows," a Wall Street cliché for "I have no idea."

I developed the Great Companies investing strategy, and wrote this chapter, for times like this. While the Great Companies portfolio has delivered excellent returns during good times, the key to any core strategy's success is preservation of capital during bad times. GCA had been hurt, and our returns were down dramatically from what they had been six weeks before. However, the GCA portfolio was still outperforming both the Dow and the S&P 500 for the year, and that is precisely what it was designed to do.

While on a short-term basis the market moves in strange ways with irrational twists and turns, the people who make money in the market follow logical principles and strategies that have been proven over time. Most of the investing principles in this book are based on fact, and a few are based on experience. In no case are the principles based on emotion.

In order for these principles to work for you, it is critical that you develop the proper investing mindset, a mindset that will control how you react to and manage your portfolio during market gyrations. It's imperative that investors adopt a mindset that will enable them to control the most dangerous of all investor emotions, fear and greed.

Fear stems from the underlying concern that the next market correction will be the "big one," and that if you remain invested in the market, you might lose a huge amount of your principal. In this regard, you are no different from the person who has survived minor earthquakes but always has it in the back of his mind that the next earthquake will be devastating.

Investor fear is built in exactly the same way. When the market has a sharp decline, it seems that every television channel has someone willing to predict that this is the beginning of the next stock market crash. Visions of 1929 come into your head, with people jumping out of windows or standing in line at soup kitchens. At this point, you want to forget about retirement and simply cut your losses. As the market declines, fearful investors begin to sell in an effort to cut their losses. As the market continues to drop, fear turns to panic. At this stage the panicked investor becomes one of the masses reacting in an emotional rather than a logical manner, caught up in the belief that this really is the "big one." Like the earthquake victim leaving California, you leave the market, vowing never to return. Fear is a very dangerous but very real part of investing.

The other dangerous emotion that investors must control is greed. Greed works in the opposite way from fear but is equally dangerous. The greedy investor sees the market begin to take off in small-cap stocks. Day after day the market in small caps roars, up 5 percent, up 10 percent, up 20 percent. The greedy investor can't stand it any longer; he sells his large-cap holdings or cashes in his bonds and pours this money into small caps. Without warning, the small-cap market reverses itself and tumbles. Since the investor wasn't in for the ride up, but only for the ride down, his losses are significant. Had this investor properly allocated his funds, managed for the long term, and controlled his emotions, these losses would not have occurred.

In order to control these very dangerous emotions, you need to develop an investing mindset that encompasses the following six elements:

1. *The market will go down.* During the past ninety-six years the market has had fifty-two declines of 10 percent or more. There have been fifteen periods when the market declined 25 percent or more. This pattern of declines will continue whether you are invested in the market or holding your money in a bank. The longer you are invested in the market, the greater the odds are that you will experience a 25 percent market correction. Many experienced investors view these declines as opportunities to purchase stocks at bargain prices. However, emotional investors view this as the end of the world. They are so concerned about selling that they can't possibly consider buying. As the market drops, the bears will be cheering wildly and shouting "I told you so." Meanwhile, the fearful investors are biting their nails and unable to sleep. When it gets really bad, remember the next point.

2. *The market goes up more than it goes down.* Historically, an investment in the market has increased between 10 percent and 11 percent per year. Over the past two centuries stocks have increased at an after-inflation compounded rate of 6.7 percent.

This means that the investor's purchasing power for stock investments doubles every ten years and six months. We doubt that average returns will radically change over the next hundred years. As noted in chapter 3, all other investment options have lagged behind the returns of the stock market.

3. *There will always be events that have a short-term impact on the market; however, almost none of them will have a long-term impact.* The Federal Reserve may raise the interest rate, sending investors into bonds and the economy into a recession. A world leader may be assassinated and stocks in a particular region drop. A currency in some part of the world may fail. An emerging market may develop a new and better technology that experts predict will eventually dominate the world market. A freeze may impact crops. There will always be something happening that could have either a negative or a positive short-term impact on the market. Long term, however, almost none of these events will have a lasting effect.

4. *There is absolutely nothing you can do to change the previous three points.* The market doesn't know or care that you are invested in stocks. These trends will continue just as surely as the tide changes. When the tide is out, sailors don't return to port. They study their charts, plan their course so that they avoid dangerous reefs and shoals, and carefully monitor their progress. They know they are exposed to more dangers when the tide is low, and they plot a course that minimizes these ever-present dangers.

   The investor must prepare for market changes the same way that the sailor prepares for shifts in the tide and weather. First, have a sturdy boat (a sound core investing strategy and the stocks of the Great Companies) that can sail in a variety of conditions. Second, get a good set of charts (facts about the companies, including their performance in down markets). And finally, chart a safe course (an investment plan for allocating your resources). With these elements in place, the patient long-term investor has nothing to fear.

5. *You are a long-term investor.* You know that over time the market has provided wonderful returns to rational investors with sound strategies. You know that there is no place else you can invest that will provide equivalent returns at low risk. You know and

understand the wisdom of your investing strategy, and are quite familiar with the stocks in your portfolio. This knowledge and confidence will be of immense comfort to you when things look bad.

A key to reducing market volatility is investing in stocks for the long term. Over the long term large-cap stocks are not much more volatile than bonds; however, in the short term volatility increases. Therefore, in times when the market is plunging, remember that you can minimize market volatility by holding on to your stocks for the long term.

6. *You are following a wonderful core investing strategy.* Core strategies form the foundation on which you build your net worth. Therefore, they are the most important strategies that you will employ, for the funds that you allocate to these core strategies will represent a significant percentage of your net worth. Core strategies are appealing to virtually everyone regardless of their age, income, net worth, or investing mindset. Core strategies shouldn't change unless your investing objective changes dramatically.

Core strategies support your other investing strategies. Because they are so important, a core strategy *must* meet the following criteria:

- *Proven over time.* Most importantly, a core strategy must be time tested. You should examine portfolio performance over periods of at least five and ten years. Don't fall for the "newest" strategy or the "hottest" money manager. Seek out core strategies that have endured the test of time across a variety of market cycles, not investing fads.
- *Disciplined/Model driven.* The best core strategies are based on logical guidelines (like our twelve traits of Great Companies) that will endure. While these models may occasionally be fine tuned for subtle market changes, they should endure over time. These model-driven strategies ensure that the manager is using a consistent investing approach, a key to long-term investing success.
- *Low risk.* While the core strategy should outperform the indexes, it

should also protect your capital. Remember that your core strategy will represent a significant portion of your net worth, and you want to adopt a strategy that effectively manages risk. Portfolio volatility is typically measured by standard deviation. A core investing strategy should produce a portfolio that ideally has a low standard deviation but yields high returns. It's important to note that portfolios with high deviations don't necessarily yield high returns. The chart on the next page compares three-year average annual returns with the three-year standard deviations of the top-performing, five-star, large-cap, growth funds in Morningstar, the Great Companies portfolio, the *Built to Last* and *In Search of Excellence* portfolios, the stocks held in Berkshire Hathaway's portfolio, and Berkshire Hathaway A. Investors should be aware of how much risk they can tolerate. As you can see from the chart, higher standard deviations don't always produce higher returns.

- *Comprehensible.* You must be able to understand the core strategy. If you don't understand it, don't use the strategy. Also, don't use "black box" investing strategies that sound sophisticated and are being used by "everyone" as a core strategy. Likewise, if a money manager won't take the time to explain a core strategy to you in detail, don't invest with that manager.

- *Logical.* If the core strategy doesn't sound right to you, stay away from it. Whenever I have encountered a money manager with a complex strategy that doesn't hang together, I have found over time that the money manager is using a flawed strategy.

- *Diversification.* The core strategy should provide diversification among the stocks in the portfolio as well as from your other core strategy. Many people rely on two core strategies; one that is growth oriented and one that is value driven. This provides diversification from both a portfolio and strategic perspective.

- *Tax efficient.* The core strategy should deliver index-beating, tax-efficient returns. The key measure of performance is how much you have left over after taxes.

- *Cost effective.* The best core strategies also have low management costs.

Finally, depending on your situation, an ideal core strategy **might** meet the following criteria:

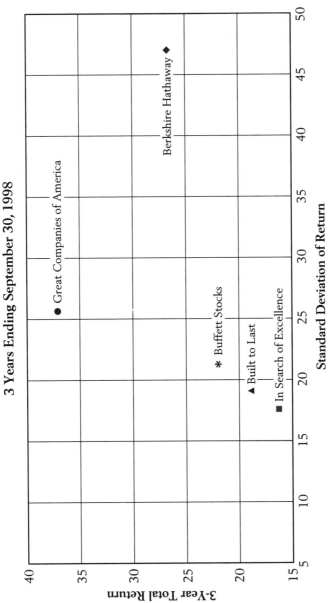

Berkshire Hathaway, S&P 500, Buffett Stocks, Built to Last, and In Search of Excellence Comparison with GCA

3 Years Ending September 30, 1998

3-Year Total Return (vertical axis): 15, 20, 25, 30, 35, 40

Standard Deviation of Return (horizontal axis): 5, 10, 15, 20, 25, 30, 35, 40, 45, 50

- ● Great Companies of America
- ◆ Berkshire Hathaway
- ✳ Buffett Stocks
- ▲ Built to Last
- ■ In Search of Excellence

Source: Standard & Poor's Compustat PC Plus & Morningstar Standard Deviation Formula

NOTE: PAST PERFORMANCE IS NOT INDICATIVE OF FUTURE RESULTS.

- *Socially responsible.* More and more investors are boycotting the stocks of companies that produce tobacco or alcohol or pollute the environment. You might want to add this criterion to your core strategy.
- *International exposure.* Many investors seek to invest overseas as a way of diversifying their portfolio. By purchasing the stocks of the Great Companies, which generate at least 40 percent of their revenues overseas, you are able to purchase U.S. stocks but participate in the growth of international markets.

The Great Companies investing strategy meets all of these criteria and certainly qualifies as a core investing strategy. When the market is crumbling around you, remember that you are following a wonderful strategy that has been tested over time. Understanding the Great Company investment strategy will provide you with the peace of mind you need to stay invested while the market declines. Remember that downturns in the market offer you the opportunity to buy Great Companies at bargain prices. Think of these stock market downturns as wonderful sales where you can stock up on companies you want to own.

If you are interested in learning more about how people react to stock market corrections, I would suggest that you read the following books:

- *Against the Gods,* Peter L. Bernstein. New York: John Wiley, 1996.
- *Crashes and Panics—The Lessons from History,* ed. Eugene N. White. Burr Ridge, IL: Irwin Professional Publishing, 1990.
- *Extraordinary Popular Delusions and the Madness of Crowds,* Charles Mackay. New York: Crown Publishing, 1980.

Your readings will prove that in the area of investing and the markets, history repeats itself.

SECTOR RISKS

The second type of risk is *business/sector risk.* These risks are associated with a specific type of business or market sector. For example, if there is an airline fare war, all major airlines may be heavily impacted, while the balance of the market seems not to even notice. In order to minimize the potential impact of business/sector risk, investors may spread their investments among a number of unrelated business sectors that do not move in the same direction at the same time. This strategy of sector diversification should be limited to those sectors that have attractive business fundamentals. For example, investing in a steel company might minimize your sector risks, but then you would be investing in an unattractive business. Investors need to balance sector diversity with business/sector attractiveness.

The Great Companies tend to fall within three different sectors:

1. *Consumer products.* Stocks within this sector are relatively resistant to downturns in the economy. Consumer products companies in the Great Companies portfolio are Procter and Gamble, Coca-Cola, and Gillette.
2. *Medical.* Companies marketing pharmaceuticals and medical devices seem to move in a different pattern from consumer products stocks. Companies in this sector include Bristol-Myers Squibb, Johnson & Johnson, Medtronic, Merck, Pfizer, and Schering-Plough.
3. *Financial Services.* This sector follows a different pattern from the other two. Stocks in this sector include American International Group, Citigroup, and Merrill Lynch.

Note that General Electric spans several of these categories. GE sells consumer products like light bulbs, has a massive financial services business, and is also becoming more involved in the medical area. Interestingly, all of the Great Companies pharmaceutical companies also market consumer products. While this sector is directionally correct, you should understand that there is significant overlap among some of the companies within the portfolio.

Sector diversification provides the Great Companies investor with an approach for minimizing the impact of any one sector on the total portfolio's returns.

INDIVIDUAL STOCK/COMPANY RISKS

These are the risks associated with owning the stock of a particular company. These risks include the following:

- *Earnings shortfalls.* If a company whose stock you own falls short of its earnings estimates, investors will "punish" the company by selling shares and lowering the stock price.
- *Low growth.* Companies that are growing more slowly and less profitably than their competitors or the market normally trade at a lower PE multiple.
- *New product failure.* The failure of a promising new product to deliver profits can also lead to a drop in the stock price.
- *Management departure.* The departure of a highly respected manager can cause the stock price to decline.
- *Major lawsuits.* Companies that have major suits filed against them and are found guilty may also get "hit" by investors.
- *Analysts' downgrades.* Whenever an analyst downgrades a stock, you typically see a decline in the stock's price.

These are examples of risks that result from owning the stock of a particular company. You can see the devastating effect these risks can have on a company's stock price. Whenever a high-growth technology stock misses its earnings estimates, the market cap of the company may decline by as much as 50 percent in one day. I am aware of a situation where a company was found guilty of patent violations and saw its stock drop from $38 to $3.125 during a six-week period. It's not unusual for an analyst's downgrade of a stock to knock 5 percent off a company's value in a day. These risks are very real and they occur on a routine basis.

The screens that I developed and used in selecting the Great Companies are designed to minimize the impact of these types of risks on the Great Companies portfolio. For example:

- *Consistency of earnings.* One of my selection criteria was that earnings of the companies in the portfolio had to be consistent from quarter to quarter and year to year. The companies in my portfolio have been acknowledged leaders in earnings consistency, taking great pride in their track records of consistently meeting the "Street's" expectations.

- *Revenue and profit growth.* The tremendous growth in the future will come from developing nations. While they will encounter problems as they develop, the opportunities for increased profits in these countries are enormous. Therefore, I developed a screen that required companies in the portfolio to derive at least 40 percent of their sales from outside the United States.

- *New product failure.* The screen that evaluates a company's research and development capabilities minimizes the risks of unsuccessful new products, and/or the lack of new products. The Great Companies have outstanding R&D departments that are focused on improving existing products and developing new ones.

- *Key management departures.* While no company is immune to the loss of key managers, even the Great Companies, I screened companies to make sure that the founder had already left the company (probably the biggest risk of all personnel departures), and that the company placed great importance on developing others within the organization. While management can't prevent people from leaving, it can minimize the impact of their departures by having capable people in position to take over on short notice.

"DO NOTHING" RISKS/PURCHASING-POWER RISKS

While the market risks that we discussed are significant, the greatest and most certain risk of all comes from doing nothing with your money. I can assure you that if you keep your money in a bank, inflation will outstrip your ability to grow capital and expose you to purchasing-power risks. For example, if an investor's portfolio grew 3 percent in a year, but inflation increased at a rate of 4 percent, the investor would have made money but lost purchasing power because inflation grew faster than the portfolio value increased. The significance of this risk was addressed by *Money* magazine when it noted, "According to Ibbotson Associates [a research firm], in each of sixty-three overlapping ten-year holding periods since 1931 [1931–1940, 1932–1941, and so on], equities have beaten the annual inflation rate. Far from being safer, an all-cash portfolio would have lost money after adjusting for inflation more than half the time." Investing totally in cash does not eliminate all investing risks. Simply put, you need to have some of your money in the market if you are concerned about inflation.

IN RETROSPECT

It is now January 1999, and August did turn out to be the worst month that the market has suffered since the crash of 1987. In fact, August was among the ten worst months since the crash of 1929. The following chart shows how volatile the market was during this time period.

DATE	DJIA POINT GAIN OR (LOSS)	DJIA CLOSE	% CHANGE
8/31/98	(512.61)	7539.07	(6.37%)
9/1/98	288.36	7827.43	3.82%
9/3/98	(100.15)	7682.22	(1.29%)
9/8/98	380.53	8020.78	4.98%
9/10/98	(249.48)	7615.54	(3.17%)
Total Change	**1,513.13**		**19.63%**

Source: Dow Jones/*Wall Street Journal*

During five trading days over a ten-day period, the total market change equaled almost 20 percent of the market's value. The headlines in the major business journals heightened investor fears and concerns during this time: "How Worried Should You Be?" *Business Week*, August 17, 1998; "Is It Armageddon . . . or October 1987 Revisited?" *Forbes*, September 21, 1998; "The Crash of '98: Can the U.S. Economy Hold Up?" *Fortune*, September 28, 1998.

The year 1998 was a very difficult one for many money managers. *Smart Money* reported that approximately 88 percent of all domestic equity mutual funds failed to exceed the S&P 500 index and a third of domestic equity funds lost money in 1998. In 1998, a number of highly speculative hedge funds run by Wall Street geniuses got hammered. Investors who thought that market-neutral hedge funds were a "safe" haven suddenly realized how vulnerable their investments really were.

Contrary to the August/September headlines, the world did not end. While the DJIA ended up slightly off its highs of the year (9181.43 vs. 9337.97), a gain of 16.10 percent, the S&P 500 index gained 26.67 percent. The Great Companies of America portfolio was up 28.75 percent for the year (detailed returns are included in the appendix). Some of the stocks in the portfolio were hit hard when the market plummeted, but as investors returned to the market, the Great Companies of America have become an investing haven.

The Great Companies strategy will endure over the long term. The August decline, while frightening at times, has served to reassure me that the Great Companies strategy is everything I hoped it would be. While the market was falling, it gave me comfort to know that I was invested in the Great Companies. Hopefully, you, too, will be invested in the Great Companies in the near future.

We offer a variety of services to investors who want to invest in the Great Companies strategy. Please contact us at our website, http://www.greatcompanies.com or call us at 1(800) 538-5111.

APPENDIX

As I reflected back on my search for a core investing strategy, I realized that I had uncovered what I refer to as the Five Truths of Investing in the Stock Market.

THE FIVE TRUTHS OF INVESTING IN THE STOCK MARKET

1. Profits on Wall Street are driven by portfolio turnover.

   Turnover for investors results in higher taxes, increased trading costs, and nullifies the power of compounding, an investor's greatest ally.

2. A fool can make investing in the stock market complex.

   The most successful investors keep it simple.

3. Long-term success in the stock market doesn't result from high portfolio turnover and complex trading strategies.

   Long-term success comes from understanding companies, businesses, and values, and sticking with a sound investing strategy over time.

4. There are very few bad companies in bad businesses (they don't last), there are a number of bad companies in good businesses

(they get acquired), and there are a group of good companies in bad businesses (their management helps them survive).

There are only a handful of Great Companies in terrific businesses that consistently increase their intrinsic values and are worthy of your investing dollars.

5. Many on Wall Street believe that great returns make great companies.

They are wrong! Great Companies produce great returns. Therefore, don't buy stocks, invest in Great Companies.

PORTFOLIO COMPOUNDED ANNUAL RETURNS
Through December 31, 1998

	1-Year Returns from 12/31/97	3-Year Returns from 12/31/95	5-Year Returns from 12/31/93	10-Year Returns from 12/31/88
Great Companies of America	28.75%	38.24%	35.99%	29.86%
Berkshire Hathaway–CLA	52.17%	29.68%	33.80%	31.01%
S&P 500 Comp–LTD	28.58%	28.22%	24.05%	19.19%
Buffett Stocks	11.02%	28.17%	27.37%	24.56%
Built to Last	22.42%	26.73%	25.10%	20.25%
In Search of Excellence	14.00%	18.20%	21.18%	16.50%
Dow Jones Industrials	18.16%	23.91%	22.30%	18.84%

eturns include price appreciation and reinvested dividends.

urce: Standard & Poor's Compustat PC Plus, Intrinsic Value Associates, LLC

tal returns on the S&P Indexes that have been calculated using PC Plus may differ from the total returns on the S&P Indexes calculated by Standard & Poor's.

OTE: PAST PERFORMANCE IS NOT INDICATIVE OF FUTURE RESULTS.

MARKET-WEIGHTED PORTFOLIO

Assumes money was invested based on market cap at the beginning
of each investing period and no portfolio adjustments were made.

Year Started on January 1

Great Companies of America

Year Ended on December 31

	1989	1990	1991	1992	1993	1994	1995	1996	1997	1998
1989	44.66%									
1990	27.09%	11.66%								
1991	39.14%	36.46%	66.77%							
1992	28.68%	23.75%	30.29%	1.78%						
1993	24.01%	19.33%	22.00%	4.34%	6.97%					
1994	22.24%	18.19%	19.88%	7.39%	10.31%	13.75%				
1995	26.43%	23.62%	26.17%	17.67%	23.50%	32.69%	54.79%			
1996	27.42%	25.13%	27.53%	20.86%	26.17%	33.31%	44.31%	34.54%		
1997	29.99%	28.26%	30.83%	25.64%	31.04%	37.87%	46.99%	43.24%	52.50%	
1998	29.86%	28.32%	30.57%	26.08%	30.66%	35.99%	42.20%	38.24%	40.12%	28.75%

Berkshire Hathaway

Year Ended on December 31

	1989	1990	1991	1992	1993	1994	1995	1996	1997	1998
1989	84.57%									
1990	19.17%	–23.05%								
1991	24.41%	2.14%	35.58%							
1992	25.74%	10.64%	32.68%	29.83%						
1993	28.28%	17.12%	34.73%	34.31%	38.94%					
1994	27.72%	18.65%	32.22%	31.12%	31.76%	24.96%				
1995	31.58%	24.37%	36.90%	37.23%	39.79%	40.23%	57.35%			
1996	28.11%	21.60%	31.24%	30.38%	30.52%	27.83%	29.29%	6.23%		
1997	28.85%	23.19%	31.75%	31.12%	31.38%	29.56%	31.13%	19.71%	34.90%	
1998	31.01%	26.11%	34.15%	33.94%	34.64%	33.80%	36.10%	29.68%	43.28%	52.17%

S&P 500 Index

Year Ended on December 31

	1989	1990	1991	1992	1993	1994	1995	1996	1997	1998
1989	31.62%									
1990	12.93%	–3.10%								
1991	18.48%	12.41%	30.40%							
1992	15.66%	10.79%	18.46%	7.61%						
1993	14.52%	10.61%	15.59%	8.83%	10.06%					
1994	12.21%	8.68%	11.85%	6.27%	5.60%	1.32%				
1995	15.52%	13.03%	16.57%	13.35%	15.33%	18.05%	37.55%			
1996	16.42%	14.40%	17.61%	15.21%	17.19%	19.66%	30.04%	22.95%		
1997	18.19%	16.61%	19.74%	18.05%	20.26%	22.95%	31.14%	28.05%	33.35%	
1998	19.19%	17.89%	20.81%	19.50%	21.60%	24.05%	30.49%	28.22%	30.94%	28.58%

Buffett Stocks

Year Ended on December 31

	1989	1990	1991	1992	1993	1994	1995	1996	1997	1998
1989	41.29%									
1990	15.46%	–5.65%								
1991	27.81%	21.57%	56.63%							
1992	24.92%	19.90%	35.16%	16.63%						
1993	21.81%	17.38%	26.24%	13.33%	10.13%					
1994	19.88%	16.00%	22.15%	12.44%	10.40%	10.67%				
1995	23.04%	20.24%	26.22%	19.59%	20.59%	26.18%	43.87%			
1996	24.37%	22.12%	27.49%	22.35%	23.82%	28.75%	38.88%	34.06%		
1997	26.16%	24.39%	29.40%	25.35%	27.16%	31.82%	39.74%	37.71%	41.47%	
1998	24.56%	22.83%	26.94%	23.19%	24.32%	27.37%	31.92%	28.17%	25.32%	11.02%

Built to Last

Year Ended on December 31

	1989	1990	1991	1992	1993	1994	1995	1996	1997	1998
1989	32.16%									
1990	14.26%	–1.22%								
1991	21.20%	16.06%	36.37%							
1992	18.34%	14.07%	22.57%	10.18%						
1993	15.59%	11.79%	16.49%	7.67%	5.21%					
1994	14.76%	11.56%	15.01%	8.66%	7.91%	10.67%				
1995	17.58%	15.31%	18.93%	14.94%	16.57%	22.69%	36.03%			
1996	18.63%	16.81%	20.13%	17.12%	18.92%	23.87%	31.06%	26.27%		
1997	20.01%	18.58%	21.71%	19.43%	21.37%	25.78%	31.26%	28.95%	31.68%	
1998	20.25%	19.00%	21.80%	19.85%	21.54%	25.10%	28.99%	26.73%	26.97%	22.42%

continued on next page…

Year Started on January 1

Search of Excellence — Ended on December 31

	1989	1990	1991	1992	1993	1994	1995	1996	1997	1998
1989	23.59%									
1990	11.73%	1.01%								
1991	15.05%	11.01%	22.00%							
1992	12.04%	8.43%	12.34%	3.45%						
1993	12.00%	9.27%	12.17%	7.56%	11.84%					
1994	11.49%	9.22%	11.37%	8.04%	10.42%	9.01%				
1995	15.78%	14.53%	17.44%	16.33%	20.97%	25.81%	45.19%			
1996	16.24%	15.22%	17.78%	16.96%	20.60%	23.67%	31.72%	19.50%		
1997	16.78%	15.96%	18.26%	17.65%	20.72%	23.05%	28.12%	20.35%	21.21%	
1998	16.50%	15.74%	17.72%	17.12%	19.57%	21.18%	24.43%	18.20%	17.55%	14.00%

Dow Jones Industrials — Ended on December 31

	1989	1990	1991	1992	1993	1994	1995	1996	1997	1998
1989	32.22%									
1990	14.68%	–0.54%								
1991	17.78%	11.17%	24.25%							
1992	15.10%	9.90%	15.52%	7.40%						
1993	15.47%	11.63%	16.00%	12.08%	16.97%					
1994	13.66%	10.27%	13.15%	9.68%	10.84%	5.02%				
1995	16.73%	14.33%	17.55%	15.94%	18.93%	19.92%	36.94%			
1996	18.18%	16.30%	19.38%	18.42%	21.35%	22.85%	32.86%	28.91%		
1997	18.91%	17.35%	20.15%	19.48%	22.06%	23.36%	30.16%	26.89%	24.91%	
1998	18.84%	17.44%	19.90%	19.29%	21.40%	22.30%	27.05%	23.91%	21.49%	18.16%

Source: S&P Compustat

NOTE: PAST PERFORMANCE IS NOT INDICATIVE OF FUTURE RESULTS.

Equal-Weighted Portfolio

Portfolio rebalanced each year using an equal weight
for each stock in each portfolio

Year Started on January 1

Great Companies of America

Year Ended on December 31

	1989	1990	1991	1992	1993	1994	1995	1996	1997	1998
1989	44.66%									
1990	26.19%	10.07%								
1991	38.19%	35.07%	65.73%							
1992	30.32%	25.87%	34.60%	9.31%						
1993	26.08%	21.82%	26.00%	9.87%	10.43%					
1994	23.80%	20.01%	22.63%	10.91%	11.72%	13.03%				
1995	27.64%	25.00%	28.22%	20.25%	24.14%	31.62%	53.27%			
1996	28.53%	26.38%	29.32%	23.06%	26.76%	32.72%	43.81%	34.94%		
1997	31.15%	29.55%	32.60%	27.77%	31.81%	37.78%	47.18%	44.23%	54.15%	
1998	30.97%	29.53%	32.20%	28.00%	31.41%	36.06%	42.51%	39.10%	41.23%	29.39%

Berkshire Hathaway

Year Ended on December 31

	1989	1990	1991	1992	1993	1994	1995	1996	1997	1998
1989	84.57%									
1990	19.17%	-23.05%								
1991	24.41%	2.14%	35.58%							
1992	25.74%	10.64%	32.68%	29.83%						
1993	28.28%	17.12%	34.73%	34.31%	38.94%					
1994	27.72%	18.65%	32.22%	31.12%	31.76%	24.96%				
1995	31.58%	24.37%	36.90%	37.23%	39.79%	40.23%	57.35%			
1996	28.11%	21.60%	31.24%	30.38%	30.52%	27.83%	29.29%	6.23%		
1997	28.85%	23.19%	31.75%	31.12%	31.38%	29.56%	31.13%	19.71%	34.90%	
1998	31.01%	26.11%	34.15%	33.94%	34.64%	33.80%	36.10%	29.68%	43.28%	52.17%

S&P 500 Index

Year Ended on December 31

	1989	1990	1991	1992	1993	1994	1995	1996	1997	1998
1989	31.62%									
1990	12.93%	-3.10%								
1991	18.48%	12.41%	30.40%							
1992	15.66%	10.79%	18.46%	7.61%						
1993	14.52%	10.61%	15.59%	8.83%	10.06%					
1994	12.21%	8.68%	11.85%	6.27%	5.60%	1.32%				
1995	15.52%	13.03%	16.57%	13.35%	15.33%	18.05%	37.55%			
1996	16.42%	14.40%	17.61%	15.21%	17.19%	19.66%	30.04%	22.95%		
1997	18.19%	16.61%	19.74%	18.05%	20.26%	22.95%	31.14%	28.05%	33.35%	
1998	19.19%	17.89%	20.81%	19.50%	21.60%	24.05%	30.49%	28.22%	30.94%	28.58%

Buffett Stocks

Year Ended on December 31

	1989	1990	1991	1992	1993	1994	1995	1996	1997	1998
1989	41.29%									
1990	13.82%	-8.31%								
1991	27.38%	20.94%	59.53%							
1992	25.61%	20.78%	38.63%	20.46%						
1993	22.73%	18.48%	29.05%	16.06%	11.83%					
1994	20.24%	16.42%	23.58%	13.49%	10.16%	8.52%				
1995	23.29%	20.52%	27.29%	20.31%	20.26%	24.71%	43.31%			
1996	24.18%	21.91%	27.83%	22.29%	22.75%	26.63%	36.79%	30.56%		
1997	26.21%	24.44%	29.99%	25.62%	26.68%	30.70%	39.05%	36.97%	43.70%	
1998	25.39%	23.74%	28.47%	24.55%	25.25%	28.12%	33.55%	30.45%	30.39%	18.31%

Built to Last

Year Ended on December 31

	1989	1990	1991	1992	1993	1994	1995	1996	1997	1998
1989	32.16%									
1990	12.79%	-3.74%								
1991	18.69%	12.48%	31.43%							
1992	18.56%	14.34%	24.62%	18.16%						
1993	18.07%	14.79%	21.72%	17.14%	16.13%					
1994	16.97%	14.14%	19.11%	15.26%	13.84%	11.60%				
1995	19.67%	17.71%	22.54%	20.41%	21.17%	23.77%	37.27%			
1996	20.59%	19.02%	23.31%	21.75%	22.66%	24.92%	32.16%	27.24%		
1997	22.20%	21.01%	25.03%	23.99%	25.19%	27.57%	33.38%	31.48%	35.87%	
1998	22.18%	21.12%	24.64%	23.70%	24.65%	26.43%	30.44%	28.24%	28.74%	21.99%

continued on next page..

Year Started on January 1

In Search of Excellence — Year Ended on December 31

	1989	1990	1991	1992	1993	1994	1995	1996	1997	1998
1989	23.59%									
1990	10.44%	−1.30%								
1991	13.92%	9.37%	21.20%							
1992	11.40%	7.61%	12.37%	4.18%						
1993	12.01%	9.29%	13.06%	9.20%	14.46%					
1994	11.57%	9.31%	12.14%	9.27%	11.91%	9.41%				
1995	16.04%	14.83%	18.36%	17.66%	22.54%	26.78%	46.92%			
1996	16.23%	15.21%	18.22%	17.63%	21.26%	23.61%	31.39%	17.50%		
1997	16.81%	15.99%	18.69%	18.28%	21.32%	23.10%	28.03%	19.52%	21.57%	
1998	17.81%	17.19%	19.73%	19.52%	22.29%	23.92%	27.83%	22.04%	24.38%	27.25%

Dow Jones Industrials — Year Ended on December 31

	1989	1990	1991	1992	1993	1994	1995	1996	1997	1998
1989	32.22%									
1990	14.68%	−0.54%								
1991	17.78%	11.17%	24.25%							
1992	15.10%	9.90%	15.52%	7.40%						
1993	15.47%	11.63%	16.00%	12.08%	16.97%					
1994	13.66%	10.27%	13.15%	9.68%	10.84%	5.02%				
1995	16.73%	14.33%	17.55%	15.94%	18.93%	19.92%	36.94%			
1996	18.18%	16.30%	19.38%	18.42%	21.35%	22.85%	32.86%	28.91%		
1997	18.91%	17.35%	20.15%	19.48%	22.06%	23.36%	30.16%	26.89%	24.91%	
1998	18.84%	17.44%	19.90%	19.29%	21.40%	22.30%	27.05%	23.91%	21.49%	18.16%

Source: S&P Compustat

NOTE: PAST PERFORMANCE IS NOT INDICATIVE OF FUTURE RESULTS.

STANDARD DEVIATION OF QUARTERLY RETURNS (ANNUALIZED)

	1-Year Standard Deviation 1998	3-Year Standard Deviation 1996–1998	5-Year Standard Deviation 1994–1998	10-Year Standard Deviation 1989–1998
Great Companies of America	45.16%	29.60%	24.88%	23.11%
Berkshire Hathaway–CLA	89.50%	47.04%	38.69%	36.52%
S&P 500 Comp–LTD	33.78%	19.77%	16.53%	14.99%
Buffett Stocks	41.34%	25.82%	20.70%	22.69%
Built to Last	39.07%	24.19%	19.30%	19.56%
In Search of Excellence	31.80%	19.78%	16.70%	17.01%
Dow Jones Industrials	30.13%	19.39%	16.06%	14.16%

Source: Standard & Poor's Compustat PC Plus, Intrinsic Value Associates, LLC

NOTE: PAST PERFORMANCE IS NOT INDICATIVE OF FUTURE RESULTS.

SOURCES

BOOKS

Adizes, Ichak, *Corporate Lifecycles*. Englewood Cliffs, NJ: Prentice Hall, 1988.

American Association of Individual Investors, *The Individual Investor's Guide to Low-Load Mutual Funds*. Chicago: NTC Contemporary Publishing Company, 1998.

Collins, James C. and Jerry I. Porras, *Built to Last*. New York: HarperCollins, 1994.

Daniels, John L. and Dr. N. Caroline Daniels, *Global Vision*. New York: McGraw-Hill, 1993.

Dent, Harry S. Jr., *The Roaring 2000's*. New York: Simon & Schuster, 1998.

Fisher, Philip A., *Common Stocks and Uncommon Profits*. New York: John Wiley & Sons, Inc., 1958.

Fucini, Joseph J. and Suzy Fucini, *Entrepreneurs, The Men and Women Behind Famous Brand Names and How They Made It*. Boston: G. K. Hall & Co., 1985.

Garten, Jeffrey E., *The Big Ten*. New York: Basic Books, Division of HarperCollins, 1997.

Gertz, Dwight L. and Joao P. A. Baptista, *Grow to Be Great*. New York: The Free Press, 1995.

Graham, Benjamin, *The Intelligent Investor*. New York: Harper & Row Publishers, 1973.

Hamel, Gary and C. K. Parhalad, *Competing for the Future*. Boston: Harvard Business School Press, 1994.

Kilpatrick, Andrew, *Of Permanent Value: The Story of Warren Buffett*. Birmingham, AL: AKPE, 1994.

Lowe, Janet, *Value Investing Made Easy*. New York: McGraw-Hill, 1996.

Lowe, Janet, *Warren Buffett Speaks*. New York: John Wiley & Sons, Inc., 1997.

Lowenstein, Roger, *Buffett The Making of an American Capitalist*. New York: Doubleday, 1995.

Mackay, Charles, *Extraordinary Popular Delusions and the Madness of Crowds*. New York: John Wiley & Sons, Inc., 1996 .

Peters, Thomas J. and Robert H. Waterman, *In Search of Excellence*. New York: Harper & Row, Publishers, 1982.

Siegel, Jeremy J., *Stocks for the Long Run*. New York: McGraw-Hill, 1994.

Slywotzky, Adria J. and David J. Morrison, *The Profit Zone*. New York: Times Business, 1997.

Stewart, G. Bennett, III, *The Quest For Value*. New York: Harper-Collins Publishers, 1991.

Taylor, John H., *Building Wealth with Mutual Funds*. New York: Windsor Books, 1993.

Treacy, Michael and Fred Wiersema, *The Discipline of Market Leaders*. Reading, MA: Addison-Wesley, 1995.

Tanous, Peter J., *Investment Gurus*. New York: New York Institute of Finance, 1997.

ARTICLES

"A Hail of Silver Bulletts," *Forbes*, January 26, 1998.

"America's Greatest Wealth Creators," *Fortune*, November 9, 1998.

"America's Most Admired Companies," *Fortune*, March 2, 1998.

"Are You on Track? Measuring the Performance of Your Total Portfolio," *AAII Journal*, July 1995.

"Analysts Face Challenges," *New York Times*, July 5, 1998.

"Big Caps, Big Edge," *Business Week*, March 1, 1999.

"Competing through Innovation, How Pfizer Turns Research into Profit," *Enterprise*, November 1993.

"Creating Cures and Shareholder Values," *Leaders*, April/May/June 1997.

"For Deal on Wrap Accounts, Just Ask," *New York Times*, December 31, 1994.

"High Price for Certainty," *Forbes*, April 14, 1997.

"How the Discount Brokers Stack Up," *Smart Money*, July 1998.

"Increasing Returns and the New World of Business," *The Harvard Business Review*, July/August 1996.

"It's Easy for Investor to Start Small," *USA Today*, January 30, 1998.

"It Was a Hit in Buenos Aires—So Why Not Boise?" *Business Week*, September 7, 1998.

"Just Concentrate," *Barron's*, April 13, 1998.

"Merck, Will the Growth Machine Keep Going?" *Business Week*, October 12, 1998.

"Michael Dell Rocks," *Fortune*, May 11, 1998.

"More Shun Fund Fees, Pick Their Own Stocks," *USA Today*, July 30, 1998.

"My Years With the Pfizer Board," *Directors and Boards*, Summer 1997.

"No Fuss Investing," *Barron's*, December 1, 1997.

"One Hundred Sixty Companies for the Price of One," *Forbes*, February 26, 1997.

"Patents Hit Record in '98 as Tech Firms Rushed to Protect Intellectual Property," *Wall Street Journal*, January 15, 1999.

"Pfizer versus Merck," *Forbes*, April 6, 1998.

"Proven Performers," *Barron's*, July 14, 1997.

"Putting Index Funds in Their Place," *Wall Street Journal*, March 12, 1999.

"Screening for Stocks Using the Graham and Dodd Approach," *AAII Journal*, August 1995.

"See No Evil, Speak No Evil," *Forbes*, December 15, 1997.

"Should You Put a SPDR in Your Portfolio?" *Investor's Business Daily*, March 15, 1999.

"Sick Process," *Red Herring Magazine*, October 1998.

"So You Think You're Diversified," *Worth*, April 1996.

"Start-Up Links Firms and Investors," *Wall Street Journal*, October 22, 1998.

"Striking Out at Wall Street," *U.S. News & World Report*, June 20, 1994.

"The Basics Haven't Changed," *Worth*, April 1996.

"The Best & The Worst Boards," *Business Week*, December 8, 1997.

"The Best Pipelines," *R&D Directions*, January/February 1997.

"The Mutual Fund Shell Game," *Worth*, March 1995.

"The 100 Best Companies to Work For," *Fortune*, January 11, 1999.

"The 500 Biggest Private Companies," *Forbes*, November 30, 1998.

"The Reckoning," *Smart Money*, February 1998.

"The Secrets of America's Most Admired Corporations," *Fortune*, March 3, 1998.

"The Top 25 Managers of the Year," *Business Week*, January 12, 1998.

"The World's Most Admired Companies," *Fortune*, October 26, 1998.

"Warren Buffett's Idea of Heaven," *Forbes*, October 18, 1983.

"What the Sales Brochure Didn't Tell You," *Forbes*, April 7, 1997.

"What We Can Learn From Phil Fisher," *Forbes*, October 19, 1987.

"Why Generic Drugs Often Can't Compete Against Brand Names," *Wall Street Journal*, January 18, 1998.

"Why Pfizer," *Fortune*, May 11, 1998.

"You Ain't Seen Nothin' Yet," *Business Week*, August 31, 1998.

SPECIAL PUBLICATIONS

Credit Suisse-First Boston Corporate Publications

"Competitive Advantage Period 'CAP': The Neglected Driver," January 14, 1997.

"EVA Primer," February 20, 1996.

"Plus Ça Change, Plus C'est Pareil," December 13, 1995.

"Thoughts on Valuation," October 21, 1997.

PaineWebber

"Continuing Patent Boom Good Sign for Productivity," Portfolio Manager's Spotlight, January 27, 1998.

"More Gorillas," Portfolio Manager's Spotlight, January 14, 1997.

Berkshire Hathaway

Berkshire Hathaway Annual Reports
1990
1993
1995
1996
Berkshire Hathaway Annual Meetings
1993
1995
1996
Berkshire Hathaway, An Owner's Manual, 1996
Warren Buffett Lecture at Stanford Law School, March 23, 1990.

ACKNOWLEDGMENTS

This book is the result of the help, support, and time of a number of people who made my initial effort as a writer a tremendous learning experience and a real joy. They encouraged me when I was down, and pointed the way when I was lost. Most of them don't know each other, but together they were an awesome force.

Let me began by thanking Gerry Bollman, a truly talented analyst who takes great pride in his profession, and is committed to objective and accurate analysis. Gerry provided valuable insights into the world of intrinsic value, and was of immense value as I screened companies and developed portfolio returns.

Bruce Marcus, a neighbor and an accomplished author who has published thirteen books and hundreds of newsletters, provided guidance during the early stages of writing this book. He helped me better understand the publishing process, and was always encouraging. He is a professional author, and I truly respect his great talents.

Peter Cowenhoven, formerly of Value Line, was instrumental in collecting, organizing, and analyzing the data that was initially used to screen the Great Companies. Peter always came up with the facts that were needed when they were needed.

Ralph Goldman, the most knowledgeable broker that I know.

Ralph was the first person to whom I explained the Great Companies investing strategy. His knowledge of the markets, extensive experience with money mangers, and practical approach to investing proved to be a great asset. His insights and guidance along the way have proven invaluable.

I am deeply indebted to the people in the Great Companies of America who welcomed me into their worlds. They willingly and openly shared their experiences and insights. They made writing this book the most significant learning experience of my life. In addition to being highly successful executives in the best companies in the world, they are genuinely sincere and dedicated people. The CEO interviews will provide you with a unique understanding of their companies, which helped me develop the qualities that are part of the core of every Great Company. Others within the companies helped provide meaningful backup materials. These executives include:

American Internation Group, Inc: Maurice R. Greenberg, Chairman and CEO; Thomas Savage, President, AIG Financial Products Corporation; John T. Wooster, Jr., Vice President, Communications.

General Electric Company: John F. Welch, Jr. Chairman and CEO; Joyce Hergenhan, President of the GE Fund; and Frank P. Doyle, retired. I want to single out Joyce's contributions in so many areas. Joyce is to the public relations community what Jack is to the business management community.

The Gillette Company: Alfred M. Zeien, Chairman and CEO; David A. Fausch, retired; Joan Gallagher, Vice President, Corporate Relations; Matthew M. Miller, Manager, Corporate Public Relations; and Bruce C. Swinsky, Senior Vice President.

Pfizer, Inc.: William C. Steere, Jr., Chairman and CEO; Brian McGlynn, Director of Corporate Media Relations; William J. Robison, Senior Vice President Employee Relations.

I also want to thank the many other executives in the Great Companies who assisted in verifying the data contained in the corporate profiles that are included in chapter 4. They include: John L. Skule, Vice President, Corporate & Environmental Affairs, Bristol-Myers Squibb Company; John M. Morris, Director, Media Relations/Corporate Affairs, Citigroup; Robert Murray, Vice President, Corporate Relations, Colgate-Palmotive Company; John McKeegan, Manager, Corporate Communications, Johnson & Johnson; Paul W. Critchlow, Senior Vice President, Communications, Merrill Lynch & Co. Inc.; Charlotte R. Otto, Global Public Affairs Officer, The Procter and Gamble Company; and Stephen K. Galpin, Jr., Staff Vice President, Corporate Communications, Schering-Plough Corporation.

A key to the book was my agent, Jim Levine. Jim helped me turn a good idea into the book that you are now reading. An avid investor who not only believes in but invests in the Great Companies strategy. Jim is a credit to his profession, and has become a friend.

Suzanne Oaks, my senior editor, was a tremendous resource. She understood the Great Companies strategy immediately, and referred to it as "The Built to Last of Investing." She was a believer in the book from the beginning, and was immensely helpful in organizing the book in a manner that made it highly readable and actionable. She was also right about the cover.

Bill Shinker, the president and publisher of Broadway Books, provided valuable counsel when it counted. I believe that Bill knows as much about publishing and marketing books as any person alive. Importantly, Bill has been smart enough to combine his two passions in life, publishing and golf. As a result he has published some really terrific golf books.

There were a number of others at Broadway who were great to work with including Kathy Spinelli, Lisa Olney, David Drake, Robert Allen, and the National Accounts Team. Bill Shinker has built a terrific team at Broadway, and it's wonderful to have their support on a project like Great Companies, Great Returns.

I would also like to thank Warren Buffett for sharing his wisdom, experience, and insight into investing via his shareholder letters, annual meetings, interviews, etc. You see, I am a shareholder in Berkshire Hathaway, and have been for years. The Owner's Manual that Berkshire Hathaway distributes refers to the shareholders as "owner-partners" and Warren Buffett and Charlie Munger as managing partners. The company does everything it can make you feel like a partner. I peronally believe that Warren Buffett is the most brillant investor of our time; however, his brilliance as an investor is overshadowed by his business ethics and attitude toward the people who invest with him. Every person in the investment management community and all investors should read the Berkshire Hathaway Owner's Manual at least once each year. The Owner's Manual is a beacon to follow. You can access the Owner's Manual on the Berkshire Hathaway website http://www.berkshirehathaway.com.

I would also like to acknowledge several good friends who listened as I endlessly rambled on about this new investing strategy. They should be given medals for their patience. You know who you are.

I also want to acknowledge the contributions of my partner, Jack Kenney. Jack is a terrific business partner and a wonderful person.

Finally, I would like to thank my wife, Marie, my biggest critic and most ardent supporter. I couldn't have done it without her.

Because of all these people, what started out as a good idea turned into a book that will prove invaluable to investors who properly use the lessons it contains. I want to thank them for helping me write this book, and lastly, thank you for reading it. Enjoy!

FREE OFFERS TO
BOOK PURCHASERS

Receive a **free** special report on intrinsic value
Receive a **free** copy of the *Great Companies Newsletter*
Receive a **free** corporate profile of a Great Company
Receive a **free** The Five Truths of Investing in the Stock Market card
Obtain the forms mentioned in the book at no charge by contacting
  our website
Contact us as follows:
Mail: Great Companies, LLC
      8550 Ulmerton Rd.
      Suite 101
      Largo, FL 33771
Internet: www.greatcompanies.com
Telephone: (800) 538-5111
Fax: (800) 572-0150